No More Secrets

No More Secrets

Open Source Information and the Reshaping of U.S. Intelligence

HAMILTON BEAN

**Foreword by
Senator Gary Hart**

Praeger Security International

 PRAEGER

AN IMPRINT OF ABC-CLIO, LLC
Santa Barbara, California • Denver, Colorado • Oxford, England

Library of Congress Cataloging-in-Publication Data

Bean, Hamilton.
   No more secrets : open source information and the reshaping of U.S.
intelligence / Hamilton Bean ; foreword by Senator Gary Hart.
      p. cm. — (Praeger security international)
   Includes bibliographical references and index.
   ISBN 978-0-313-39155-2 (alk. paper) — ISBN 978-0-313-39156-9 (ebook)
1. Open source intelligence—United States.   I. Title.   II. Series.
   JK468.I6B396   2011
   327.1273—dc22   2011008505

ISBN: 978-0-313-39155-2
EISBN: 978-0-313-39156-9

15   14   13   12   11   1   2   3   4   5

This book is also available on the World Wide Web as an eBook.
Visit www.abc-clio.com for details.

Praeger
An Imprint of ABC-CLIO, LLC

ABC-CLIO, LLC
130 Cremona Drive, P.O. Box 1911
Santa Barbara, California 93116-1911

This book is printed on acid-free paper ∞

Manufactured in the United States of America

Contents

Foreword

"There are no secrets," a friend said some years ago. Though he was forecasting the disappearance of personal privacy, he might well have been predicting the tsunami building off the shores of those peculiar islands of secrecy known as intelligence agencies that emerged in the post–World War II Cold War years.

Efforts by governments to collect and hoard secrets—regarding both the intentions of their enemies and possible treachery by their own citizens—surely date to the Greek city-states if not also to a variety of oligarchies before them.

Elizabeth I's principal secretary, Sir Francis Walsingham, is generally considered 16th-century England's charter member of the Western world's intelligence services and is credited with recruiting the dramatist Christopher Marlowe into the enterprise. Whether Marlowe's violent death in 1593 was directly traceable to his spying sideline is still a matter of conjecture, but it certainly started a trail leading more or less directly to his fellow countryman David Cornwell (a.k.a., John Le Carré) some four centuries later.

What few in this long, complex, and murky history could have foreseen, however, was an age in which there were few, if any, secrets. Technology, the hallmark of the early 21st century, is credited with cracking the vault of mystery and concealment. The silicon chip, digital compression, wireless intercepts, wall-penetrating listening devices, ultra-long-range camera lenses, and so on have all combined to ensure that Wikipedia would inevitably become WikiLeaks.

It was by no means accidental that those deputized to plug the many leaks mounting to a virtual river of secrets during the Nixon era were given the colorful designator "plumbers." This would prompt Norman Mailer to compare plumbers to rocket scientists in that both were tasked with the prevention of treachery in closed systems.

Daniel Patrick Moynihan commented extensively in the late Cold War years on bureaucracy's predictable response to the erosion of secrecy— create more secrets. Thus, an increasing army of security bureaucrats, in and out of uniform, armed itself with the most dangerous of weapons— rubber stamps, in this case marked "Secret." But, if everything is secret, as Senator Moynihan shrewdly observed, then nothing is secret.

At the turn of this century, technology, the engine of "open sources," swept away burgeoning warehouses of secrets faster than they could be built and filled. And this fact is central to Hamilton Bean's remarkable and critically important pioneering work. What happens to the mysterious world of intelligence, he asks, when the content of its hidden vaults shrinks and melts before our very eyes? What happens when there are few, if any, secrets?

An image of this intelligence revolution comes to mind: a small crew tunneling diligently to come up under an epic vault of secrets only to discover upon surfacing that they are in the New York Public Library. But this transformation did not arrive without warning. As early as 1969, a Central Intelligence Agency study said, "A virtual tidal wave of publicly printed paper threatens to swamp almost all enterprises of intellectual research." And by 1975, the movie *Three Days of the Condor* featured a CIA researcher, Joe Turner (Robert Redford), who, by simply reading books, uncovers a complex CIA plot to dominate Middle Eastern oil fields.

Interestingly, and importantly, in between these dates the so-called secret bombing of Cambodia during the Vietnam War made it clear that secrecy was a two-edged sword. The Cambodians surely knew they were being bombed. The secret was being kept from the American people. The pattern of using instruments of intelligence to collect secrets from the American people and to prevent them from discovering the perfidies their own government was carrying out would lead to congressional investigations requiring substantial reforms in the vast U.S. intelligence community. Though the Cold War has been over for two decades, today that community is much more vast.

If one were to date the dramatic shift from too little intelligence to too much, documented here in Dr. Bean's groundbreaking work, one might arbitrarily select the inauguration of the World Wide Web in 1990. Ironically, this was within months of the collapse of the Soviet Union. Before that, the intelligence world dramatized by John Le Carré was tedious, dreary, and mundane. Now that world approximates the political image of drinking from a fire hose.

Dr. Bean recognizes that a democracy must protect its citizens and that the collection of information and the conversion of it to intelligence are crucial to that duty. But he also knows that a democracy that violates the rights and privacy of its citizens and conceals its activities from them edges dangerously near something other than a democracy.

The most radical of our founders, Thomas Jefferson, held that the best guarantor of the American republic was the good judgment and common sense of the American people, a people fully informed of the activities of its government on their behalf. Thanks to the advent of open sources converting intelligence to information, we may be restoring that ideal.

Gary Hart

Scholar in residence, University of Colorado; charter member of the U.S. Senate Intelligence Oversight Committee; co-chair of the U.S. Commission on National Security/21st Century

Preface

I arrived for my first day of work at Intellibridge Corporation on May 21, 2001. Intellibridge was located in Washington, DC, in a modern, red brick building at the corner of 33rd and M streets near Georgetown University. When I arrived, the wall between Intellibridge's second-floor office and an adjoining apartment had been hastily torn down to make room for more desks. Even that did not provide enough space, however, so analysts were soon working from computers perched atop the apartment's kitchen counter. When walking into Intellibridge during the months before the September 11, 2001, terrorist attacks, one encountered a series of small, dimly lit rooms filled with more than two dozen analysts gazing intensely into their desktop computer screens. These analysts—in their 20s, 30s, and 40s—possessed government work experience, foreign language skills, and advanced degrees from prestigious colleges and universities. Typically working 10-hour shifts (spread across the day), these analysts scoured the Internet, looking for information in nearly a dozen languages that responded to the defined needs of Intellibridge's clients.

My image of intelligence up to that point had been mostly informed by Hollywood movies, so I was shocked to see analysts supporting U.S. naval intelligence crammed into a darkened, debris-strewn Georgetown apartment. Intellibridge provided what it called "open source intelligence and analytical services" to its clients. This meant that Intellibridge employed policy, security, and business experts to search and analyze online sources of information about geopolitical trends and events deemed of interest to Fortune 500 corporations and U.S. government agencies. Promising insight and advantage to clients, Intellibridge's motto claimed to provide

"Not Just What You Need to Know, But What It Means." Intellibridge was an early purveyor of what has come to be known as outsourced or private intelligence.

In the years following the 9/11 terrorist attacks, I strode the corridors of power in Washington, DC, attempting to persuade national security officials to purchase the open source information and analytical support services of Intellibridge. In the process, I became fascinated by how people talked about open source. Some argued that open source was in no way new, unique, or important. Others, however, argued that open source would be the catalyst for a radical reshaping of U.S. intelligence and national security. It became clear that if I wanted to understand the dynamics of open source, I needed to analyze processes of institutional communication, organizational culture, and organizational change. Thus, in 2005, I left the business of U.S. intelligence in order to investigate the reshaping of this institution. This book represents the culmination of that investigation.

By investigating the institutionalization of open source, this book exposes the inner workings of the U.S. intelligence bureaucracy: its organizational assumptions, imperatives, and turf wars. This book provides case studies of institutional change within settings where the stakes for officials, policy makers, and citizens are extraordinarily high. Intelligence stakeholders confront a complex environment characterized by risk, urgency, competing priorities, changing assumptions, and new and unfamiliar open source technologies and practices, yet there has been little discussion of how these conditions influence the production of intelligence or relate to the deliberative principles of a democratic society. By investigating how open source laws, policies, and practices are developed, maintained, or transformed, this book enhances public understanding of contemporary U.S. intelligence and national security affairs. I have written it for students and researchers in the fields of communication, intelligence studies, public administration, political science, and security studies. The book provides an example of scholarship conducted at the *intersection* of communication, organization, and intelligence studies.

My professional background and ongoing interaction with members of the U.S. intelligence community require that I reflect on the claims, selection of evidence, and interpretations I present herein. Specifically, in 2008, anonymous Department of Homeland Security (DHS) officials determined that my exploration of the relationships among organizational culture, discourse, and homeland security information sharing were worth supporting through a research grant. As a researcher, however, I do not analyze an objective world for government officials; rather, I am responsible for representing a particular view of that world—one that is always a selective and partial attempt to shape meaning. I am committed to the principle that the voices of the marginalized should be explored in organizational studies. In this book, I attempt to enact that principle by representing not only managerial voices but also the often-muted voices of intelligence analysts and citizens.

In undertaking this research, I have been gripped by simultaneous impulses to defend and criticize U.S. intelligence community officials. The impulse to defend comes from recognizing that we ask much of the men and women who serve within intelligence and national security organizations and who work under intensely stressful conditions dealing with life and death. I have witnessed firsthand how this work can take its toll on one's health, well-being, and relationships. By contrast, the impulse to criticize comes from my impulse to see democratic principles of transparency, accountability, and participation extended to the national security arena in order to ameliorate some of the error, waste, and abuse that often characterize this sector. Because intelligence institutions possess immense power to control and extinguish human lives, I believe officials have an obligation to use open sources to challenge taken-for-granted assumptions, engage a wide array of stakeholders, improve planning and decision making, and adequately assess the actual and potential consequences of policy decisions. We can and should do better.

I also believe that to the extent possible, open source products (translations, reports, databases, and analyses) should be widely shared with citizens so interested parties can be more aware of national security issues and better equipped to deliberate about them. It has long been argued that a strong democracy requires an informed and influential citizenry; however, determining what the U.S. intelligence community's role should be in supporting the development of that citizenry is no easy task. Intelligence agencies generally have no direct responsibility to support the public; agencies do so indirectly through the support of the executive branch. The advent of whistleblower websites, such as WikiLeaks, places some secret information directly into citizens' hands. How these events will influence the trajectory of intelligence reform or relate to the development of informed and influential citizens remains to be seen. Nevertheless, if open source is, as many have argued, a means of both avoiding national security disasters and strengthening institutional transparency and accountability, then stakeholders ought to better understand how language promotes or impedes competing visions of open source's development and use. In short, this book is intended to spur critical discussion of the institutional and public dimensions of open source discourse in order to explore its democratic potential.

Hamilton Bean

Denver, Colorado
January 2011

Acknowledgments

I am indebted to the people who have assisted me in this effort, especially Steve Catalano at Praeger for his guidance during the publication of this project. I am grateful for the members of various 9/11 family organizations and other citizen groups who agreed to participate in this research. I am also grateful for the participation of dozens of current and former government officials, analysts, and contractors, at federal, state, and local levels, whom I interviewed. These men and women spoke to me on the condition that neither their names nor their specific organizational affiliations would be disclosed.

Special thanks go to the Department of Communication at the University of Colorado Denver (where I am employed), the Department of Communication at the University of Colorado at Boulder (where I earned my Ph.D.), the National Consortium for the Study of Terrorism and Responses to Terrorism (START) at the University of Maryland, and the U.S. Department of Homeland Security. These organizations directly or indirectly supported this research through generous financial assistance.

Drs. Stephen Hartnett, Lisa Keränen, Timothy Kuhn, and Karen Tracy provided essential guidance during this project. I want to especially thank Bryan Taylor for his influence and expertise. I am also thankful for the work of other scholars in the fields of communication, organization studies, and intelligence studies, including Drs. Joshua Barbour, Stanley Deetz, H. L. Goodall Jr., Cynthia Hardy, Arthur Hulnick, Robert Ivie, John Lammers, Gordon Mitchell, Robert Newman, Nelson Phillips, and Amy Zegart. These scholars' work has served as both a model and resource, especially in how I have conceptualized the institution of intelligence, processes of organizational change, the shifting meanings of open source, and the role of citizens in national security affairs. Additionally, thanks are due to colleagues in the Department of Communication at the University of Colorado Denver. Special thanks are due to Senator Gary Hart, whose participation in this project kept me attuned to how my theoretical concerns could be translated into practical guidance for national security officials and policy makers.

This book would not have been possible without the support of Brooke Evans. I wish to acknowledge my former colleagues at Intellibridge, as well as dozens of Washington, DC, and Colorado friends and acquaintances whose identities and useful contributions on open source issues will, paradoxically, be kept secret in these acknowledgments. I can acknowledge, however, the support of Matt Sanders, Krista Belanger, Margaret Durfy, John McClellan, Erica Delgadillo, Mary Gray, Susan Brink, and Lauren Strand. I am forever indebted to my parents, Halimah Ashley and Reynold Bean, who have always been my most trusted sources of information and advice. Thank you to Max for being the motivation for this project. Finally, a portion of the proceeds from the sale of this book will be given to veterans' charities in honor of their service.

Abbreviations

ADDNI/OS	assistant deputy director of national intelligence for open source
CIA	Central Intelligence Agency
CIRA	Central Intelligence Retirees Association
COSPO	Community Open Source Program Office
DCI	director of central intelligence
DDNI/A	deputy director of national intelligence for analysis
DDNI/C	deputy director of national intelligence for collection
DHS	Department of Homeland Security
DIA	Defense Intelligence Agency
DNI	director of national intelligence
DoD	Department of Defense
EO	Executive Order
FAS	Federation of American Scientists
FBIS	Foreign Broadcast Information Service
FBMS	Foreign Broadcast Monitoring Service
FMA	foreign media analysis
FMSO	Foreign Military Studies Office
FSC	Family Steering Committee

GWOT	Global War on Terror
HUMINT	human intelligence
IAFIE	International Association for Intelligence Education
IC	intelligence community
ICD	Intelligence Community Directive
IMINT	imagery intelligence
INT	intelligence discipline
IO	information operations
IP	internet protocol
IRTPA	Intelligence Reform and Terrorism Prevention Act of 2004
ISE	Information Sharing Environment
JICPAC	Joint Intelligence Center, Pacific
JMIC	Joint Military Intelligence College
JTTF	Joint Terrorism Task Force
NASA	National Aeronautics and Space Administration
NATO	North Atlantic Treaty Organization
NGO	nongovernmental organization
NIB	National Intelligence Board
NIC	National Intelligence Council
NIE	National Intelligence Estimate
NIO	national intelligence officer
ODNI	Office of the Director of National Intelligence
ONI	Office of Naval Intelligence
OSC	Open Source Center
OSS	Office of Strategic Services
OSIF	open source information
OSINT	open source intelligence
PDB	President's Daily Brief
SARS	Severe Acute Respiratory Syndrome
SCI	Sensitive Compartmented Information
SIGINT	signals intelligence
SIPRNet	Secret Internet Protocol Router Network
SOUTHCOM	U.S. Southern Command

TQM	Total Quality Management
UAV	unmanned aerial vehicle
USG	United States government
WMD	weapons of mass destruction

CHAPTER 1

The Coming of Age
of Open Source

The need for a centralized agency to administer the growing exploitation of all foreign open sources of information is . . . already evident to rationalize the numerous efforts, all with similar objectives, going on simultaneously within and outside of the intelligence community.
　　—Central Intelligence Agency (CIA) *Studies in Intelligence* article, 1969[1]

I have seen an unprecedented increase in open-source awareness and in capabilities across the enterprise, and perhaps, most importantly, open source is starting to be institutionalized with formal plans, explicit budgets, and policy guidance across the various enterprises.
　　—Senior Director of National Intelligence (DNI) official, 2008[2]

The U.S. intelligence community has long acknowledged the need to institutionalize the collection, analysis, and dissemination of open source information derived from "newspapers, journals, radio and television," and, more recently, the Internet.[3] However, it was only in 2007 that U.S. officials formally declared the "coming of age" of open source at the inaugural DNI Open Source Conference, held July 16–17 at the Ronald Regan Building and International Trade Center in Washington, DC.[4] According to organizers, the conference was the first ever open to the public in the U.S. intelligence community's 60-year history.[5] Even Eliot Jardines, who became America's first assistant deputy director of national intelligence for open source (ADDNI/OS) in 2005, seemed surprised to be speaking at the conference, telling the audience, "Over the past years . . . I frequently felt like Kevin Costner in the movie 'Field of Dreams.' Believe me, proposing to the intelligence community that we have a free conference open to the general public and the media was something just as strange for my colleagues as building a baseball diamond in the middle of an Iowa cornfield."[6] The conference brought together more than 1,000 members of the U.S. intelligence community, academia, think tanks, media organizations, commercial firms, and governmental and nongovernmental organizations from the United States and abroad. These stakeholders came together to discuss the opportunities and challenges of gathering, analyzing, and disseminating information in a world saturated with communication technologies, 24/7 global media, and whistleblower websites—conditions that bolster the assertion of the CIA's Don Burke, who claimed in 2008 that "in 15 years, there will be no more secrets."[7]

There are, of course, plenty of secrets left for governments to uncover or conceal; the massive growth of classified U.S. intelligence programs in the wake of 9/11 demonstrates that secret intelligence endures.[8] Additionally, websites such as WikiLeaks have attracted public attention because they reveal information governments, corporations, and nongovernmental organizations would rather keep secret. The 2007 Open Source conference nevertheless underscored an identity crisis facing the U.S. intelligence community. Specifically, there has been an unprecedented increase in the amount and quality of publicly-available open source information, yet the U.S. intelligence community's response to this development has been characterized, alternately, by engagement, ambivalence, and outright conflict among government agencies and between those agencies and their private sector contractors. For intelligence contractor and commentator Ronald Marks, the reasons are clear: "The U.S. Intelligence Community is a first generation business lost in a new market; like the old IBM hanging on to mainframes in a PC world. Information was the Intelligence Community's game. Control of information was its business. And unique access to others' secrets was its advantage. Sadly, the Soviet Union is gone and the information technology explosion of the 1990's happened. Twitter has replaced teletypes."[9] These dynamics have led to new challenges.

For example, four months after the inaugural DNI Open Source Conference, in November 2007, the U.S. DNI released declassified portions of a National Intelligence Estimate (NIE) regarding Iran's nuclear intentions and capabilities. The NIE judged "with high confidence that in fall 2003, Tehran halted its nuclear weapons program."[10] Some of the evidence supporting that conclusion came from open sources. According to an MSNBC report, two pieces of publicly available video played a role: One piece showed former Iranian president Mohammad Khatami visiting the Iranian uranium enrichment facility in Natanz in March 2005; the other piece of video, from the same time frame, described the Iranian nuclear power program.[11] Both pieces of video helped officials gauge the progress of Iran's uranium enrichment program. The 2007 NIE's controversial findings sent shockwaves through the U.S. national security arena and continue to complicate U.S. policy toward Iran. Intelligence analysts use newspapers, journals, and radio and television broadcasts, as well as databases, commercial satellite imagery, blogs, and academic studies, to track states' nuclear activities.[12] This information helps analysts understand a state's energy needs, political and economic conditions, the perceptions of elites, and how these factors might influence a state's nuclear ambitions. Occasionally, technical information about specific facilities, materials, and research programs surfaces in open source reporting as well. For example, an analyst could determine from public records, reports, and subject matter experts the properties and specifications of the materials used during the construction process for a particular facility, the companies that helped build the facility, and the personnel involved. Challenges include open source's limited availability within closed societies and technical domains, its overwhelming abundance in other areas, its diversity in terms of language, and its uneven quality, reliability, and credibility.[13]

Despite these challenges, former assistant to the president for homeland security and counterterrorism, Frances Fragos Townsend, has noted, "Much of what is known about our enemies is derived from their own statements, blogs, videos, and chat sessions on the Internet."[14] Similarly, then CIA director Michael Hayden bluntly stated in 2008, "Secret information isn't always the brass ring in our profession. In fact, there's real satisfaction in solving a problem or answering a tough question with information that someone was dumb enough to leave out in the open."[15] Accordingly, much of what adversaries know about the United States is also derived from open source material. For example, in planning the 9/11 terrorist attacks, Khalid Sheikh Mohammed relied on information from "Western aviation magazines, telephone directories for U.S. cities, airline timetables, and . . . Internet searches on U.S. flight schools . . . supplemented by flight simulator software and information gleaned from movies depicting hijackings."[16] While open source contributions were not the deciding factor in the conclusions reached in the 2007 NIE on Iran's nuclear program, nor the success of the 9/11 attacks, these cases illustrate how open source information has become a critical resource for intelligence in the 21st century.

Prominent 9/11 and 2003 Iraq War inquiries have come to similar conclusions. The Weapons of Mass Destruction (WMD) Commission asserted in 2005, for example, "The Intelligence Community does not have an entity that collects, processes, and makes available to analysts the mass of open source information that is available in the world today."[17] According to a 2007 Congressional Research Service report, "Intelligence analysts have long used [open source] information to supplement classified data, but systematically collecting open source information has not been a priority of the U.S. Intelligence Community."[18] Writing about post-9/11 changes within Canada's intelligence sector, the former head of intelligence analysis noted in 2009, "The use by analysts of unclassified, freely available information from the internet or other open sources was not just desirable but essential. . . . However, getting access to open sources from within 'secret organizations' required a range of changes in longstanding methods, attitudes, rules, structures and processes and these took time."[19] Responding to similar conditions within the United States, officials established the DNI Open Source Center (OSC) in 2005 and simultaneously created the position of ADDNI/OS to coordinate and oversee the institutionalization of open source across the intelligence community.

The OSC built upon the CIA's Foreign Broadcast Information Service (FBIS), which was established in 1947. The OSC currently defines itself as the U.S. government's "premier provider of foreign open source intelligence."[20] The password-protected website supplies authorized government and contractor personnel with information on "foreign political, military, economic, and technical issues beyond the usual media from . . . more than 160 countries in more than 80 languages."[21] This information is derived from websites, press, broadcasts, television, radio, maps, databases, gray literature, photos, and commercial satellite imagery. A 2008 brochure stated that the OSC covers 2,000 periodical publications, 300 radio stations, and 235 television stations. In 2008, the OSC had more than 13,000 active customers—ranging from the president's national security team to municipal police officers. A 2009 DNI report stated, "OSC produces over 2,300 products daily, including translations, transcriptions, analyses, reports, video compilations, and geospatial intelligence, to address short-term needs and longer-term issues. Its products cover issues that range from foreign political, military, economic, science, and technology topics, to counterterrorism, counterproliferation, counternarcotics, and other homeland security topics. OSC also collects 'gray literature,' which is material with very limited distribution, such as academic papers, brochures, leaflets, and other publicly distributed materials."[22] The immense output from the OSC raises the question of whether any intelligence agency—or group of agencies—can effectively analyze it.

Nevertheless, in 2010, the stated vision of the OSC was the following: "We are the nucleus of a global information enterprise serving U.S. national security interests." Its stated mission was, "We apply our expertise in searching, acquiring and analyzing the world's publicly available information to inform and enable those who make US policy and defend our nation."[23] Given its mission, only some of the OSC's translations are made available to the general public through the subscription service World News Connection; the majority of its analytical products are available only to authorized government and contractor personnel.[24] The Federation of American Scientists' (FAS) Steven Aftergood notes, "Open source intelligence products . . . are often withheld from public disclosure, for

various reasons. These include habit, the cultivation of the mystique of secret intelligence, the protection of copyrighted information, and the pres-
ervation of 'decision advantage,' i.e. the policy-relevant insight that open
source intelligence at its best may offer."[25] Thus, a key theme explored in
this book is the extent to which open source reports are and/or should be
openly available.

Much of the information and analysis available to the OSC's users
comes from private sector information providers and experts. In 2008,
the OSC hosted material and analysis from 95 external organizations.[26]
These information suppliers included the Economist Intelligence Unit,
LexisNexis, Jane's industry publications, ProQuest, STRATFOR, Thom-
son Reuters, and Oxford Analytica, among others. In its effort to "build
a global state-of-the-art technical infrastructure to acquire, filter, process,
deliver, and protect the intelligence advantage [of the United States],"
the OSC also delivers an "extended community workforce of experts and
professionals."[27] While OSC experts and professionals are not spies—they
conduct their work mostly from behind their desks using the Internet—
their objectives are more-or-less similar to their clandestine counterparts.
Specifically, the job of these experts and professionals is to obtain information that might yield the U.S. government some strategic advantage or
protect its interests.[28]

For example, in early 2003, prior to the establishment of the OSC, Dan
Silver, a China analyst working for the open source contractor Intellibridge Corporation, was scanning Hong Kong's *Ming Pao* newspaper
online when he noticed an unusual story about an outbreak of atypical
pneumonia in the region.[29] Silver believed there was something odd about
the way the story was reported, so he immediately notified his client, the
U.S. Navy's Joint Intelligence Center, Pacific (JICPAC), as well as a handful of U.S. health officials. Silver was later given an award by the medical
information provider ProMED-mail for his reporting, which contributed,
in part, to the successful containment of what would later become known
as the global health epidemic SARS (severe acute respiratory syndrome).[30]
Numerous anecdotes like this one have helped mark the coming of age
of open source. This book explains why and how that coming of age occurred and explores the implications of these developments for national
security stakeholders, including officials, policy makers, contractors, and
citizens. I argue that the coming of age of open source is the result of post–
Cold War political, economic, and technological transformations and the
use of national security and commercial discourses by a handful of policy makers, officials, and executives who have worked to institutionalize
open source in ways that align with their strategic interests. Analyzing
how these policy makers, officials, and executives have used speech and
writing to promote and/or impede competing visions of institutional
change offers a unique way of understanding the post-9/11 reshaping of
U.S. intelligence.

WHO DRIVES OPEN SOURCE DEVELOPMENTS: GOVERNMENT OR INDUSTRY?

To understand how open source has risen to become a key plank within U.S. intelligence strategy, it is necessary to understand three converging events: the end of the Cold War; the innovation and global diffusion of information and communication technologies—especially the Internet; and the rise of private intelligence contractors at the end of the 1990s. Most commentators trace the U.S. government's first effort to formally collect and analyze open source information to World War II and the creation of the Foreign Broadcast Monitoring Service (FBMS). Under the National Security Act of 1947, the FBMS was renamed the Foreign Broadcast Information Service and placed within the CIA. Since that time, open source information has been known by many names, including "nonsecret information," "open information," "overt information," "overt intelligence," "public information," "unclassified information," and "white intelligence."[31] For most of the Cold War, the U.S. intelligence community was unable to analyze the bulk of *real-time* foreign news reporting and open source information because immediate access to those sources was limited. This situation changed dramatically toward the end of the 20th century.[32]

The dissolution of the Soviet Union in 1991 called into question established beliefs about U.S. national security. In a series of *New York Times* articles published in February 1992, for example, commentators questioned whether the demise of the Soviet Union undermined the need for the continued existence and expense of the CIA. One reporter noted that then director of central intelligence Robert Gates stated during his confirmation hearings that the CIA had been so narrowly focused on the Kremlin that the agency relied on travelers for information about other Soviet republics besides Russia.[33] In 1996, the Aspin-Brown Commission emphasized the need for improved open source collection and analysis in response to the post-Soviet geopolitical environment.[34] In 1998, the chairman of the National Intelligence Council (NIC), John Gannon, elaborated the consequences of the post-Soviet environment and the need for improved open source capabilities during a speech before the World Affairs Council: "Critical expertise we need to inform our analysis will increasingly be found outside the Intelligence Community, and our professionals will need to be out there to engage it. Technology will challenge us in every area of our business to be smarter, more agile, more customer focused, and more collaborative with experts, wherever they may be found. In a nutshell, we face some big challenges."[35] In this speech, Gannon linked the post-Soviet geopolitical environment with the rapid diffusion of information and communication technology, a development that created both problems and prospects for the U.S. intelligence community. Technology posed a problem for the intelligence community by intensifying the requisite speed of intelligence production, as well as increasing—*to nearly unmanageable levels*—the amount of available, and potentially useful, information for analysts to consider. This problem occurred as U.S. intelligence agencies experienced personnel cuts of 30 percent as a result of the initial post–Cold War "peace dividend."[36] As Gannon indicated, however, technology also offered the prospect of efficiently tapping sources of information and expertise outside the intelligence community, as well as potentially managing the surge of information entering the analytical process. Contracting with and/or outsourcing to private sector corporations possessing specialized expertise in information collection, analysis, and management thus became a way for the intelligence community to keep pace with rapid political, economic, and technological transformations.

The private sector has long been at the forefront of open source developments. For example, G. M. McGill, then vice president of government information services for LexisNexis, wrote this statement in the foreword to a 1994 volume concerning open source: "At the same time that intelligence communities were relying more and more on expensive compartmented technical collection systems with narrow focus . . . the private sector in general and the information industry in particular has literally exploded with an almost incomprehensible plethora of open sources, systems, and services."[37] Nearly 20 years later, the private sector has deepened its integration with the intelligence community. For example, Jardines, then owner of Open Source Publishing, Inc., in testimony before Congress in 2005, responded to one representative's question about why intelligence analysts did not simply conduct their own open source collection and analysis activities: "The reality is," Jardines stated, "if all-source analysts [had] the time and the expertise to do effective open source exploitation, I would be standing in the unemployment line right now."[38] Nine months after this hearing, Jardines would be named America's first assistant deputy director of national intelligence for open source and assume responsibility for the institutionalization of open source collection and analysis across the entire intelligence community. Jardines, of course, knew much about the private sector's open source activities within the intelligence community, having directly participated in them himself.

According to intelligence scholar William Lahneman, outsourcing within the intelligence community "refers to the practice of . . . turning over entire business functions to an outside vendor that ostensibly can perform the specialized tasks in question better and less expensively than [the intelligence community] can."[39] In the case of open source, a company may take over day-to-day responsibility for collecting, analyzing, and perhaps disseminating information on behalf of a government agency. These services are often provided through a combination of specialized analysts, experts, and technologies. The decision to outsource is based on the assumption that a given agency does not possess equivalent resources or expertise. Officials may assume that an open source contractor can provide services more cost-effectively than were the agency to try to re-create the contractor's analytical or technological capabilities in-house. The reality is more often that outsourcing open source can lead to exorbitant costs as providers rack up managerial fees and assign high-paid staff members to conduct mundane tasks in order to increase the overall bill to the government.

There are dozens of North American and European companies claiming to support U.S. government clients; consider just a handful of the exhibitors at the 2008 DNI Open Source Conference: AT&T Government Solutions, Google Enterprise, LexisNexis, Oracle USA, Inc., SAIC, and Sun Microsystems. Add to these some of the open source data mining and visual analytics companies exhibiting at a 2010 conference: Abraxas, Bivio Networks, BrightPlanet, Cray, DMC Worldwide, EON, Ercom, ExecutiveAction, iJet, Intelligence Rose Systems, Infosphere AB, Institute for Intelligence Studies, IPBank, MarkLogic, Narus, NICE Systems, OSINT Solutions, Oxford Analytica, Packet Forensics, Qosmos, SAIL Labs Technology, Sandstone, Silobreaker, TradeBytes Data Corporation, Verint Systems, Visual Analytics, and Xerobank/IPBank. Many of these companies offer specialized search engines and discovery tools designed to separate the open source wheat from the chaff—in other words, the policy-relevant information about people, events, and objects from the immense noise found within the online public sphere.[40]

There are no publicly available statistics regarding the level of outsourcing in the open source arena.[41] Depending on how open source is defined, the multimillion-dollar industry employs thousands of analysts, experts, technicians, and marketers worldwide.[42] The OSC's budget was estimated at around $100 million in 2005—still just a fraction of the more than $40 billion U.S. intelligence community budget.[43] According to investigative journalist Tim Shorrock, the rise of open source can be linked to the late 1990's growth of the intelligence-industrial complex—a distinct-yet-related counterpart to the military-industrial complex. Shorrock defines the intelligence-industrial complex as a secretive army of private sector intelligence collectors, analysts, and operators serving both government agencies and international corporations.[44] Prior to 9/11, this army consisted of major defense contractors including Booz Allen Hamilton, BAE Systems, CACI, ManTech, Northrop Grumman, SAIC, and many others. Intellibridge Corporation belonged to a subset of this group of companies known colloquially as "boutique intelligence shops."[45] Such shops tended to rely on open source information from the Internet, television, publications, archives, and experts as the foundation of their various intelligence services. The value-added content provided by these intelligence shops was, ostensibly, access to proprietary (but nonetheless unclassified) sources of information, translation services, and the customized analysis their in-house analysts and outside (subcontracted) experts provided to clients.

Today, such companies include Control Risks, Eurasia Group (which acquired the assets of Intellibridge in 2005), iJET, Jane's Information Group, Kroll, Oxford Analytica, STRATFOR, SITE Intelligence Group, and Total Intelligence Solutions, among others. One of these companies, SITE (Search for International Terrorist Entities), gained public attention in October 2007 when it was widely reported in mainstream news media that the company had provided U.S. intelligence agencies with exclusive access to a newly obtained videotape of Osama bin Laden. Unfortunately for SITE, Bush administration officials leaked the videotape with attribution to SITE to cable television news networks, thereby destroying SITE's surveillance operation, which had been used to intercept and pass along messages, videotapes, and warnings of suicide bombings to its clients.[46] SITE's experience demonstrates how open source often strikes a precarious balance with secrecy. Total Intelligence Solutions, in contrast to SITE, bills itself as a company that "brings the intelligence gathering methodology and analytical skills traditionally honed by CIA operatives directly to the board room."[47] Led by the former director of the CIA's Counterterrorist Center, Cofer Black, and executives formerly affiliated with the private military contractor Blackwater USA, Total Intelligence Solutions claims to "fuse" information from thousands of open and proprietary sources to create "predictive intelligence" for its clients.[48] Thus, the end of the Cold War and the diffusion of information and communication technologies contributed to the rise of a group of companies that most Americans have never heard of, but that nonetheless influence official decision-making processes within U.S. national security organizations and the world's elite corporations.

The intelligence community has acknowledged that contract employees populate roughly one-third of its ranks.[49] In its 2010 "Key Facts about Contractors," the DNI states, "Core contract personnel may perform activities such as collection and analysis; however, it is what you do with that analysis, who makes that decision, and who oversees the work that constitute the 'inherently governmental' functions."[50] The fact sheet is silent, of course, concerning how the revolving door between government agencies and private sector contractors actually works. At Intellibridge, I became familiar with this process. Intellibridge was established in 2000 by three former Clinton administration officials: National Security Advisor Anthony Lake, Director of Central Intelligence John Deutch, and a deputy undersecretary at the Department of Commerce, David Rothkopf. In 2001, the current U.S. ambassador to the United Nations, Susan Rice, along with Gayle Smith, currently special assistant to the president and senior director for development on the U.S. National Security Council, worked to sell Intellibridge services to African government clients. John Gannon (former NIC chairman) joined the company in 2002. When I joined Intellibridge in May 2001, I was immediately assigned to support the company's newest and largest client, Enron—the Houston-based, global energy and commodity-trading firm. Intellibridge had been hired to provide open source intelligence and public relations services to executives of the corporation that *Fortune* magazine named six times as "America's Most Innovative Company." When I arrived, however, Intellibridge was struggling to meet the exhausting demands of Enron's top managers. In a twist of fate, within six months, several of those managers would be under investigation by the U.S. Securities and Exchange Commission, and Enron would be well on its way to bankruptcy. Intellibridge, by contrast, would be positioning itself to profit from changes within the U.S. national security arena resulting from the 9/11 terrorist attacks.

Following 9/11, Intellibridge began hiring retired military officers who maintained ties with their former colleagues inside government agencies. These officers suggested to their former colleagues that it would be in their best interest to arrange a meeting with Intellibridge managers in order to receive a briefing on the capabilities of the company. Contractors, of course, hire former government and military officials precisely because those officials possess extensive connections across a range of the company's potential clients. At Intellibridge, government personnel usually agreed to a meeting, if only out of respect for their former colleagues. At these meetings, Intellibridge representatives attempted to persuade officials that the company possessed unique sources of information and unmatched analytical capabilities in support of their agency's mission. Occasionally, officials agreed to a test phase of Intellibridge's services, with the enticement of a larger contract pending a successful trial run.

Unnoticed by most commentators is a mechanism by which a preferred corporation can be steered a government contract. To comply with the Federal Acquisition Regulation, a government agency must generally distribute a contract solicitation for competitive proposals among qualified firms. These solicitations are distributed through public websites such as Federal Business Opportunities or via selected contracting vehicles, whereby only a handful of preapproved contractors are able to view and respond to the government's solicitation. By the time a solicitation appears on Federal Business Opportunities or another solicitation website, it has often been so narrowly tailored to a particular company's capabilities that other firms are effectively eliminated from consideration because those firms cannot adequately meet the government's specialized requirements. The goal of contractors is to shape the solicitation process itself so that it is difficult for competitors to meet the government's tailored requirements.

One example of how this process occurs is illustrated using the case of the U.S. Southern Command (SOUTHCOM). In 2004, Intellibridge personnel made repeated visits to command headquarters in Tampa, Florida, to showcase Intellibridge's analytical reports concerning geopolitical, economic, technological, and social trends and events within the SOUTHCOM Area of Responsibility. Impressed, SOUTHCOM officials agreed to develop and issue a solicitation for open source support. In practice, there is nothing that prevents a government agency from simply dropping a company's marketing materials or sample statement of work wholesale into its own solicitation, thereby ensuring that a preferred company will be the most likely winner of the competitive selection process. Pinpointing such soft abuses of power is difficult for intelligence stakeholders because it requires having access to the marketing materials used by a given corporation to woo potential government clients. Only by tracing the degree of overlap between a given statement of work and a corporation's tailored sales pitch is it possible to determine whether work had been steered to a preferred company via an inappropriately skewed contracting process.

These dynamics raise the following questions: How have competing national security and commercial imperatives influenced the development of open source plans, policies, and practices? How have these developments contributed to the reshaping of U.S. intelligence? What are the actual and potential consequences of this reshaping for officials, policy makers, and citizens? These are among the core questions explored in this book; their answers hinge on the way stakeholders construct the meaning of open source.

"INFORMATION TO INTELLIGENCE" AND THE MEANING OF OPEN SOURCE

In 1992, the CIA's open source coordinator asked a question in an article published in the *American Intelligence Review*: "But what, precisely, is the meaning of open source?"[51] Who is permitted to answer that question and how it is answered are critical for understanding the reshaping of U.S. intelligence. Edward Schiappa argues that shaping the meaning of a concept is a political act. Such a perspective turns attention away from the "is" of a concept toward the "ought" of its rhetorical constitution.[52] For example, the OSC's tagline is "Information to Intelligence," and among its objectives is to "redefine 'open source' as one of the 21st Century's most important sources of intelligence."[53] In the chapters that follow, I examine the specific ways officials and commentators have promoted that redefinition in different contexts, the impediments these individuals have faced in doing so, and the opportunities such a redefinition may offer citizens seeking to participate in national security deliberations through a variety of means and methods. Studying the post-9/11 institutionalization of open source provides a window into a paradoxically secretive and closely defended world, offering researchers a chance to scrutinize its dynamics without unduly exacerbating those traits. Illustrating the paradox of open source, then ADDNI/OS Jardines stated in 2006, "The number of open source items provided in the President's Daily Brief have increased . . . I would say we're scoring some wins with our most important customer."[54]

Jardines later stated, however, "I can't get into detail of what [open source reporting goes into the President's Daily Brief]."[55] Certainly, there are limits to the openness of open source.

It is important to clearly explain that this book investigates open source not to assert a preferred definition of the term, nor to explain how open sources can best be gathered and used to support U.S. government interests (i.e., whether open source could improve prediction- and/or threat-based intelligence analysis). Readers interested in these questions should consult this book's bibliography for practitioner-oriented literature. This book instead explores the struggle over the *meaning* of open source and the implications of that struggle for officials, policy makers, and citizens. For example, if open source is the "bread and butter of analysis," as one commentator asserts, then slighting it as an intelligence resource makes little sense.[56] Likewise, if open source is defined as material that any member of the public can lawfully obtain, how does that complicate the relationship between intelligence agencies and citizens? Due to these ambiguities, the concept of open source has become contested within institutional reform. As the Congressional Research Service states, "In recent years, given changes in the international environment, there have been calls, from Congress and the 9/11 Commission among others, for a more intense and focused investment in open source collection and analysis. However, some still emphasize that the primary business of intelligence continues to be obtaining and analyzing secrets."[57] How various meanings of open source are constructed, disseminated, and interpreted will determine whether and how this situation will change.

In the aftermath of 9/11 and Iraq, U.S. intelligence and national security organizations have grappled with numerous reforms aimed at preventing terrorist attacks and avoiding intelligence failures. Among the most high profile of these reforms are the institutionalization of open source collection and analysis within the intelligence community and the sharing of intelligence and information with new international and domestic partners. Former DNI official William Nolte argues that these changes, along with the broad definition of intelligence contained within the Intelligence Reform and Terrorism Prevention Act of 2004 (IRTPA), "may provide a significant opportunity to rethink intelligence: what it is, what we want its instrumental role in American society to be, and how we as citizens want to operate within the broader framework of American laws and values."[58] Responding to Nolte, this book engages three specific open source developments: (1) the influence of open source vis-à-vis the trajectory of post-9/11 institutional reform; (2) the relationship between open source and organizational culture within the context of U.S. homeland security; and (3) the democratic dimensions of open source; specifically, the relationships among open source, institutional reform, and deliberation of U.S. national security affairs. Each of these themes is introduced in the following, returning to my work with Intellibridge as a guide.

Open Source and U.S. Intelligence Community Reform

The U.S. intelligence community is nominally a federation of executive branch agencies and organizations that conduct activities necessary for the performance of U.S. foreign affairs and national security. These activities include intelligence collection, analysis, and dissemination, as well as "such other intelligence activities as the President may direct from time to time" and "special activities"—in other words, clandestine operations.[59] By formal standards, the U.S. intelligence community is relatively small, comprising just 16 agencies. The official members of the U.S. intelligence community include Air Force Intelligence, Army Intelligence, Central Intelligence Agency, Coast Guard Intelligence, Defense Intelligence Agency, Department of Energy, Department of Homeland Security, Department of State, Department of the Treasury, Drug Enforcement Administration, Federal Bureau of Investigation, Marine Corps Intelligence, National Geospatial-Intelligence Agency, National Reconnaissance Office, National Security Agency, and Navy Intelligence. Congress created the position of the director of national intelligence in 2004 to serve as the head of the intelligence community; oversee and direct the implementation of the National Intelligence Program; integrate foreign, military, and domestic intelligence; and act as the principal advisor to the president and the National Security Council. The intelligence community would be ranked roughly 50th in the Fortune 500 if its annual budget were analogous to revenue. However, hundreds of commercial organizations provide the intelligence community with technology, information, and management systems; analysts; and support staff among other goods, services, and personnel. It is thus more useful and accurate to view the U.S. intelligence community as a significant economic sector comprising both government agencies and their private sector partners.

My work for Intellibridge from 2001 to 2005 brought me into contact with numerous national security officials within the CIA, the White House, the Pentagon, and intelligence organizations. I witnessed firsthand how institutional imperatives—the "constraints, organizational premises, plans, expectations, acceptable justifications, and traditions inherited from predecessors"—shaped the actions of national security officials.[60] For example, Defense Intelligence Agency (DIA) officials routinely sought specialized open source information (on issues, for example, surrounding adversaries' military facilities, personnel, and weapons systems and programs) from private sector organizations in order to increase the contributions that DIA's subunits made to the War on Terror. It is reasonable to assume that DIA officials sought such outside support, in part, because their successful demonstration of innovative intelligence contributions to national security planning and decision making increased the likelihood of larger annual budget appropriations for their respective subunits. These dynamics may help explain why, in one meeting I attended, a DIA official agreed to a million-dollar contract with Intellibridge on the basis of a colleague's recommendation and the evaluation of only *one* of Intellibridge's written reports. As a result of similar experiences during my interactions with other officials, I became concerned with how open source advocates were influencing—for better and worse—the unfolding of post-9/11 intelligence reform.

Let me be clear here: open source can certainly make useful contributions to national security planning and decision making. The language surrounding open source, with its emphasis on "openness," "competing perspectives," "cost-effectiveness," and "public-private collaboration," seems to challenge some of the secretiveness and insularity of the U.S. intelligence community. As a result, I have become interested in how national security institutions change, the role of communication and culture within these processes, and the prospects of increased democratic deliberation of U.S. national security policy. These issues have directed my attention to institutional discourse—the constellations of talk and text that constitute particular understandings and practices as "popular, important, and widely applicable" within U.S. intelligence and national security affairs.[61] During my work for Intellibridge, I observed the critical importance of official and unofficial documents—such as reports, plans, directives, and correspondence—for developments within the intelligence sector. For example, from 2002 to 2005, a handful of open source contractors were locked in fierce competition for intelligence officials' patronage. The strategic production and distribution by these contractors of numerous and diverse texts—emails, letters, presentations, reports, and marketing materials—became the principal method for them to gain clients' attention, influence their thinking about the value of open source, and persuade them to procure open source services. Communication uniquely shapes the open source arena.

By 2005, Intellibridge's market had shifted almost exclusively to the government sector. The company had supported clients such as the Armed Forces Medical Intelligence Center, Chief of Naval Operations, Defense Intelligence Agency, Missile and Space Intelligence Center, Missile Defense Agency, Office of the Secretary of Defense, U.S. Pacific Air Forces, Air Force Intelligence and Analysis Agency, Commander Naval Forces Europe, Department of Agriculture, Foreign Broadcast Information Service, JICPAC, Naval War College, Office of Naval Intelligence, and SOUTHCOM. During this period, overall intelligence contracting and outsourcing for personnel, equipment, and services climbed and by 2007 accounted for roughly 70 percent of the $44 billion U.S. intelligence budget.[62] The rapid growth of open source contracting and outsourcing activities throughout the intelligence community prompted, in part, the creation of the ADDNI/OS in 2005. The ADDNI/OS was established to oversee and manage the institutionalization of open source throughout the intelligence community. The ADDNI/OS reports to the deputy director of national intelligence for collection (DDNI/C), who, in turn, reports to the DNI. The first case study in this book, in chapter 4, centers mainly on the activities of the ADDNI/OS and the various officials across the intelligence community involved in the ADDNI/OS's initiatives. I have obtained copies of key texts produced and disseminated by the ADDNI/OS, as well as various speeches and media reports. Additionally, since 2007, there have been two major open source conferences sponsored by the DNI, both of which I attended.

Open Source, Cultural Change, and U.S. Homeland Security

In early 2002, recognizing that the Internet could be leveraged to spur tighter integration and collaboration among organizations possessing a newfound homeland security mandate, Intellibridge was among the first companies to market a daily electronic newsletter—*Homeland Security Monitor*—to officials who suddenly found themselves responsible for preparing for a new array of perceived security threats. Dozens of governmental and commercial organizations distribute homeland security newsletters and other information services to officials.[63] Chapter 5 examines how the meanings of open source are reconfigured within the context of homeland security information sharing. Information sharing between federal, state, and local agencies is a key element of the U.S. government's post-9/11 homeland security strategy. Recently created fusion centers operated by state agencies integrate, analyze, and disseminate federal, state, local, tribal, and private sector homeland security information. These fusion centers have been established in most U.S. states in order to "provide a more accurate picture of risks to people, economic infrastructure, and communities [that] can be developed and translated into protective action."[64] The collection, analysis, and dissemination of open source information are central fusion center tasks. However, questions remain concerning the effects of lingering negative attitudes toward open source. As Frank Cilluffo, director of the Homeland Security Policy Institute, stated in testimony before Congress in 2008, "I think some of the better [homeland security intelligence] products are actually open source. . . . If [an intelligence product] has that marking with a code word on it [meaning that the information is classified], we think it is better. That doesn't mean it is better."[65] During the same hearing, however, Matthew Bettenhausen, executive director of California's Office of Homeland Security, stated, "Open source is very important because you can pull a lot of this [information] together. Sometimes we get more timely information from reading the news reports than we do in getting the [official intelligence] products.

I mean, you know, the National Intelligence Estimate—we were reading about what was in there in the paper for a week before we ever even got a briefing from DHS on it. That is frustrating, and that has to change."[66] These comments illustrate the ambiguity surrounding how open source information sharing is actually understood and conducted by those responsible for preventing and managing homeland security emergencies.

One reason for this condition is that commentators have largely overlooked the institutional dynamics that shape the meanings of open source. After 9/11, these institutional dynamics have involved cultural change initiatives. For example, the DNI has called for a shift from a "need to know" culture of secrecy to a "responsibility to provide" culture of sharing.[67] Therefore, a second theme explored in this book is the relationship between institutional discourse and organizational culture. As intelligence scholar Gregory Treverton says, there is perhaps no greater truism within reform discourse than that effective collaboration and "real" reforms require changing not just institutional structures, but the *cultures* of intelligence, law enforcement, and emergency management organizations.[68] In the aftermath of 9/11, cultural change has been repeatedly asserted and codified as an institutional reform strategy—recently appearing as a central plank of the White House's *National Strategy for Information Sharing* in 2007 and the Information Sharing Environment's (ISE) *Annual Report to the Congress* in 2010. While top-down prescriptions for cultural change are politically appealing, the actuality of cultural change remains theoretically contentious and empirically complex.[69] This book thus scrutinizes how language mediates cultural change in organizations relying on open source collection and analysis to support homeland security information-sharing activities.

Open Source and Citizen Participation in National Security Affairs

Nolte argues that the institutionalization of open source, improved information sharing among agencies, and the review of security practices represent the "iron triangle" (i.e., the three most important components) of U.S. intelligence reform.[70] This book modifies that triangle by revising the component of security practices as "the public dimensions of intelligence." By public dimensions, I mean questions concerning what information ought to be shared with the public. I was largely unaware of such concerns while working at Intellibridge; I assumed, like most Americans, that intelligence was the business of national security elites. Nevertheless, while I marketed Intellibridge's open source services to organizations within the U.S. intelligence community throughout 2002 and 2003, four 9/11 widows from New Jersey were simultaneously conducting their own open source collection activities. These widows, who later joined with others to become known collectively as the "9/11 families," used the Internet to collect detailed information about the 9/11 attacks and institutional responses, helping them achieve what appeared to be an unprecedented level of participation in U.S. national security affairs.[71]

The 9/11 Commission was established on November 27, 2002, and ceased operations on August 21, 2004. Americans followed the 9/11 Commission hearings as witnesses, the 10 commissioners, and the commission's staff attempted to uncover the facts surrounding the attacks. The commission's work culminated in its *Final Report*. Through the subsequent reorganization of U.S. intelligence based on the 9/11 Commission's recommendations as codified in IRTPA and the Implementing Recommendations of the 9/11 Commission Act of 2007, the 9/11 Commission's work endures. Most commentators agree that the 9/11 Commission would not have been formed without the efforts of the Family Steering Committee (FSC) for the 9/11 Independent Commission.[72] The FSC organized 9/11 victims who were lobbying Congress to create an independent commission to investigate the 9/11 attacks. A leader of the FSC, Kristen Breitweiser, recounts in her memoir, "As the battle for a 9/11 commission began, we gathered mountains of information while patched together on the phone each night. In the midst of conversation, one of us would shout out some new tidbit of information, which would then lead to all of us researching that particular topic over the Internet for hours, sometimes days, at a time."[73] Despite opposition from the Bush administration, the FSC successfully worked with lawmakers to establish a commission to investigate the 9/11 attacks. In the process, the 9/11 families appeared to achieve a remarkable level of direct (although temporary) participation in national security affairs.

More recently, the controversial whistleblower website WikiLeaks rocketed to headlines in 2010 when it released the Afghan War Diary, the Iraq War Logs, and U.S. Embassy Cables, respectively. These unauthorized disclosures of secret information prompted myriad responses from officials, commentators, and citizens concerned with their influence within national security affairs. Thus, the cases of the 9/11 families and websites such as WikiLeaks provide opportunities to speculate, in chapters 6 and 7, how open source developments could contribute to opportunities for more citizens to actively participate in U.S. national security dilberations.[74]

ORGANIZATION OF THE BOOK

The WMD Commission asserted in 2005 that "many open source materials may provide the critical and perhaps only window into activities that threaten the United States."[75] This book, therefore, engages open source and the reshaping of U.S. intelligence in order to assess the institutionalization of open source within three areas: (1) the U.S. intelligence community, (2) the homeland security sector, and (3) the citizen activism arena. I continue this discussion in chapter 2 by highlighting the U.S. government's effort to formally collect and analyze open source information during World War II and the subsequent Cold War and immediate post–Cold War periods. This chapter sets the stage for post-9/11 open source developments discussed later in the book. Chapter 3 develops the inter-connections among institutions, organizational discourse, and national security rhetoric. This chapter advances a discourse-oriented perspective to interpret the case studies of open source that follow. This perspective is used, in part, because institutional secrecy generally prevents schol-ars from immersing themselves within intelligence and national security agencies. However, the sites chosen for this research yielded accessible materials of sufficient quantity and variety to permit an examination of the complex dynamics of institutional change.

Chapters 4, 5, and 6 provide three case studies of the post-9/11 reshaping of U.S. intelligence and national security. Specifically, chapter 4 examines the development of open source within the U.S. intelligence community in order to explore the relationships among institutions, discourse, and change. Chapter 5 sustains discussion of these issues by investigating how open source is reconfigured in the context of homeland security. Chapter 6 engages the normative dimensions of open source through exploring how its development could potentially bolster citizen participation in national security affairs. Chapter 7, the final chapter, describes public intelligence websites and the challenges of developing a more democratic intelligence sector, as well as summarizes the contributions of this book for stakehold-ers such as institutional members, policy makers, scholars, and citizens. An appendix discusses specific open source contexts and practices in order to provide readers an overview of what open source–related work can include.

SOURCES, METHODOLOGIES, AND THEORETICAL PERSPECTIVES

Intelligence scholar James Wirtz notes that "compared to other na-tions . . . Americans appear to be remarkably open about discussing poli-cies, procedure, failure and even tradecraft employed by their intelligence organizations."[76] Although securing interviews with institutional mem-bers remains challenging, the public archive of relevant information and reasonably accessible research sites and stakeholders creates adequate op-portunity for scholarly work. In conducting this work, I relied on pub-licly available documents, the remarks of officials concerning internal government documents, and interview data. Materials obtained for this book include transcripts of speeches, directives, strategic plans, policy memoranda, congressional hearing transcripts, commercial documents, conference materials, memoirs, books, articles, documentaries, archival material, news coverage, and interviews with current and former gov-ernment officials, corporate executives, law enforcement officials and an-alysts, scholars, and citizen activists. Therefore, the reader should have confidence that the research presented herein adequately accounts for key institutional documents under existing constraints.

My direct engagement with open source issues spans from 2001 to 2010—the four-year period prior to the establishment of new open source organizational structures in 2005 and (subsequently, as a scholar) through the first five years of open source's formal institutionalization under the guidance of the ADDNI/OS. Open source as a concept has existed in one form or another since the formation of the U.S. intelligence community. Nevertheless, my professional background and training in communication studies provides me with a unique perspective on open source at a critical juncture in its development. From 2007 to 2009, I conducted semi-structured interviews with more than 50 current and former national security and homeland security officials, analysts, contractors, citizen activists, and other stakeholders in order to understand their perspectives concerning the institutionalization of open source. All these figures were in some way central to the questions explored in this book and/or possessed specialized knowledge of intelligence, national or homeland security, and open source issues. I identified participants based on my prior work experience, books, articles, and websites, and the "Participant Contact Information" booklet distributed during the 2008 DNI Open Source Conference. The methodologies used in conducting this research included discourse analysis, rhetorical criticism, interviews, and observations.[77] By critically contrasting institutional members' understandings with officials' intentions, discourse analysis, rhetorical criticism, and interviews complement one another.[78] While I conducted participant observation at two public open source conferences during the course of this study, I used field notes primarily to supplement my interpretations of document and interview data.

As a communication scholar, I am generally concerned in this book with three overlapping dimensions of discourse: (1) textual practice, (2) discursive practice, and (3) social practice.[79] Textual practice involves the study of the production of texts. Here, I examine how open source documents and speeches draw on other texts and discourses to establish the legitimacy of open source, as well as the authority of the actors responsible for its institutionalization. Discursive practice involves the study of how language and images are used to reproduce or transform the identities, relationships, and belief systems of institutional members. Here, my focus is on how representations across texts work to establish officials' preferred understandings of open source and national security more broadly. I study how official open source texts draw on powerful national security themes and neoliberal assumptions to construct the concept of open source in specific ways. Finally, social practice, as the term is used here and in other studies, involves an assessment of how institutional members actually respond to texts.[80] Here, I assess how stakeholders make sense of open source developments within their everyday organizational routines and practices. I gauge to what extent official open source texts appear to influence the thoughts and behaviors of institutional members.

These three levels of practice should be viewed as interrelated and mutually influential. The authors of texts, as well as audiences, bring different backgrounds and perspectives to the production and reception of discourse, thereby rendering clear-cut or stable claims about cause and effect awkward. A person may passively accept—in whole or in part—a text's preferred representation of open source; however, that same person may also challenge or resist aspects of that representation, thereby potentially influencing subsequent textual, discursive, and social practices. Given the context, scope, and objectives of this book, it is neither possible nor desirable to fully examine all three dimensions of discourse within each case study. By focusing primarily on textual and discursive levels of practice in the first case study in chapter 4 and social practice in the second and third case studies in chapters 5 and 6, I am able to offer a richer assessment of open source developments. Additionally, the examples of textual practice explored in the second case study are similar to those analyzed in the first. In other words, the official texts involved in open source discourse within the homeland security sector are generally the ones that influence open source's diffusion across the broader U.S. national security apparatus. Additionally, there are no official open source texts within the citizen activism arena; therefore, my understanding of these groups' discourse is derived from archival material and interview data.

The discourse-analytic scheme advanced herein follows studies that have investigated the connections between discourse and institutional change.[81] Discussion of the texts that I have selected for analysis is provided in the associated case studies. Institutional texts were selected based on their importance as identified by statute, directive, or strategic plan; the frequency of their appearance within the discursive milieu; and institutional members' statements concerning their influence. During the past nine years, I have collected hundreds of fragments of open source discourse in digital and material form. My analysis centers on inductive and deductive categorization of the multiple depictions of open source circulating within the field; identifying vocabularies, logics, and underlying theories of change; pinpointing key processes of textual production and dissemination; and, finally, assessing the influence of these processes on the beliefs and practices of institutional members at multiple levels.

Finally, my aim in this book is to provide an example of communication scholarship that combines a concern for the internal, institutional dynamics of intelligence with the broader, public dimensions of national security discourse. I do this by developing what I term an institutional discourse perspective (elaborated in chapter 3), which combines insights primarily from the fields of organizational discourse and rhetoric. Organizational discourse scholars investigate patterns in the production, distribution, and consumption of texts to understand processes of stability and change within organizations and institutions. These texts may take a variety of forms but are generally symbolic expressions that are meaningful to the people who make and interpret them, rule in and/or rule out ways of thinking about phenomena, are accessible to others, and *construct*—rather than simply reflect—social reality.[82] In this way, organizational discourse scholarship complements rhetoric's traditional focus on public statements, the actual or potential effects of these statements, processes of identification and persuasion, and how these phenomena enhance or degrade possibilities for ethical communication.[83] By pursuing this combination, I am able to more effectively trace open source discourse across institutional and public spheres and assess the implications of its development for officials, policy makers, and citizens.

Despite the popularity of discourse-centered research, the study of intelligence remains largely overlooked by organizational theorists and organizational communication scholars. Christopher Grey writes: "Agencies relating to intelligence, counter-terrorism, warfare, defence procurement, policing and so on can be understood as organizational apparatuses which could be studied in similar ways to any other organization. In fact, such studies are rare when compared to almost any other sector . . . Security agencies, with perhaps the exception of the police, are notably absent from the [organization studies] repertoire."[84] Responding to Grey, this book places intelligence studies and organization studies in conversation in order to invigorate both. I agree with Grey when he writes, "The issues of human security, broadly conceived, are pressing and complex . . . They are also in no small measure organizational. An organization studies that matters should have something to say about them."[85] This book's approach enables me to simultaneously explain how language organizes the institutional complexities of post-9/11 intelligence reform and explore what these developments could portend for the future of U.S. national security.

This book also brings the fields of organizational discourse and rhetoric together to explore the interrelationships between internal/organizational and external/public communication. In doing so, I respond to calls from scholars to develop interdisciplinary perspectives in order to study institutions that cut across the domains of science, national security, public policy, and citizen activism.[86] The case of open source provides a useful example of how texts are imbued with organizing properties, become distributed and interpreted by actors, and both influence and are influenced by broader public discourses.[87] In studying open source discourse across institutional and public spheres, this book is similar to the work of communication scholars including H. L. Goodall Jr., Gordon Mitchell, Robert Newman, and Bryan Taylor. These scholars' body of work displays an exemplary mobility in shifting between the contexts of organizational/institutional communication and public/cultural rhetoric. Scholars who work at the boundaries of established fields face the challenge of maintaining fidelity to each field while simultaneously integrating their perspectives to generate new knowledge. Despite the challenge of integration, boundary-spanning studies are increasingly needed within the field of communication in order to account for complex sites of meaning making—where the influence of political forces, managerial discourses, citizen activism, and cultural values cannot be easily bracketed. This book thus illustrates one boundary-spanning approach for scholars working at the intersection of communication, organization, and security.

CHAPTER 2

The Origins of the
Open Source Debate

The Defense Communications Board recommends a substantial expansion in monitoring activities of the Federal Communications Commission to include continuous recordings of foreign press and propaganda broadcasts which can he heard within the United States.
—U.S. Defense Communications Board, 1940[1]

Everyone is by now aware that a virtual tidal wave of publicly printed paper threatens to swamp almost all enterprises of intellectual research.
—CIA *Studies in Intelligence* article, 1969[2]

In CIA alone, the amount of open source information has grown by a factor of ten over the past four years.
—Aspin-Brown Commission, 1996[3]

Espionage has been called the world's second-oldest profession.[4] In biblical times, spies gathered both secrets and openly available information.[5] Elizabethan England spymasters treated "news" and "secret information" as synonyms.[6] Commentators, however, generally identify World War II as the catalyst of contemporary open source developments.[7] Specifically, in the United States, the onset of World War II spurred the creation of the Foreign Broadcast Monitoring Service.[8] Figure 2.1 is a timeline of open source history provided by the OSC on its public website.

As both the timeline and the chapter epigraphs make clear, officials have long acknowledged the necessity of gathering and analyzing open source information in support of U.S. national security interests. For just as long, commentators have questioned the adequacy of the government's

Figure 2.1:
History of the Open Source Center

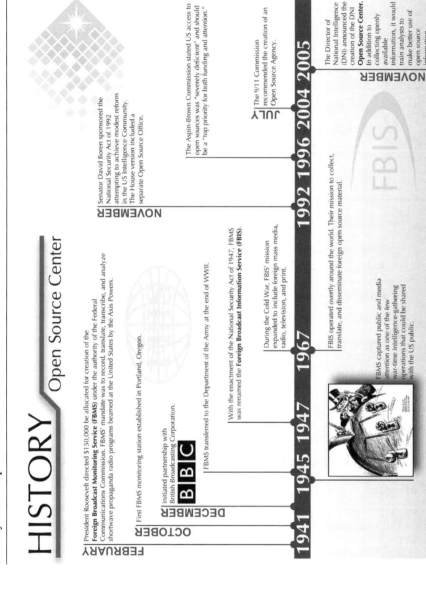

Source: Open Source Center.

open source plans, policies, and practices. The aim of this chapter is not to provide a comprehensive history of open source but instead to identify key themes and developments in order to place post-9/11 events in context. Other commentators have written about the history of FBMS/FBIS; that material is only summarized here.[9] This chapter instead examines World War II–era challenges using the case of the U.S. Navy's chief public information officer from 1941 to 1943, William W. Drake. Drake's wartime experiences evoke questions that any contemporary open source stakeholder would recognize: What should be the role of the press in U.S. intelligence affairs? What are the dangers of open source's availability to U.S. adversaries? How can stakeholders pinpoint the specific contributions that open source makes to national security planning and decision making? Answers to these questions suggest that although open source technologies have radically changed since World War II, associated ambiguities and dilemmas have remained remarkably stable.

Cold War open source developments were characterized by a steady increase in the amount of publicly available information and the government's struggle to effectively obtain and analyze it. However, geopolitical and technological conditions limited the scope and scale of formal open source initiatives. As former NIC chairman, John Gannon, recalled in 2005, "[Prior to the mid-1980s, it] used to take me . . . about 14 days to get a newspaper from the Caribbean and Latin America where I was covering, and policymakers were quite willing to wait for me to finish my analysis and fill the very large information gaps with my judgments and my expertise."[10] As a result of these conditions, the drumbeat for a more deliberate approach to open source exploitation became much louder in the post–Cold War period, when the diffusion of global media and information technology rapidly accelerated.

Several figures have uniquely influenced post–Cold War open source developments: among the most notable are open source advocate Robert David Steele; former Connecticut congressman Rob Simmons; the first ADDNI/OS, Eliot Jardines; and the director of the OSC, Doug Naquin. Perhaps more than any other figure, Steele has done more in the past two decades to advance public awareness of open source issues. Yet Steele's vision of open source organizational structure has remained largely outside of official policy. This chapter explains some of the reasons for this situation and sets the stage for the post-9/11 institutionalization of open source described in the remainder of this book.

THE CATALYST OF WORLD WAR II

The events of December 7, 1941, drew the United States into the war and forever changed the global political order. William W. Drake covered that story and participated in its unfolding. As maritime reporter and editor for the *Los Angeles Times*, Drake chronicled the rise of Japan's power throughout the 1930s by closely following the movements of the Japanese fishing fleet and merchant ships from Southern California. His articles described ship movements and cargo and tracked Japan's rush to stockpile oil, chemicals, cotton, and scrap metal. With his extensive knowledge of the world's naval and commercial vessels, plus his connections with naval, press, and civilian officials, the Intelligence Office of the 11th Naval District and members of the Office of Naval Intelligence (ONI) inevitably approached Drake as a source of information.[11]

The Office of Strategic Services (OSS)—the precursor to the CIA—also gathered public and secret information to support U.S. intelligence activities during World War II. Historian Kathy Peiss notes, "Despite its reputation for glamorous exploits, much of its work, perhaps a majority of it, involved prosaic tasks of gathering and analyzing published materials. Its founder, William 'Wild Bill' Donovan, believed that intelligence could be learned from open sources, and he sought broad-based, contextualizing information about, for example, industrial production, transportation patterns, and the psychology of the enemy."[12] Along these lines, Drake was the ideal contact for ONI: a respected maritime editor who had carte blanche access to ships coming in and out of Southern California's ports. As an officer in the U.S. Naval Reserve, Drake knew most of the officers in the U.S. Pacific Fleet, and he knew many of the captains of the commercial ships that regularly visited the port of San Pedro.[13]

The 11th Naval District was headquartered in San Diego but covered the area from above Los Angeles to Baja, California. U.S. Navy officials had become increasingly suspicious of the first- and second-generation Japanese living and working near military installations and defense plants in Southern California. In his capacity as maritime editor, Drake likely passed any rumors of Japanese espionage activities along to ONI.[14] In 1940, ONI stepped up its counterintelligence operations against the Japanese, and Drake, who had served 19 years with the *Los Angeles Times,* took a leave of absence in order to take charge of the Los Angeles District Naval Intelligence Office.[15] Thus Drake, who had gained his vast knowledge of maritime issues through open sources, became a key player in attempts to thwart alleged Japanese espionage in Southern California.

In May 1941, Drake was called to active duty. He received orders to report to Admiral Arthur J. Hepburn, director of naval public relations in Washington, DC.[16] Drake spent several weeks in Washington attending meetings and briefings and was told that he would assume the title of press relations officer for the entire Pacific Fleet, which in 1939 had been moved from the West Coast to Pearl Harbor, Hawaii. Drake found himself in Pearl Harbor on the eve of the Japanese attack consolidating Navy public relations and serving as the link between the American people and the Pacific Fleet. Drake censored and released stories to the press and planned pictures and articles to humanize the Navy. In other words, Drake generated favorable press so that officials in Washington would allocate funds to supply the Navy with needed materials for its buildup in the Pacific.

On the morning of December 6, 1941, at 8:00 A.M., Drake met Joseph C. Harsch, a correspondent for the *Christian Science Monitor*, in the reception area of Pacific Fleet's headquarters.[17] Admiral Kimmel, the commander of the Pacific Fleet, had agreed to an interview with Harsch, and Drake was there, as usual, to oversee press matters. Harsch was somewhat puzzled by the relaxed atmosphere: there was no hint of an impending crisis. Once he was able to, Harsch wasted no time in asking Kimmel the question that was on everyone's mind: "Admiral, is there going to be a war out here?" "No," Kimmel replied confidently, "the Japanese cannot attack us in the Pacific without running the risk of a two-front war. The Japanese are too smart to run that risk. No, young man, I don't think they'd be such damned fools!" Following the interview, Kimmel called Drake into his office and asked him to show Harsch "around Wheeler Field and the Army area over the hill."[18] While Drake showed Harsch around the military areas of Oahu, open source developments reached a milestone.

Foreign Broadcast Monitoring Service

Specifically, on this day, the newly established FBMS, headquartered in Washington, DC, issued its first analytical report based on the previous week's monitoring of Japanese radio transmissions conducted from its bureau in Portland, Oregon. FBMS's December 6 report warned readers: "Japanese radio intensifies still further its defiant, hostile tone; in contrast to its behavior during earlier periods of Pacific tension, Radio Tokyo makes no peace appeals. Comment on the United States is bitter and increased; it is broadcast not only to this country, but to Latin America and Southeastern Asia."[19] The FBMS report was the culmination of two years of organizational changes within the U.S. government. A declassified *Studies in Intelligence* article describes how the United States, following the United Kingdom's growing concern over German propaganda beamed via shortwave radio, began efforts to monitor foreign transmissions.[20] The first organized effort to analyze the content of foreign radio broadcasts was established at Princeton University (the "Princeton Listening Post") in 1939, followed by Stanford University's monitoring of Asia-based broadcasts.[21] Government officials within the State Department, increasingly concerned about foreign propaganda, began pushing for a more formal monitoring organization. President Roosevelt allotted $150,000 from an emergency fund to support the effort, and, on February 26, 1941, FBMS commenced operations.[22] By September 1941, numerous publications were being produced, including a daily digest of broadcasts to North America and Latin America and special reports published as events dictated.[23]

In some ways, the work of FBMS analysts would be familiar to anyone involved in open source exploitation in the 21st century. Like their contemporary counterparts, FBMS analysts were well educated and multilingual; possessed knowledge of foreign affairs, social psychology, and political science; and had the ability to write well. Also similar to today's

obstacles in the open source contracting sector, FBMS officials were more
or less dissuaded from hiring foreign nationals possessing extensive language skills and deep cultural understanding and background due to
counterintelligence concerns.[24] FBMS officials also confronted the need to
conceal open source reporting and analysis from the public while simultaneously expanding FBMS's utility among key government stakeholders.
FBMS generally did not provide its information to persons or organizations outside the government.[25]

Concealing the Success of the Pearl Harbor Attack
from the Open Press

Drake likely did not see the December 6 FBMS report, having chap-
eroned Harsch around Oahu that day. The following morning, Sunday,
December 7, Drake's two young sons, who had heard on the radio that the
Japanese were attacking Pearl Harbor, awakened him. He rushed to the
scene; he would not see his wife and children again for 10 days.[26] From
the window of his office on the third floor of the Navy's headquarters,
Drake could see the devastation: the battleships *Oklahoma* and *Arizona* had
been badly hit, the *Pennsylvania* and *Tennessee* were also damaged, and the
California rested on the shallow harbor bottom. Drake also learned that
the *Nevada*, the *West Virginia*, and 18 other ships had also been damaged;
many hangars and other buildings had been hit; nearly 200 planes had
been destroyed; and thousands of Americans has been killed or injured.[27]

In his role as public information officer, Drake had to conceal the full
extent of the damage from the Japanese. Officers believed that if the Japanese military learned how successful their attack had been, they might
consider an invasion of the island.[28] Therefore, immediately following the
attack, Drake issued a communiqué to the press describing how the *Oklahoma* and a few other ships had been damaged. The Japanese, of course,
knew this already; anyone looking down on Pearl Harbor from the surrounding heights could see this clearly. In other words, Drake's communiqué gave only information that was openly available to someone viewing
the scene. The next day's headlines in the major U.S. newspapers made
no mention of the heavy fleet losses. It would be several weeks before the
American public knew the full extent of the damage.[29] Drake successfully
prevented the Japanese from learning, via open source reporting from the
American press, just how successful their attack had been.

Turning the Tables: Open Source's
Availability to Adversaries

In the early days of the war, FBMS monitored foreign radio broadcasts
for items of interest to officials and policy makers, while Drake, through
censorship activities, worked to limit the dissemination of U.S. military

information that could find its way into open sources. Despite Drake's efforts, this situation occurred following the Battle of Midway, when, on June 7, 1942, the *Chicago Tribune* ran the headline "Navy Had Word of Jap Plan to Strike at Sea."[30] Navy officials feared that readers of the story would be able to deduce that U.S. ciphers had cracked Japan's naval codes, thus alerting the Japanese to stop using them. Officials considered prosecuting the *Tribune's* editor under the Espionage Act of 1917 but soon reconsidered, assuming that associated news coverage would ensure that Japan stopped using the codes. However, Japanese officials either ignored or discounted the *Tribune's* reporting and continued to use a version of the codes throughout the war.[31]

In the *Tribune* case, Drake was unable to prevent the disclosure of critical information via the open press. The dilemmas that Drake faced in his roles as a reporter and the Navy's chief PIO therefore demonstrate that the "downsides" of open source have a long history.[32] Specifically, Drake's need to conceal both the success of the Pearl Harbor attack and U.S. code-breaking capabilities underscores that one's own leaked secrets can become an adversary's open source nuggets. Additionally, it is unclear whether Drake received FBMS reports or found them useful. The difficulty of discerning what open source material is valuable and what is simply inane chatter persists. Specifically, intelligence scholar Stephen Mercado notes FBMS's many successes during the war, including more timely reporting than commercial news providers, real-time monitoring of foreign leaders' speeches, in-depth analysis of trends, coverage of far-flung locales, and the occasional gleaning of technical details from foreign broadcasts.[33] Yet, speaking of OSS's open source activities during World War II, Peiss notes that officials "began to supplement microfilmed publications with their own observations and reports on conversations and rumors. Some [officials] became downright skeptical of the value of what is now termed 'open-source intelligence,' arguing that publications had to be actively combined with agents' assessments of people and events."[34] Peiss explains that OSS field representative George Kates wrote this statement from China in 1944: "Much of this general plan for omnivorous and utopian book gathering . . . has no great bearing on the winning of the war."[35] Kates argued, "Some of the most vital information that this organization can gather is not in printed form, nor does it seem likely that it will become so."[36] We thus find in Kates's assertion the seeds of some intelligence community members' ambivalent attitudes toward open sources—attitudes that would be in place more than 60 years later.

A "PUBLICATIONS EXPLOSION" DURING THE COLD WAR

A declassified *Studies in Intelligence* article written by Herman Croom in 1969 entitled "The Exploitation of Foreign Open Sources" describes Cold

War–era institutional responses to open source challenges.[37] Croom notes that an internal CIA study from 1957 found that 75 to 90 percent of the agency's "total economic, scientific, and geographical knowledge of the Soviet Bloc was based on analysis of open source material."[38] In 1961, the State Department and the CIA were designated as the primary collectors of foreign publications, press, radio, and television broadcasts. During this time, FBIS produced 80 periodicals including its daily report for the Soviet Union, Eastern Europe, communist China, Asia and the Pacific, the Middle East and Africa, Latin America, and Western Europe.[39]

In language eerily similar to contemporary open source commentary, Croom likens "publicly printed paper" to a "tidal wave" threatening to swamp the U.S. intelligence community. He offers readers guidance for dealing with the volume of and means of obtaining and processing open source material from the foreign press. Croom notes, however, that the "reliability" of open source is an ever-present concern, and he reminds readers that useful analysis involves multiple, high-quality sources. In addition to concerns about reliability, Croom identifies problems such as the inability of analysts to find and retrieve open source material; no uniform filing and indexing system had yet been established. Croom therefore asserts, "The use of machine records methods will be mandatory in the future."[40] Interestingly, Croom suggests, in ways all-too familiar to some contemporary open source advocates, the need for an open source agency. For Croom, such an agency would "allow more efficient disposition of intelligence talent and budget."[41] Nearly 40 years later, stakeholders are still debating this issue.[42] FBIS, of course, was not the sole provider of open source material during the Cold War. Other providers included the Foreign Military Studies Office, State Department, Library of Congress, Defense Intelligence Agency, Atomic Energy Commission, and National Aeronautics and Space Administration (NASA).[43]

Although open source providers within the government expanded their operations during the Cold War, it remains difficult to pinpoint exactly how such material contributed to U.S. planning and decision making during that era. For example, intelligence scholar Glen Hastedt has examined whether NIEs produced during the 1958 China Straits Crisis provided decision makers with significantly different or better information than could be obtained from open sources.[44] Hastedt found that both NIEs and the public press accurately assessed the Chinese government's goals: "In each, repeated reference is made to concerns of prestige, influence, enhanced regional standing, and testing U.S. intentions, rather than Peiping's desire for war."[45] However, Hastedt found significant differences in how each source depicted the underlying dynamics of the situation. Open sources considered a wider array of possible underlying causes of the crisis—for example, domestic politics and military balance of power—while NIEs relied almost exclusively on a rational actor model of deterrence. As a result, Hastedt argues that NIEs advanced a more "constricted" image of the Chinese government's decision-making process. Yet the broader perspective found in open sources did not necessarily provide U.S. decision makers with a clearer course of action. Both sources, Hastedt implied, are vulnerable to "cherry picking" by officials, whose biases lead them to ignore repeated caveats about the uncertainty of the information presented. The most consequential difference between open sources and NIEs related to the issue of transparency. While the open press generally identified sources of information, according to Hastedt, "[NIEs] did not identify either the source of the analysis presented to policymakers or the source of the information used for analysis. Neither dissenting footnotes nor in-text dissents were included. True to the notion of NIEs as the considered conclusion of the entire Intelligence Community, information was presented in summary, although detailed, fashion."[46] Hastedt acknowledges that presenting summarized analysis saves decision makers time, yet it potentially "leaves analysts vulnerable to the charges of tilting evidence or acting on the basis of bureaucratic imperatives rather than the best interest of policymakers."[47]

Intelligence scholar Robert Pringle is even more cautious about the role of open sources during the late Cold War.[48] Analysts of the Soviet Union, referred to as Kremlinologists, often relied on Soviet media and speeches to understand power dynamics within the Politburo and the likely course of Soviet policy. When Mikhail Gorbachev became general secretary in 1985, his private statements to Soviet and foreign leaders occasionally contradicted public accounts of his positions on issues, such as the pullout of Soviet forces from Afghanistan. Multiple and conflicting public accounts of the USSR's intentions created challenges for open source analysts in making predictions. Indeed, Pringle (a recipient of the CIA's Distinguished Intelligence Medal) asserts, "Not one government or academic observer of the Soviet Union foresaw the collapse of the Soviet government."[49] Pringle therefore concludes, "Open source intelligence is a double-edge sword for the government analyst. During the Cold War it was of tremendous value to those doing 'Kremlinology.' . . . But reassessing the use of OSINT in the Gorbachev years suggests that open source information can be more ambiguous than analysts, historians, and diplomats are willing to admit."[50]

Ambiguity surrounding the use and effectiveness of open source information during the Cold War may have spurred Jan Herring and George Marling to begin to survey and enhance the intelligence community's access to open sources in the 1970s. According to Robert David Steele, Herring, the first national intelligence officer for science and technology, and Marling, then a member of the intelligence community staff, pioneered institutional open source reforms.[51] Steele claims, "Generally, the S&T analysts rather than the managers, collectors, or covert operators, have understood the extreme importance of access to open sources in all languages."[52] Yet according to Steele, "Herring and Marling failed [to adequately institutionalize open source] for the same reason that later reformists failed: the management mindset is closed, narrow, and completely unwitting of the dereliction of duty attendant to ignoring open sources in all languages."[53] Nevertheless, Herring and Marling would soon be joined by other advocates whose efforts to improve open source exploitation gathered momentum in the post–Cold War period.

POST–COLD WAR OPEN SOURCE ADVOCACY

The dissolution of the Soviet Union in 1991 accelerated the development of new open source plans, policies, and practices. According to a 1993 article written by Paul Wallner, then the CIA's open source coordinator, "3,000 new newspapers in the former Soviet Bloc [had emerged] that were not on the market only three years ago."[54] Rapid geopolitical and technological changes prompted Wallner to declare, "The hard, cold reality . . . is that the Intelligence Community is facing a fundamental restructuring of the way we go about our business."[55] These conditions set the stage for open source advocates to audition their preferred approaches to open source collection and analysis, and no single figure is more associated with open source advocacy than Robert David Steele.[56]

A former Marine Corps infantry and intelligence officer and CIA clandestine case officer, Steele organized and conducted numerous international open source conferences throughout the 1990s and early 2000s. Steele has written several books, dozens of academic articles, and hundreds of commentaries on open source. He has produced open source handbooks for the North Atlantic Treaty Organization (NATO) and the U.S. Joint Military Intelligence Training Center, and he maintains the most comprehensive archive of open source–related material available at his website, OSS.net. For more than 20 years, Steele has both shaped and critiqued institutional responses to open source developments. According to Steele, from 1988 to 1992, he unsuccessfully "made the rounds within the government attempting to secure interest in both redirecting half of the National Intelligence Topics (NIT) away from the Soviet Union and toward the Third World; and in creating the open source exploitation capabilities that the Marine Corps Intelligence Command demonstrated were so lacking at the national level."[57] However, Steele would soon gain more visibility and allies.

Both Steele and the OSC note that, in 1992, Senator David Boren (D-OK) and Congressman Dave McCurdy (D-OK) proposed national security reform legislation; the House version described an "Office of Open Source Information" to be placed under a newly created deputy director for national intelligence for estimates and analysis. The proposed legislation stated, "This office, headed by a director, will coordinate the collection of openly available information of potential intelligence value within the intelligence community. It is anticipated that this office will serve as the sole agent within the intelligence community for the procurement of open source material. All existing intelligence community open source entities will be consolidated in this office upon implementation of this act."[58] Although the proposal did not come to fruition, that year the DCI did establish an open source coordinator within the CIA that, two years later, was superseded by the Community Open Source Program Office (COSPO). The objectives of COSPO were to oversee a process for users to receive open source information, engage in advocacy, ensure funding for open source activities, and oversee a process for establishing open source requirements.[59] COSPO's 1995 *Strategic Plan* stated the following:

The Community Open Source Program will enable users and customers to have timely access to all open source information pertinent to their needs in their work environments. The Program will improve in a cost-effective manner, the use, usefulness, and usability of open source information. It will improve acquiring, accessing, processing, distributing, disseminating, and exploiting open sources and make it easier to use more focused open source information. The Community will thereby be able to make more effective and efficient use of its unique, classified assets in support of its customers by ensuring that we "do not send a spy where a schoolboy can go."[60]

During the 1990s, COSPO was one of several interconnected open source forums that formed, merged, and disbanded in the wake of the Cold War. These forums included the Scientific and Technical Intelligence Committee's Open Source Subcommittee, the Open Source Steering Committee, numerous agency-specific task forces on open source, and technical efforts such as the Open Source Information System (OSIS) portal. These groups generally performed advocacy functions to focus officials' attentions on open source issues and opportunities. According to Wallner, "My job as the DCI's Open-Source Coordinator was brought about by the realization among the Community's leadership and political masters that the information explosion, and the profusion of automated tools and systems to handle it, must be more effectively incorporated into the intelligence process."[61] These were largely the same challenges that confronted Joseph Markowitz, who headed COSPO in the 1990s.

During this time frame, two events appear especially important for understanding how Steele emerged as a key figure within open source debates. First, the National Intelligence Council's *Open Source Task Force: A Vision for the Future,* written in 1992, became a central focus of Steele's commentary.[62] *A Vision for the Future* was intended to be "something more concrete than a simple vision statement" and, therefore, "leans closer to a system description . . . to lend some credibility to the reality of a vision."[63] The report noted that the intelligence community's systems were "designed to function most efficiently against the closed Soviet Union" and that "there are significant shortfalls for this new world."[64] These shortfalls included the quantity of open source data that analysts were able to access, an awareness among analysts of what kinds of materials were available, timeliness, poor presentation of materials, and an inability to incorporate value added (presumably notes and commentary from other analysts). The report indicated that, in 1992, "There [was] no way to get printed material scanned and entered into the electronic holdings" and "there [were] no . . . capabilities to store and make available to the user images, graphs, or voice materials."[65] Nearly simultaneously to the release of the NIC's *A Vision for the Future,* Steele issued a 52-page commentary.[66] Significantly, Steele asserted that the NIC report did not "integrate the perspectives of a very broad community of military, non-military, and private sector consumers," and he urged the creation of a new taskforce under the guidance of the Defense Technical Information Service, rather than the NIC.[67]

Three years later, in 1995, Steele testified before the Aspin-Brown Commission about the value of open source. The commission directed Steele to go head-to-head against the intelligence community in what has come to be known, colloquially, as "the battle-of-the-INTs [intelligence discipline]."[68] According to *Wired* magazine's Noah Shachtman:

The subject would be the tiny and generally dismal nation of Burundi. The battle was engaged at 17:00 on a Thursday and the delivery deadline was 10:00 the next Monday. On Monday morning Steele showed up with: The names of the top 10 journalists covering Burundi (ripe for debriefing); The names of the top 10 academics covering Burundi (ripe for debriefing); 20 two-page executive-level political-military summaries on Burundi; Burundi order-of-battle information down to the tribal level; 1:50 maps of the country; 1:50 cloud-free imagery of the country that was less than 3 years old.[69]

The CIA, by contrast, provided "a PowerPoint chart of nominal value and a regional—not country-specific—economic study."[70] The Burundi case sparked controversy among intelligence stakeholders, with some accusing Steele of exaggerating his company's performance and misrepresenting the conditions surrounding the event.[71] The Aspin-Brown Commission concluded, however, that "Given the amount of open source information that is readily available to the public over computer networks, the effort of the Intelligence Community to structure and make available to analysts pertinent open source data bases seems inexplicably slow."[72] Regarding the battle-of-the-INTs, the commission concluded, "Information obtained from open sources was substantial and on some points more detailed than that provided by the Intelligence Community. On the other hand, the information that came from open sources took longer to produce, required validation, and failed to cover many key aspects of the situation important to policymakers."[73] Echoing Croom's observation written in 1969, the commission stated, "An adequate computer infrastructure to tie intelligence analysts into open source information does not appear to exist. In the view of the Commission, the creation of such an infrastructure should be a top priority of the DCI and a top priority for funding."[74]

Following the Aspin-Brown Commission, Steele's increasingly blunt critique of the intelligence community, along with his idealistic vision of reform, led one official to assert that he belonged on the "lunatic fringe"— a label that Steele later embraced as evidence of his reformist credentials.[75] Commentators have also argued that Steele's claims would benefit from more detailed evidence. For example, reviewing Steele's *The New Craft of Intelligence*, Frederick Wettering wrote, "Mr. Steele makes conclusion after conclusion without developing his arguments for each or showing proofs. Rather he directs readers to his earlier work, *On Intelligence*, or to the many authors in his magnificent annotated bibliography for more detailed exposition and reasoning. This methodology is unsatisfactory and frustrating."[76] According to intelligence scholar Arthur Hulnick, "[Steele's] zeal in support of OSINT is so overwhelming, it is much like being confronted with a relentless used-car salesman. Conversations with him tend to be very one-sided, in that he leaves few openings for rejoinders to his rather intense presentations."[77] Despite the tone of Steele's rhetoric, he is among the most knowledgeable commentators—if not *the* most—regarding the intelligence community's attempts to institutionalize open source.

Steele shares the commitments of private sector open source contractors, including these elements: (1) establishing open source as a legitimate intelligence discipline, (2) perpetuating the belief that open source can meet the bulk of intelligence requirements cost-effectively and without the need for secret collection systems, (3) establishing new organizational structures within the government to facilitate the expanded and improved use of open source, and (4) ensuring that the private sector plays a central role in the open source arena. Yet, since 2005, Steele has largely shifted his attention away from institutional efforts and toward public or collective intelligence concerns. For example, in 2008, Steele published *Collective Intelligence: Creating a Prosperous World at Peace*, edited by Mark Tovey. In that volume, Steele signaled his abandonment of institutional reform, stating, "In the USA, the recent issuance of [a] disappointingly incomplete and misleading Congressional Research Service (CRS) report . . . [is] the final nail in OSINT's coffin."[78] As a result of his stance, institutional open source developments have moved forward largely without Steele's influence.

Steele is undoubtedly at the center of post–Cold War open source advocacy, yet former congressman Rob Simmons (R-CT) joins him there. Simmons served in Congress from 2001 to 2007, during which he helped vault open source to the forefront of U.S. national security reform debates. According to a biographical sketch, Simmons is a former U.S. Army Reserve military intelligence officer with more than 37 years of active and reserve service; he also worked for the CIA, serving as an operations officer for a decade.[79] In the 1990s, Simmons was a commander of the 434th Military Intelligence Detachment in New Haven, Connecticut, where he led the writing of the "Open Source Intelligence Guide for the Military Intelligence Officer."[80] In 1995, Simmons completed a master's

degree from the Joint Military Intelligence College (JMIC), where he wrote
a thesis entitled, "Open Source Intelligence: An Examination of Its Exploitation in the Defense Intelligence Community."[81] In that thesis, Simmons
declared, "At the Defense Intelligence Agency (DIA), the analytical components are ill-prepared and ill-supported to make full use of any information outside of the small, restrictive and limited domain of classified
intelligence sources."[82] Through surveys and interviews conducted with
nearly 400 analysts, Simmons determined that "DIA analysts spend only
a small fraction of their time and resources on the open sources that can
potentially provide the vast majority of their final intelligence product."[83]
Simmons did not specify what time and resources should be devoted to
open source efforts, however.

Simmons's thesis included five citations of Steele's writings, along with
interview material. Simmons, in turn, has written forewords for Steele's
books, including *Information Operations: All Information, All Languages, All
the Time* and *The Smart Nation Act: Public Intelligence in the Public Interest.*
In the foreword to *Information Operations* in 2006, Simmons wrote, "It is no
longer enough to have spies and diplomats—we are engaged in a 100-year
six-front Global War, and nothing less than universal information coverage will meet our needs"[84] Simmons echoed Steele's idealism when he asserted, "As we develop our IO [information operations] capabilities, we
must focus on the ethics of openness, not the manipulation of opinion. We
must strive to deliver the tools for truth to all peoples everywhere, and
nurture democratic elements from the bottom up as well as the national
level."[85] Whether senior intelligence community officials shared this idealism is unclear.

In his role as chairman of the Subcommittee on Intelligence, Information Sharing, and Terrorism Risk Assessment, Simmons was instrumental
in raising the visibility of open source. Specifically, Simmons claims that
he was successful in inserting language into the 2006 National Defense
Authorization Act that legally defined open source intelligence and required the Department of Defense to establish a formal open source program.[86] Simmons has also advocated for an open source agency outside
the CIA. In 2006, Simmons remarked, "Every discipline needs a home and
the current open source center . . . is still part of the CIA, so it's still the
ugly stepchild of the intelligence community."[87] Furthermore, Simmons
explained, "I think the time is right for open source. I think we know the
benefits. We still know it's the ugly stepchild but at least the ugly stepchild
is getting a chance to go to the dance."[88] We can interpret "the dance" as
meaning open source budgets, inclusion in high-profile intelligence products, and increased acknowledgment from senior officials of open source's
contribution to intelligence.

Simmons shares the commitments of policy makers concerned with
intelligence reform. These commitments include cultivating public trust
by demonstrating leadership in the intelligence arena and ensuring that

taxpayers receive value for money from government agencies. His third commitment perhaps distinguishes Simmons from other policy makers; he promotes an antisecrecy ethic in order to increase information sharing between the intelligence community and members of Congress and the public. Simmons supports the development of open source in ways that private sector contractors, like Steele, cannot. Specifically, through legislative acts, public statements, and interactions with senior government officials, Simmons was able to directly press stakeholders to formally address open source issues. A statement that Simmons made at one of Steele's open source conferences in 2006 sums up his perspective: "In my assessment, the Intelligence Community is afraid of open source. . . . It seems to me [that open source is] the 'ugly stepchild' of the Intelligence Community, getting the least money, getting the least recognition, always pushed aside for secret products. I think it is time to change that paradigm."[89] Simmons enlisted a long-time colleague to help do just that.

Eliot Jardines, a former open source contractor, became the first ADDNI/OS in 2005. Both Simmons and Jardines attended Fairfield High School in Connecticut. Jardines was also a member of the Army's 434th Military Intelligence Detachment, then commanded by Simmons. One may speculate what role this relationship played in Jardines being named to the position of ADDNI/OS. Then CIA director Hayden stated, "We brought in Eliot Jardines from the private sector. . . . Using a community open source steering committee, Eliot will foster collaboration, drive strategy and policy development and enhance our ability to leverage capabilities that exist outside the community."[90] Jardines was previously the president of Open Source Publishing, Inc., an open source contracting firm he founded in 1996. In his role as ADDNI/OS from 2005 to 2008, Jardines balanced the commitments of various stakeholders within the intelligence community. These commitments included securing resources for open source exploitation by acknowledging the importance of open source while simultaneously maintaining facets of the bureaucratic status quo. In 2006, Jardines stated, "Getting the [intelligence community] to accept open source as the source of first resort is my number one goal. . . . In the past we tended to value information in proportion to how hard it was to get."[91] At a June 21, 2005, congressional hearing, when Jardines was still a contractor, he stated, "We must establish OSINT as an equal partner with human intelligence, signals intelligence, imagery intelligence and measurement and signatures intelligence. For too long, open source exploitation has been delegated as merely an additional duty for intelligence analysts. This is simply a ridiculous notion. No one would seriously propose that intelligence analysts be required to collect their own signals or imagery intelligence. However, that is precisely what we do with open source intelligence."[92]

Jardines thus echoed Wallner, who wrote in 1993, "We will have to convince a lot of people that just because a piece of information is unclassified and publicly available . . . does not mean that it is inherently useless."[93]

Getting the intelligence community to use open source as a source of first resort required funding for programs. To persuade decision makers to provide larger open source budget allocations, Jardines had to identify the level of funding for open activities across the intelligence community. At Steele's 2006 conference, Jardines stated that he was working to identify all open source programs and the level of funding for each. He stated that the information would help officials decide "whether [budgets] need to be right-sized or adjusted."[94] Statements such as this may have caused concern among contactors who feared consolidation of their market. For example, Steele recommended in 2005 that "all funds that might be confused with OSINT missions should immediately be labeled, more accurately, Information Operations in order to prevent the DNI from trying to confiscate funds earmarked for OSINT within other elements of the IC [intelligence community]."[95] Steele's recommendation illustrates the critical importance of control over the meaning of open source: Jardines had to not only manage open source programs but also successfully track and shape the shifting meanings of the term.

Jardines was also placed in the awkward position of having to publicly champion open source while downplaying Simmons's antisecrecy ethic within the intelligence community—where such an ethic is at best quixotic and at worst abhorrent. Jardines's support of Simmons's antisecrecy ethic seems to have shifted somewhat when he moved from the private sector to the intelligence community. Prior to being appointed ADDNI/ OS, Jardines was a vocal advocate of information sharing. At a 2005 congressional hearing, he stated, "In my hope, we would be disseminating [open source] down to a very diffuse level, down to local police departments. . . . That's the thing about open source . . . we can't hide it; it's unclassified."[96] At Steele's 2006 conference, however, journalist Kent Bye questioned Jardines about whether the government's open source products would be made available to the public. Jardines responded, "The issue of whether we are going to be able to push information out to the general public is one that I think that we will be able to expand, a bit. . . . The bottom line is that even though it is open source, in some instances, we still need to be able to protect sources and methods. . . . We have to be careful."[97]

At FBIS, Steele, Simmons, and Jardines confronted another powerful open source advocate, Doug Naquin, who joined FBIS in 1979 and became its director in 2002; he subsequently became the head of the OSC in 2005 and chairman of the National Open Source Committee in 2008. Naquin's long tenure with FBIS positioned him to be at the forefront of open source developments. Yet as interest in private sector open source capabilities grew during the 1990s, FBIS saw its fortunes decline. In remarks before the Central Intelligence Retirees Association (CIRA) in 2007, Naquin recalled, "The 1990s was not a good decade for FBIS."[98] Between 1993 and 2002, FBIS staff shrunk by 50 percent. Naquin characterized this time frame as "marked by downsizing, serious morale problems, and general lack of appreciation."[99] The events of 9/11 changed all that. Naquin noted, "9/11 was a sort of watershed for us."[100] Citing the importance of the 9/11 Commission and the WMD Commission's recommendations, Naquin explained how open source advocacy reached its zenith when, in 2005, FBIS was "rebranded" the OSC and given additional capabilities and authorities. Rebranding has been among Naquin's main concerns: "We quickly went to work to build an organization around what we wanted our 'brand' to be: our identity."[101] This rebranding involved changing perceptions about open source that have persisted since World War II; namely, FBIS needed to communicate that it could do much more than simply translate foreign language broadcasts and information. Among Naquin's goals were to ensure that audiences valued the OSC for its analytical and technological capabilities and for providing information beyond what one could read in a newspaper.

During his CIRA presentation, Naquin noted, "My biggest challenge . . . has not been resources as much as it's been awareness of what we can do with open sources and how open source exploitation contributes to the intelligence mission. I encounter a lot of unproved assumptions about what open sources can and cannot do."[102] Naquin lamented, "On the one hand, we have what I call the Open Source zealots. I don't mean that pejoratively, because it's nice to have cheerleaders." Naquin characterized the zealots as believing that "Open Sources can solve all our problems."[103] Naquin explained how over two decades, he has confronted many armchair quarterbacks who believe that they can manage open sources more effectively than FBIS/OSC: "It's as if they say: 'Well I got an "A" on a term paper once in college, so I know how you guys can run Open Source better.' "[104] On the other hand, Naquin acknowledged that many institutional members still ignore open sources, which Naquin has tried to overcome through educating his colleagues about what open sources can contribute to the intelligence mission. Naquin's Facebook profile in 2010 indicated that among his favorite movies was *Last of the Mohicans.* That is an apt analogy given that Steele's influence has faded, Simmons recently failed to win a Senate primary for Connecticut and remains on the sidelines, and Jardines has returned to the private sector. In many ways, Naquin is the only post–Cold War open source advocate whose influence continues to grow.

In summary, the history of open source reveals consistent dilemmas in its acquisition and analysis, long stretches of institutional stability, periods characterized by urgent transformations, and ambiguity surrounding its use and effectiveness. Throughout this history, an underlying question has remained: what is the meaning of open source? The remainder of this book focuses on that question primarily in the post-9/11 period of open source's development. Chapters 4 through 6 take up where this chapter leaves off. Specifically, the public remarks of these figures—Steele,

Simmons, Jardines, and Naquin—are a central focus for understanding the post-9/11 reshaping of U.S. intelligence. To understand why these remarks are important to processes of institutional change, the next chapter advances a discourse-centered perspective.

CHAPTER 3

A Discourse-Centered Perspective on Open Source Developments

> Now, only the intelligence community could come up with [that] sort of a name and call [publicly available information] "open source intelligence" as opposed to "information." If you call it "information," you don't get any money. If you call it "open source," somebody will want to fund that.
> —Deputy Director of National Intelligence for Analysis (DDNI/A)
> Thomas Fingar, 2007[1]

Scholars and commentators have attempted to explain why U.S. intelligence agencies are slow to change in response to shifting political and technological conditions.[2] However, explanations of *how* such changes occur (or not) remain rare.[3] As the chapter epigraph suggests, a discourse-centered perspective views conflicting meanings of open source as a driver of institutional change. Consider, for example, the influential book *Spying Blind: The CIA, the FBI, and the Origins of 9/11*, written by political scientist Amy Zegart.[4] In this book, Zegart argues that flawed organizational routines, structures, and cultures led to U.S. intelligence agency "adaptation failure" in the post–Cold War period—culminating in the tragedy of 9/11. Zegart found that between 1991 and 2001, 12 different blue-ribbon commissions, think tank task forces, and governmental initiatives recommended 340 reforms for U.S. intelligence agencies. Only 10 percent of these recommendations, however, were implemented before 9/11.[5]

The Aspin-Brown Commission's recommendations in 1996 regarding open source were similarly overlooked.[6] According to Zegart, the post-9/11 institutional environment appears equally hostile to reform: "Future prospects for reforming the U.S. intelligence community are not promising. Although there is consensus about what problems need to be fixed and a greater sense of urgency since September 11, intelligence reform has only begun. The road ahead will be long. And it will be filled with the same obstacles—internal resistance, entrenched interests, and institutional barriers—that have blocked reform efforts for years."[7] Along these lines, at the 2007 DNI Open Source Conference, DDNI/A Fingar lamented, "We have some [analysts who] say it's good to use open sources, but don't cite them. People won't believe [the analysts who use open sources]. If we haven't paid for it or stolen it, it's not the same credible information."[8] Fingar's observation drew knowing laughter from the audience, prompting him to add, "I think that is kind of silly, and yet it's part of the reality."[9] If Zegart and Fingar are correct, then a perspective that conceptualizes reform as a *discursive* phenomenon would help identify the specific ways stakeholders use speech and writing to promote or impede competing visions of reform.

For organizational communication scholar Timothy Kuhn, conflict and contradiction within speech and writing is "a site for observing battles for control and an important source of change."[10] A discursive perspective examines the taken-for-granted statements that construct the *meanings* and *relationships* among concepts such as open source and intelligence, objects such as intelligence reports, and roles such as intelligence analyst or contractor. For example, if intelligence is conceptualized as secret information, then it makes sense that analysts would be reluctant to cite open source contributions in their reports. This narrow conceptualization of intelligence may subtly undermine outreach efforts to media, law enforcement, and academic communities, thereby reducing that range of useful perspectives that ultimately reach decision makers. In this way, discourse is important because it constitutes "the substrate for organizing by providing sets of representations, statements, narratives, images, and codes that produce ways of seeing objects and events."[11] Rarely, however, do intelligence scholars and commentators acknowledge the complex relationship between communication and reform.

To the extent that communication is discussed at all, political science and public administration scholars tend to treat communication as a variable *within* intelligence organizations rather than productive *of* them and the broader institutions of which they are a part.[12] This chapter explains why a discursive perspective is useful for understanding possibilities for institutional change vis-à-vis open source. To do this, I integrate resources from institutional theory, organizational discourse, and rhetoric to develop a discourse-centered perspective on institutional change. This chapter briefly outlines the features and illustrates the value of this perspective before applying it to the case studies of open source in the chapters that follow.

INSTITUTIONAL THEORY

The U.S. intelligence and national security sector can be understood as an institutional field, one constituted by intelligence consumers (e.g., the president, the NIC, intelligence officials, military commanders, and other policy makers), suppliers (e.g., intelligence agencies and associated vendors/contractors comprising the intelligence-industrial complex), regulatory agencies (e.g., congressional oversight committees, special courts, and inspectors general), competitors (e.g., sources of information outside the intelligence community that vie for officials' and policy makers' attention), and other stakeholders associated with civil society (e.g., media and nongovernmental organizations).[13] Conceptualizing the U.S. intelligence and national security sector as an institutional field draws attention to the influence of stakeholders well beyond the 16 official members of the U.S. intelligence community.

The term *institution* is also a sociological concept, one possessing a long and complex history within the fields of economics, political science, and organizational studies. Institutional scholars share a concern for the ways in which cultural forces—social mores, constitutions, or informal systems of control—influence human behavior.[14] "Neo-institutional theory" generally focuses on *meaning systems* and the ways that institutions are constructed and perpetuated in human interaction.[15] For example, in their landmark essay, sociologists John Meyer and Brian Rowan sought to explain why convergence toward organizational similarity within a field could occur even in the absence of shared problems of coordination and control.[16] The authors found that certain organizational structures, such as a human resources unit, could serve as a "rational myth." By rational myth, the authors meant that the primary purpose of certain structures is to "signal" an organization's legitimacy to other institutional members and stakeholders. In other words, organizations may adopt formal structures that possess little relevance and value for performance ("myth") simply in order to secure and/or maintain institutional legitimacy (a "rational" goal). For example, in the context of U.S. national security, the OSC may not necessarily require its current level of secrecy to operate effectively, but that secrecy encourages intelligence stakeholders to view the OSC as legitimate. As intelligence scholar Stevyn Gibson observes, "Regrettably, 'need to know' has become a debate complicated more by issues of organizational culture and personal vested interest than operational security."[17]

Recognizing the interconnections between communication and institutions, organizational communication scholars John Lammers and Joshua Barbour have recently advanced an "institutional theory of organizational communication" designed to assist scholars in understanding interorganizational phenomena.[18] For Lammers and Barbour, the defining features of institutions are their endurance, formal (written) knowledge, rationality, and independence. U.S. intelligence evinces each of these features. First, intelligence involves shared and well-established practices based on formalized beliefs. U.S. intelligence has existed in its modern form since 1947. Second, written rules, laws, regulations, directives, guidelines, and contracts are a defining characteristic of this institution. Third, intelligence exhibits a rational, means-ends orientation. This does not mean that rational behaviors always obtain; nevertheless, rules are developed and asserted as practical guides for members in their decision making. Finally, intelligence is independent of and larger than any single organization. The formal relationships *among* members of different organizations within the U.S. intelligence community are often as important as interactions among members *within* a given organization.

Additionally, Lammers and Barbour view institutions as manifested in practices. Practices are observable routines and behaviors that are consistent across a range of settings—for example, monitoring jihadist websites and chat rooms may occur across intelligence agencies and private sector firms. Institutions are also manifested in beliefs—cognitive and emotional elements—that influence their members' decision-making processes. For example, intelligence agency members are generally socialized to believe that secrecy is necessary to protect sources and methods of intelligence. Institutions enroll their individual members as carriers of preferred beliefs. Institutions are also characterized by low rates of change. Institutional practices relevant to organizational communication are often formalized—that is, written, stored, and used as precedents and guides for action. Lammers and Barbour's theory suggests that to understand the institutionalization of open source, scholars and commentators should examine stakeholders' beliefs, practices, and production and dissemination of formal texts. The role of talk and text in establishing, maintaining, or transforming institutions points to the concept of organizational discourse.

ORGANIZATIONAL DISCOURSE

Organizational discourse can be defined as "the collection of texts, produced through the practices of talking and writing, that bring organizationally-related objects into being as these texts are produced, disseminated, and consumed."[19] This definition implies that what open source "is" is uniquely shaped by how stakeholders write and talk about it; open source is not a phenomenon with fixed attributes and expressions. In other words, without the global infrastructure that sustains the Internet, contemporary open source discourse would sound very different— but it (or something like it) would nevertheless exist as a consequence of stakeholders' persistent bifurcation of "secret" and "open" information in deliberating U.S. intelligence policy and conducting operations. While Internet search engines, social networking sites, email alerts, web crawlers, semantic algorithms, and innumerable new and evolving technologies make many versions of open source practice possible, these practices can, alternately, be kept behind the veil of institutional secrecy, occur within established and/or new organizational structures and configurations, support the executive branch exclusively, inform congressional and/or public debate more broadly, remain within the federal arena, be diffused to the state and local level, involve ordinary citizens, and so forth. Open source is thus an ambivalent socio-technical apparatus that is capable of being configured in multiple (but not infinite) forms.[20]

There are numerous and diverse texts that describe open source within the institution of U.S. intelligence. As noted earlier, "textual contradiction" can be "a site for observing battles for control and an important source of change."[21] Studying this battle helps identify "the key organizational discourses by which ideas are formulated and articulated and to show how, via the variety of discursive interactions and practices, these go on to shape and influence the attitudes and behavior of an organization's members."[22] Official plans, policies, and directives "bear down" on institutional members, circumscribing their thoughts and actions in ways that define and perpetuate institutional norms.[23] A discourse-centered perspective, however, also considers the role of human agency in the processes of institutional creation, maintenance, and transformation. The term "institutional entrepreneurship" captures the friction created when institutional forces collide with human agency.[24] This friction centers on the question of how new institutional forms and practices can emerge if members are already embedded within institutions that structure their thoughts, actions, and identities. One answer to this question lies in conceptualizing human agency as distributed within structures that actors themselves create, maintain, and transform.[25] In this way, organizational structures both constrain and facilitate action. Drawing on these structural resources, some officials work to defend the institutional status quo from others seeking to change it. As a result, "institutional entrepreneurs must be skilled actors . . . who can draw on existing cultural and linguistic materials to narrate and theorize change in ways that give other social groups reason to cooperate."[26] In the vocabulary of neo-institutional theory, institutional entrepreneurs must be skilled at performing institutional work— fostering institutional change through the processes of advocacy, defining, vesting, constructing identities, changing normative associations, constructing normative networks, mimicry, theorizing, and educating.[27]

These nine types of institutional work can be grouped in terms of three broad categories: political work, technical work, and cultural work.[28] These categories are illustrated in an extended example later in this chapter, but briefly, *political work* involves influencing the development of institutional rules, property rights, and boundaries in the attempt to anchor an institution within a social system. This work includes advocating, defining, and vesting. *Technical work*, by contrast, involves mimicry, theorizing, and educating in order to develop diffuse mental models of how an institution functions. In order for political and technical work to endure, however, institutional entrepreneurs must also engage the normative pillar of institutions through cultural work. *Cultural work* involves presenting an institution in a way that appeals to a broad audience, shapes identities, and grounds practices within normative frameworks. These categories help us understand how a popular management fashion—for instance, Total Quality Management, Knowledge Management, or, indeed, open source—becomes institutionalized within a field rather than simply fades away.

Management scholars Markus Perkmann and André Spicer have advanced three propositions concerning institutional work: (1) "a management fashion is more likely to be institutionalized if it is propagated via a combination of political, technical and cultural work compared to a single type of institutional work"; (2) "a management fashion is more likely to be institutionalized if it is propagated by actors bringing together several types of institutional skills compared to a reduced range of such skills"; and (3) "a management fashion is more likely to become an institution through the cumulative results of different kinds of institutional work over time, compared to conjoint expenditure of institutional work at specific points in time."[29] Testing these propositions requires examining the talk and text that stakeholders use to perform institutional work. Here, the concept of rhetoric helps us anticipate the persuasiveness of particular forms of institutional talk and text and how these relate to cultural discourses and public debates.

RHETORIC

Some scholars treat the terms *discourse* and *rhetoric* as synonyms.[30] For others, rhetoric is specifically concerned with the actual or potential effects of messages, social situations beyond the interpersonal arena, the use of symbols, inductive reasoning, formal and public texts, identification, and persuasion.[31] Rhetorical critics have scrutinized U.S. national security speeches and documents in order to spur more democratic intelligence practices. For example, 36 years ago, Robert Newman argued, "When one looks at the American intelligence apparatus as a series of communication systems, three pathological conditions become apparent. Our intelligence suffers inexorably from mission involvement [politicization], it carries secrecy to risible extremes, and it overloads both the capacity of communication channels to carry it and the ability of decision makers to digest it."[32] Newman's observations seem prophetic in light of public disclosures surrounding the intelligence failures preceding 9/11 and the 2003 Iraq War. For example, Gordon Mitchell has shown how the institutionalized practice of "competitive intelligence"—which is ideally based on cooperative argumentation between intelligence professionals—becomes distorted through a phenomenon Mitchell terms "Team B intelligence coups."[33] This phenomenon involves funneling "alternative" (read "preferred") intelligence analysis by interested parties directly to policy makers, thus bypassing intelligence community peer review. In his analysis of the controversy surrounding intelligence preceding the Iraq War in 2003, Mitchell demonstrated how a "boutique intelligence shop" residing in the Pentagon, yet outside the formal U.S. intelligence community, was able to circumvent institutional norms by "stovepiping"—or selectively funneling—dubious intelligence assessments to senior administration officials. Administration officials then used those assessments to justify public pronouncements on the need for military action in Iraq. Similarly, Stephen Hartnett and Laura Stengrim analyzed declassified intelligence documents in their rhetorical critique of how the Bush administration fabricated evidence of national security threats in its run-up to the Iraq War.[34]

While not focusing on intelligence issues per se, scholars associated with Arizona State University's Consortium for Strategic Communication have highlighted the role of communication and open source information in fighting terrorism, strengthening national security, and engaging in public diplomacy. One of these scholars, H. L. Goodall Jr., argues that fundamentalism is the antithesis of democracy in that it closes down productive debate, dehumanizes and disregards the Other, and treats dissent as a form of treason. Winning the War on Terror, Goodall argues, entails countering fundamentalism through the creation of meaningful debate and dialogue both within the United States and abroad. Goodall argues that the real battleground in the War on Terror is not the Middle East; rather, it is the rhetoric of fundamentalism, wherever it is manifested. Thus, Goodall underscores rhetoric's traditional concern for humanistic ideals and deliberative democracy in the context of sustaining adequate national security.[35]

The study of national security rhetoric complements neo-institutional theory and organizational discourse perspectives in attending to the role of texts in processes of change. For example, Thomas Goodnight's essay, "Strategic Doctrine, Public Debate and the Terror War," demonstrates how rhetorical scholars and critics traditionally emphasize and critique the influence of public texts vis-à-vis the development of national security policy. For example, a key instrument of national security policy is the U.S. *National Security Strategy*, a document created and distributed by the executive branch. The *National Security Strategy* articulates strategic doctrine, which sets in place the overall guidelines for an administration and informs U.S. publics of the costs and sacrifices that they should be prepared to bear for the sake of national security. For Goodnight, presidential address enacts strategic doctrine and results in ideographs (such as "the cause of freedom") that are powerful motivators and shapers of public opinion. Goodnight analyzes a set of public speeches and texts in order to track the unfolding of the G. W. Bush administration's preemptive military doctrine.[36]

However, Goodnight generally does not address how institutional and organizational dynamics enable and constrain the influence of texts such as the *National Security Strategy* within the intelligence bureaucracy. There is an implicit assumption in Goodnight's argument that strategic doctrine, once articulated, can be rapidly, uniformly, and successfully diffused throughout the national security apparatus. Organizational discourse scholarship compels scholars to reconsider this assumption and assess the *relative* influence of both people and texts. As we have seen in controversy surrounding the release of declassified portions of the 2007 NIE concerning Iran's nuclear weapons intentions and capabilities, institutional actors can and do present challenges to unfettered presidential rhetoric. Additionally, Zegart notes that in 1999 then DCI George Tenet issued a memorandum declaring war on al Qaeda and requiring all agencies to make fighting terrorism their top priority.[37] By Zegart's account, Tenet's memo was all but ignored by institutional members. Therefore, a tension surrounding modernist rhetorical approaches to the study of national security is the impulse to cast the institution of intelligence as overly coherent and controllable, thereby discounting its members' abilities to resist and/or reshape elite rhetoric. In other words, this book departs from traditional criticism of national security rhetoric by examining the "suasory" features of texts, as well as their actual circulation, reception, and enactment among institutional audiences.

Moving closer to the perspective on rhetoric used in this book, Bryan Taylor and his collaborators have focused on the overlapping spheres of organizational and public communication produced in and around the nation's pre- and post-9/11 nuclear-weapons production complex.[38] Taylor and colleagues argue that public deliberation concerning nuclear weapons should ideally lead not only to the shaping of public opinion, but should also influence official decision making. The authors' approach to the public sphere emphasizes the ethics and politics surrounding the framing of issues, the selection of speakers, and the interpretation of evidence in controversies. In studying and critiquing the history of U.S. nuclear weapons production, the authors reveal a public sphere "constricted and degraded by technocratic domination."[39] Crucial here, the authors note, are "institutional dynamics that function pragmatically to shape the terms of discussion, the scope of actors' involvement, the legitimacy of particular speakers and speech acts, the rate, sequence, and duration of decision making, and the ways in which technical and nontechnical discourses are articulated."[40] Rhetorical scholar Robert Ivie similarly demonstrates how the rhetoric of national security elites is often developed in direct opposition to democratic ideals and practices.[41] The fragility of democracy imagined by these speakers underlies their anxiety about the vulnerability of democratic institutions to threats both foreign and domestic. Elites draw on these threats to promote their policy objectives, which usually involve the suppression of democratic deliberation ("demophobia").

In summary, intelligence and national security can be viewed as deeply rhetorical phenomena. Contemporary cultural and critical theory establishes that language organizes meaningful configurations of material and symbolic resources used by citizens and officials in their conceptualization and defense of core, cherished elements of their shared (imaginary) national existence. In other words, statements about national security phenomena influence how people act (both materially and symbolically) toward those phenomena. "National security" also evokes relational practices as identities are constituted through the deployment of oppositional-yet-interdependent terms (e.g., self/other, native/foreigner, patriot/traitor, and, in the case of open source—open/secret, U.S-person/non-U.S.-person, institutional member/citizen, and decision maker/analyst).[42] "National security" is therefore not an objective, universal, or stable phenomenon with fixed assumptions or expressions; rather, "national security" serves as a site of discursive struggle over the meanings and consequences of ambiguous events.[43] Both the 9/11 terrorist attacks and the 2003 Iraq WMD intelligence failure created situations in which key symbolic elements of traditional "national security" and "intelligence" became—at least partly and temporarily—unstable. This instability created the conditions for the rise of open source that were unavailable during the reform attempts of the 1980s and 1990s. Thus, rhetoric, as the term is used here, directs our attention to interconnecting cultural and organizational codes, stories, and scripts that organize and reproduce values, attitudes, and beliefs about intelligence, national security, and democracy.

SUMMARY

Scholars traditionally depict the institution of intelligence as built upon the strictures of secrecy and a preference for classified information.[44] Neo-institutional theory encourages scholars to examine the extent to which members' adherence to these strictures and preferences is the result of calculated reflection, the forces of inertia, or simply the inability to conceive of alternatives.[45] A neo-institutional perspective also asks to what extent the institutionalization of open source serves as a "rational myth" to bolster the legitimacy of U.S. intelligence in the wake of failures related to 9/11 and Iraq. Whether or not new open source organizational structures serve this purpose, open source advocates have performed institutional work to establish, maintain, and/or advance open source's legitimacy.

Scholars and commentators interested in open source phenomena have largely overlooked these dynamics, preferring to focus instead on open source as an input within the intelligence cycle. Such a perspective is unable to account for the ways stakeholders construct preferred meanings of open source in order to promote or impede competing visions of reform. In other words, my investigation of open source follows studies of government reform that are concerned "less about how things are done than about how things are to be thought of, a much more potent prospect."[46] This perspective focuses attention on how the practice of intelligence variously reflects the pursuit of rational interests, the exercise of conscious choice, or conventions, routines, and habits.

One objective of this research is to determine whether various open source stakeholders "feed from the same discursive sources."[47] Do open source stakeholders use the same codes, stories, and scripts to advance their interests? This is important to assess because open source discourse at operational levels within some organizations appears to differ significantly from its official representation within U.S. intelligence community strategy documents. In other words, within the upper echelons of the U.S. intelligence community, open source discourse appears relatively *consistent*, yet contested. Within and across operational levels of some homeland security organizations, by contrast, open source discourse appears relatively *inconsistent*, yet still contested. Thus, the overall system of statements that forms open source objects, concepts, roles, and the relationships among these may vary in terms of their meaningful, rule-like, and constitutive qualities. This is partially a result of the specific organizational context in which a system of statements circulates. The case studies in this book are thus presented in a sequence that illustrates the diminishing strength of open source discourse across three interrelated contexts. As a result, chapters 4 and 5 emphasize processes of institutional discourse, while chapters 6 and 7 move toward discussions of open source within the realm of citizenship. The appearance of incongruity among the case studies, however, usefully illustrates the benefits of a discursive perspective on institutional change: it underscores how communication produces the qualities of standardization and coherence across internal/public spheres that are often required for successful institutional transformation.

INSTITUTIONAL DISCOURSE: AN ILLUSTRATION

Having brought the concepts of institutions, organizational discourse, and national security rhetoric together, I briefly illustrate the benefits of this perspective. Organizational theory suggests that open source is more likely to be institutionalized if it is propagated via a combination of political, technical, and cultural work.[48] Perkmann and Spicer argue that "institutional change is not brought about by design but emerges as the result of the collective yet uncoordinated actions of distributed actors."[49] Institutionalization occurs when actors consistently reproduce preferred beliefs and practices in settings removed from the control of the institutional entrepreneurs who originally articulated those beliefs and practices.[50] However, viewing institutionalization as a largely uncoordinated activity risks underestimating the ability of institutional entrepreneurs to amplify discourse-centered forms of institutional work within a tight time frame in order to achieve their objectives.

Specifically, in 2005, open source advocates faced the formidable challenge of rapidly increasing awareness, appreciation, and use of open source within an historically insular and secretive institution. As one official remarked, "[The ADDNI/OS] was told, 'Go out and make open source something important.' There wasn't a whole lot of vision in terms of what [senior DNI officials] wanted to do with open source. . . . [The ADDNI/OS] was pretty much left to his own devices to figure out what he was going to do. There was no explicit, 'Here are your marching orders. Go out and do this.' "[51] Given the absence of a roadmap for open source's institutionalization, one way officials amplified their efforts was through the strategic use of genre. Specifically, in the case of open source, the genre of annual conference served a critical role. Organizational scholars Nelson Phillips, Thomas Lawrence, and Cynthia Hardy argue that "texts that take the form of genres, which are recognizable, interpretable, and usable in other organizations, are more likely to become embedded in discourse than texts that do not."[52] Genres are defined here as "recognized types of communication characterized by particular conventions invoked in response to a recurrent set of circumstances, such as letters, memos, meetings, training seminars, resumes, and announcements."[53] According to Phillips and colleagues, texts associated with relevant and recognizable genres are more likely to be incorporated into institutional members' own actions, texts, and discourses. To be effective, a genre must be appropriate to an institutional setting.

Conferences and genre interrelate on two levels. First, conferences enable institutional entrepreneurs to write and disseminate texts with various characteristics, thereby increasing the likelihood that at least some of those texts will be relevant, recognizable, and consumed by participants gathered at the conference. At the DNI Open Source conferences in 2007 and 2008, such texts included brochures; copies of Intelligence Community Directive (ICD) 301, which established the ADDNI/OS; information packets; panel presentations; websites; blogs; multimedia presentations; vendor promotional materials; training sessions; and transcripts. The distribution of these texts accompanied the ceremonial and symbolic functions of the conferences. Second, the conference form *itself* constitutes a genre of organizational communication within the U.S. intelligence community. For example, then DDNI/A Fingar stated during his speech at the 2007 DNI Open Source Conference, "We hold a lot of conferences. . . . We do hundreds of conferences, thousands of outside experts every year. Admonition at every one of these that I attend is, make sure that the connections live on after the session. Exchange email addresses. Exchange phone numbers. Be in contact. Give as well as receive."[54]

The organizing principle of the inaugural 2007 DNI Open Source Conference was the legitimation of open source, which involved the articulation and embedding of preferred meanings of open source throughout the intelligence and homeland security sectors.[55] The requirement of the conference reflected the need for the U.S. intelligence community to publicly demonstrate adequate response to legislation and directives calling for the increased and effective use of open source. The stylistic characteristics of the conference included the regional site location, high-tech venue, theatrical lighting, audiovisual effects, vivid presentations, speeches given by institutional celebrities, interactive training sessions, eye-popping vendor booths, promotional materials, and demonstrations—all of which created a spectacle that reinforced the authority, credibility, and legitimacy of the ADDNI/OS and his preferred vision of open source. Between featured speakers, for example, a PowerPoint presentation displayed on the large overhead screen scrolled through slides alternating between official photos of the speakers and quotations concerning the value of open source.

The 2007 and 2008 DNI Open Source conferences demonstrate how conferences can both signal the emergence of a new institution, as well as advance that institution to a sturdier position within an organizational field. Of course, not every conference (inaugural or otherwise) marks the emergence of a new institution or successfully ensures its viability. Moreover, conferences in mature fields can certainly facilitate the creation of new institutional arrangements. However, the relevant question here is how conferences, as a genre of organizational communication, have shaped the institutionalization of open source within the U.S. intelligence community. My argument is that conferences are uniquely suited for amplifying discourse-centered forms of institutional work in that they allow actors to efficiently perform—simultaneously and within a tight time frame—nearly all nine types of institutional work identified by organizational theorists, thereby encouraging the rapid diffusion of new values, attitudes, beliefs, and practices. I indicate in the following how institutional work was performed during the 2007 and 2008 DNI Open Source conferences.

Open Source Political Work

Political work—advocating, defining, and vesting—was prominent during the conferences. Advocacy involves the mobilization of political support, agenda setting, and lobbying for resources through deliberate and persuasive messages. It is not surprising, then, that the conferences were open to the media, as this helped facilitate the dissemination of key messages to influential audiences. In order to spur the reallocation of institutional resources in 2007, ADDNI/OS Jardines asserted, "It is time for open source to be the source of first resort, and that time is now."[56] Other speakers during the conferences echoed Jardines's advocacy and sense of urgency. For example, referencing the U.S. intelligence community's *Vision 2015* document, the ADDNI/OS in 2008, Dan Butler, stated, "No aspect of collection requires greater consideration or holds more promise than open source information. Transformation of our approach to open sources is critical to the future success of adaptive collection."[57] Here, Butler illustrated the official strategy of relying on authoritative institutional documents to justify new structures, funding, and practices. However, then DDNI/A Fingar stated, "For me, the use of open source is not one of those things that the WMD Commission or IRTPA or others told us to do. It's not in the nice-to-do category. It's absolutely essential."[58] Interestingly, Fingar's advocacy of open source simultaneously acknowledged and diminished the importance of official documents. In other words, Fingar's statement revealed his assumption that official texts are, in fact, generally critical for reform, yet insufficient for generating adequate commitment to new open source practices.

While open source advocacy was prominent during the conferences, it was certainly not confined to that setting: officials have incorporated advocacy as a permanent function of the OSC. For example, the director of the CIA commented in 2008, "The Open Source Center was designed to be a production line in terms of creation of knowledge of use to American policymakers. But it was also designed to be an advocate, a spokesperson, a facilitator for the open source enterprise, for the open source discipline beyond the fence line, beyond the confines of the Open Source Center itself."[59]

In contrast to advocacy, definitional work involves "constructing rule systems that confer status or identity, define boundaries of membership or create status hierarchies within a field."[60] In 2007, then DDNI/A Fingar attempted to define the parameters of open source: "[Open source]'s more, though, than going out and Googling the Internet. It's a lot more than digesting what dribbles into an electronic inbox because of a profile that has been set up to capture information on a particular range of subjects. It's a lot more than checking a Wiki entry."[61] Fingar defined open source as involving sophisticated data collection and analysis tools and outreach to experts beyond the confines of the intelligence community. In attempting to define open source, then DDNI/C Mary Margaret Graham recounted a meeting she attended during which officials crafted the organizational structure of the newly formed ODNI (Office of the Director of National Intelligence). Graham stated, "And we had quite a discussion about where we should site it (open source) in the DNI. And at the end of the day, for me, the most persuasive argument was that at its essence, [open source] is a discipline of collection."[62] Graham, however, acknowledged ongoing debates when she stated the following: "Some of my colleagues in the open source world, I know, don't agree with my characterization. . . . To me, open source—and maybe my view is a product of where I grew up [in the secret intelligence arena]. . . . For me, open source is not an INT, but is, more importantly, an enabler of intelligence."[63] Graham's position allowed her to define open source in ways that maintained its inferior status compared to other INTs (e.g., signals intelligence or human intelligence). This definitional move has created considerable problems for open source's institutionalization in that insufficient material resources appear to have been dedicated to its diffusion within the Department of Defense (DoD) and DHS. For example, a senior DoD official stated, "I would be remiss today if I told you that everything is working well, because it is not. We still face a number of challenges in the open source arena, not the least of which is moving open source out of the closet as an afterthought and making it an integral 'INT' discipline. . . . I ask all of you this morning, is open source a standalone discipline or not? Are we treating it as a source of first resort or are we still turning to, and more importantly, funding other INTs first before investing in open source?"[64] Another official further stated, "While open source is not a new discipline within defense, our biggest challenge is defining the programmatic structure to make it coequal with the other collection disciplines, intelligence disciplines."[65] Still another stakeholder interviewed for this study observed, "Every discipline has its own patron agency except for [open source]."[66] Although the conferences did not resolve debates surrounding the disciplinary status of open source, they allowed DNI officials to assert a preferred definition and advocate for its widespread adoption.

In contrast to defining, vesting involves the creation of rule structures that confer property rights. The size of an agency's budget is often interpreted by institutional members as a concrete sign of that agency's prowess. A DNI official stated during the 2007 conference that it was a result of "vast funding" that "we have formal recognition" of open source.[67] Additionally, ADDNI/OS Butler stated in 2008, "In 2007, I would say if you had to capture in one word what we started to do it would be invest."[68] Material support thus functions symbolically to put open source on equal footing with other types of intelligence collection and analysis. In response to one participant's question concerning how equal footing for open source would be achieved within the CIA, then Director Hayden stated, "It's a challenge, you know, truth in lending among friends, these are not easy budget decisions."[69]

Open Source Technical Work

Technical work—mimicry, theorizing, and educating—were also prevalent during both conferences. Mimicry involves leveraging existing assumptions, practices, and rules to support the adoption of new forms and practices. The OSC's products are provided on classified intelligence networks and apparently mimic traditional classified resources in their presentation. Then DDNI/C Graham stated during her 2007 speech, "The perfect world is when . . . open source data resides on the same space at the same time [as secret information], with the information protected on both sides of that line, so that [analysts] can look at the classified information and the open source information at the same time."[70] Additionally, the Open Source 101 and Accessing Open Sources training sessions offered to conference participants mimicked the intelligence community's well-established Analysis 101 program. In mimicking secret intelligence, however, open source is less able to preserve those attributes that make it open. As CIA director Hayden stated, "One irony of working the open source side of the intelligence business, not unlike every other part of the intelligence business, is that the better we do, the less we can talk about it."[71] Nevertheless, for most stakeholders, open source's mimicry of secret intelligence is desirable in that it facilitates institutionalization.

Theorization involves naming "new concepts and practices so that they might become a part of the cognitive map of the field."[72] Officials attempted to define open source concepts under the monikers of "source of first resort," "open source discipline," "decision advantage," and others.[73] Educating, by contrast, involves conveying to members a set of institutional skills and knowledge. During the conferences, the Open Source 101 and Accessing Open Sources training sessions served this purpose. The conferences' emphasis on mimicry and educating is unsurprising in light of the finding that "creating institutions through work that changes abstract categories of meaning (i.e., mimicry, theorizing and educating) . . . hold[s] the greatest potential for institutional entrepreneurship on the part of relatively small, peripheral, or isolated actors."[74] Indeed, in 2010, ADDNI/OS Butler announced that his office would begin implementing a certification program for open source practitioners. Butler said, "We want to be able to certify a subset of the intelligence community as true open-source intelligence professionals."[75]

Open Source Cultural Work

Conference participants' communication often focused on identities, associations, and networks—in other words, "the roles, values, and norms that underpin institutions."[76] Constructing identities involves describing the relationship between actor and field. For example, one official stated, "Look all around you because you are making history. . . . This is our community, our open source community, and you are part of that community, and the experts who are sitting in this audience, you, too, those that reside outside the traditional intelligence community, you, too, are part of our community."[77] Changing normative associations involves "re-making the connections between sets of practices and the moral and cultural foundations of those practices," while constructing normative networks involves building "interorganizational connections through which practices become normatively sanctioned."[78] Conference sessions, including Media as the Open Source, Academic Outreach, Private Sector Partnerships, International Partnerships, and Outreach to State, Local, and Tribal Partners, focused on creating new associations and interconnections between institutional insiders and outsiders. The endorsement of key institutional leaders also supported normative changes. For example, CIA director Hayden declared, "In fact, we saw the establishment of this center, the Open Source Center, as one of the three most important objectives of the ODNI in its first year."[79] Officials also claimed that the president was regularly receiving intelligence branded with the OSC's logo, as well as that 15,000 federal, state, and local officials and policy makers regularly used opensource.gov.[80]

In summary, the DNI Open Source conferences (especially the inaugural conference) served as a genre of organizational communication that enabled officials to perform the types of discourse-centered institutional work needed to create a new institution. These forms of work do not, of course, *ensure* that the institutionalization of open source will be adequate or endure. One stakeholder made the following comment:

I think Doug Naquin [director of the OSC] has done the most that he can, in the sense that he has put people down range in these organizations; he has made sure that he is gathering as much information as he can in a usable fashion. I don't think that Doug is the problem here. The problem here lies outside of Doug in the sense that Doug needs top cover for [open source's institutionalization], which means that you need to have a DNI who fundamentally acknowledges that in analytical transformation, and collection transformation, that open source is not just an INT, but in a way, it is the place to start.[81]

The hypothesis that conferences serve as a genre of organizational communication that facilitates institutionalization would appear to be supported if DNI officials no longer host conferences once they determine that a sufficient level of institutionalization has been achieved. As one stakeholder observed, "You can only put [open source] 'information sharing' into everybody's heads so many times. I think, for the most part, people 'get' open source. I mean, they will by now, and if they are not getting it, that's on them."[82] Indeed, there has not been a DNI Open Source Conference since 2008, indicating that perhaps the two conferences fulfilled their institutionalization objectives.

Finally, this illustration underscores that institutionalization occurs not primarily through action (behavior not widely written or talked about), but through the production, circulation, and consumption of talk and text that describe and communicate those actions.[83] A discourse-centered perspective on open source focuses attention on the taken-for-granted assumptions that undergird the concept of intelligence, the ways stakeholders attempt to maintain or transform those assumptions, and the persuasive arguments, stories, and images designed to achieve strategic objectives. The next chapter provides an expanded and more detailed example of this process and how it underlies the reshaping of intelligence.

CHAPTER 4

"The Source of First Resort": The Intelligence Community

I work for the CIA. I am not a spy. I just read books!
—Joe Turner in *Three Days of the Condor*

In the 1975 film *Three Days of the Condor*, Robert Redford plays the role of CIA open source analyst Joe Turner (code name "Condor"), who inadvertently uncovers—through publicly available sources—a rogue CIA operation designed to ensure U.S. control of Middle Eastern oil fields.[1] Turner's job is to analyze foreign books, newspapers, and journals to develop insights for his CIA bosses. A few days after filing a particularly intriguing report with CIA headquarters, Turner returns to his New York City office to find that his colleagues have all been murdered. The film centers on Turner's quest to solve the mystery while avoiding being killed by CIA operatives who are involved in the plot. During one scene, CIA mandarins question Turner's handler ("Higgins") about him during a meeting at headquarters:

CIA official: "This Condor isn't the man his file says he is." [Another official asks] "So where did he learn evasive moves?"

Higgins: "He reads."

CIA official: "What the hell does that mean?"

Higgins: "It means, Sir, that he reads everything."

Turner is an unlikely hero who uses open sources and his superior reasoning and creativity to uncover—and later foil—a CIA conspiracy. Decades later, far from Hollywood, a handful of officials, policy makers, and corporate executives have endeavored to craft a rather different depiction of the ideal open source practitioner. This practitioner is an intelligence agency analyst, contractor, or even an ordinary citizen who uses open sources and overcomes bureaucratic obstacles to help thwart defined *external* threats to U.S. national security. How this depiction of the ideal open source practitioner is produced and disseminated, and why it matters for the reshaping of U.S. intelligence, is the focus of this chapter.

In the years following 9/11, the U.S. Senate and Congress's Joint Inquiry (2002), the 9/11 Commission (2004), and the WMD Commission (2005) all concluded that the intelligence community needed to increase its collection and analysis of open source information in order to improve national security planning and decision making. As a result, the ADDNI/OS and a handful of officials, policy makers, and executives have subsequently attempted to make open source "the source of first resort."[2] Using the theoretical perspective developed in chapter 3, this chapter analyzes the open source discourse circulating within the U.S. intelligence community in order to investigate the connection between that discourse and the institutionalization of open source. Institutionalization involves conflict over the words, or vocabularies, that stakeholders use to describe open source, the underlying logics that give rise to those words, and overarching ideas about how institutional change should unfold. At root, this conflict occurs because officials define open source in ways that attempt to simultaneously hold the ideals of secrecy and openness in tension.

To better understand the implications of this tension, I explain in this chapter how officials author, circulate, and invoke documents in order to establish the legitimacy of open source across the U.S. intelligence community. I assess how these documents are intended to reproduce or transform certain beliefs, practices, and the identities of institutional members. I elaborate the competing logics of open source, and I describe how a dominant, institutional logic of open source has thus far been constructed using the neoliberal language of enterprise. Framing intelligence as a business enterprise hinders alternative paths to open source's development that may better respond to the idealized principles of a democratic society. Understanding the reasons for this situation first requires examining the competing logics of open source.

THE LOGICS OF OPEN SOURCE

Within open source discourse, stakeholders hold two conflicting logics in tension.[3] The first logic relates to secrecy, while the second logic relates to openness. This finding is unsurprising given that, etymologically, the term "open source intelligence" literally fuses together openness and secrecy to the extent that intelligence is synonymous with secrets. By the logic of secrecy, I refer to the assumption that governments *must* hide some information from other governments (and citizens) if they are to adequately conduct affairs of state. Commentators' assertions that open source can provide decision advantage for policy makers evokes this logic of secrecy. This logic maintains that intelligence is in no way a public good because secrecy is, in fact, what makes intelligence a special category of information. As intelligence scholar and former CIA official Mark Lowenthal states, "Secrecy does make intelligence unique. That others would keep important information from you, that you need certain types of information and wish to keep your needs secret, and that you have the means to obtain information that you also wish to keep secret are major reasons for having intelligence agencies."[4]

Open source stakeholders who agree with these premises, however, rarely acknowledge (at least publicly) how secrecy sustains difference and hierarchy among national security stakeholders in ways that are contrary to democratic ideals. For example, economist Joseph Stiglitz argues that "secrecy is corrosive: it is antithetical to democratic values, and it undermines democratic processes. It is based on a mistrust between those governing and those governed; and at the same time, it exacerbates that mistrust."[5] Possession of intelligence reinforces the image of the possessor as elite, knowledgeable, and advantaged. It is therefore natural that national security strategizing and decision making be confined to this group of actors. To ensure these privileges, the production, dissemination, and revelation of intelligence must be tightly policed.

The logic of openness, by contrast, assumes that governance is improved by the free flow of information among policy makers, officials, and citizens. As President Barack Obama stated, "Openness means more than simply informing the American people about how decisions are made. It means recognizing that government does not have all the answers, and that public officials need to draw on what citizens know."[6] The logic of openness evokes images of transparency, accountability, exchange, and trust. Thus, "open source" may not generate the same allure among intelligence professionals as "classified information" because open source is symbolically tainted by its association with open, free, or public materials. Intelligence analysts have historically discounted the inaccurate or unsubstantiated reporting thought to characterize the great bulk of open source information.[7] In the post-9/11 era, however, officials and commentators often liken this material to a vast "goldmine" filled with potential "nuggets" of intelligence.[8] Officials readily acknowledge, though, that the symbolic dimensions of open source are a primary obstacle to its institutionalization within the U.S. intelligence community. For example, in a January 10, 2006, interview with David Martin of CBS News, then ADDNI/OS Jardines stated, "One of the challenges that I have is to change the culture to value open sources more." Martin replied, "So the old attitude [is]: If it wasn't stolen, how can it be valuable?" Jardines retorted, "Correct. That's very much the old attitude"[9]

CHANGING AN "OLD ATTITUDE"

In order to change the intelligence community's organizational culture to value open sources, Jardines organized the inaugural DNI Open Source Conference in 2007. During his remarks at the 2007 conference, Jardines underscored the need for a new attitude: "Let's keep in mind that we in the intelligence community take pride in knowing things or having the ability to know things that others don't, and so there's just the natural tendency that if the document's got a fancy cover sheet that says Top Secret and all sorts of fancy code words on it, that we tend to view that as more important than, say, something that's taken just from open sources."[10] Another stakeholder interviewed for this project asserted the following:

The biggest barrier to open source [its institutionalization] is the closed source intelligence community. The closed source intelligence community is very jealous of its prerogatives. It's very jealous of its financial or budgetary resources, and over the years it . . . has interfered with the full and complete development of open source capabilities. I say that having worked for the CIA. . . . I don't have a problem with the secret side, but I will tell you that there is no question that the secret side has interfered with the development of a full and complete open source capability.

Holding competing logics of secrecy and openness in tension is challenging for intelligence officials: as an institution, U.S. intelligence and national security *require* the production of secrets—intelligence—to preserve its privileged status and authority. Open source, however, evokes egalitarian ideals that potentially undermine that status and authority. Officials have attempted to address this paradox by asserting that for open source information to become intelligence, the information in question must be formally vetted by an intelligence analyst. ICD (Intelligence Community Directive) 301 states specifically that "open source information" is "publicly available information that anyone can lawfully obtain by request, purchase, or observation."[11] "Open source intelligence," by contrast, is defined as being "produced from publicly available information that is collected, exploited, and disseminated in a timely manner to an appropriate audience for the purpose of addressing a specific intelligence requirement."[12] Here, the producer of intelligence is presumably an analyst (either an agency employee or contractor) who is both aware of a "specific intelligence requirement" and able to communicate with an "appropriate audience" (i.e., policy makers or decision makers). However, this symbolic transformation of information into intelligence is not without irony. As one senior defense official explained, "Analysts sometimes act as though I can't read the *New York Times*."[13] This official meant to underscore how widespread access to open source information complicates the relationship between intelligence analysts and policy makers. As one insider commented, "[Intelligence analysts] look upon their world as one of secrets and classification. And that's fine. They should. But they don't know what the hell is in the outside world, or they have a bare grasp on it. . . . Policymakers do not listen [to analysts] because they believe that they can get more information on their own—correctly or incorrectly. So, everybody has become their own analyst."[14]

Open source discourse thus serves as a site of struggle over the *meaning* of intelligence. This struggle occurs at a textual level, where stakeholders compete to author official documents that advance preferred concepts that constitute open source as a specific type of intelligence. For example, Simmons included the following language in the 2006 Defense Authorization Act:

(1) Open-source intelligence (OSINT) is intelligence that is produced from publicly available information collected, exploited, and disseminated in a timely manner to an appropriate audience for the purpose of addressing a specific intelligence requirement. (2) With the Information Revolution, the amount, significance, and accessibility of open-source information has exploded, but the Intelligence Community has not expanded its exploitation efforts and systems to produce open-source intelligence. (3) The production of open-source intelligence is a valuable intelligence discipline that must be integrated in the intelligence cycle to ensure that United States policymakers are fully and completely informed. (4) The dissemination and use of validated open-source intelligence inherently enables information sharing as it is produced without the use of sensitive sources and methods. Open-source intelligence products can be shared with the American public and foreign allies because of its unclassified nature.[15]

A slightly different meaning of open source is apparent in a NATO definition, authored by Steele and published in 2001: "Open Source Intelligence, or OSINT, is unclassified information that has been deliberately discovered, discriminated, distilled, and disseminated to a select audience in order to address a specific question. It provides a very robust foundation for other intelligence disciplines. When applied in a systematic fashion, OSINT products can reduce the demands on classified intelligence collection resources by limiting requests for information only to those questions that cannot be answered by open sources."[16] NATO and Steele define open source, not as an intelligence discipline in its own right, but as a foundation for other disciplines such as imagery intelligence (IMINT), signals intelligence (SIGINT), or human intelligence (HUMINT). In Congress's definition, open source achieves the status of an intelligence discipline, yet is undifferentiated from the others. Whereas Congress states that open source products can be shared with the American public, NATO makes no such assertion. As will be illustrated in the following, ambiguity surrounding the legitimacy of open source as a specific type of intelligence creates problems for its institutionalization. Legitimate intelligence disciplines are worthy of special attention and funding. Open source, however, is an ambiguous symbol, constructed from competing logics of secrecy

and openness, whose meanings and uses are struggled over by government officials, policy makers, executives, scholars, and the public.

Those who construct open source primarily in accordance with the logic
of secrecy tend to emphasize the need to protect the sources and methods
of intelligence, as well as the interests of intelligence agencies. For example, then CIA director Hayden stated during the 2008 DNI Open Source
Conference, "We are often addressing requirements or questions that are
sensitive by nature. The information is unclassified. Our interest in it is
not."[17] Nevertheless, the countervailing logic of openness maintains that
organizations and individuals outside the formal boundaries of the U.S.
intelligence community can, do, and should make contributions—albeit
indirectly—to national security. For example, ADDNI/OS Jardines declared during the 2007 DNI Open Source Conference, "We must come
to terms with the fact that the font of human knowledge resides largely
outside the intelligence community and [is] available principally through
open sources."[18] This logic permitted the conference organizers to invite
participants from commercial, nonprofit, academic, and media sectors to
contribute to the discussion.

Post-9/11 open source discourse is therefore characterized by a break
from an institutional logic that has traditionally maintained secrecy as "an
absolute way of life" within intelligence agencies.[19] Nevertheless, official
open source discourse still *privileges* the logic of secrecy—a logic that un-
dergirds the U.S. intelligence community's coherence and exceptionalism.
Privileging the logic of secrecy, while simultaneously declaring the desirability of openness, manifests itself in a number of blatant and subtle
contradictions within open source discourse. As one open source stakeholder explained, "[The 2008 DNI Open Source Conference] is a bit peculiar because the leaders of the government open source enterprise do
not otherwise have much use for public input or participation. In other
words, there was something anomalous about the conference. I can go
to the conference, but I cannot easily get most open source products."[20]
These contradictions are richly evident at the level of open source policy
documents.

OPEN SOURCE LOGICS AND POLICY

For decades, commentators and the authors of official reports have asserted that open source should be treated as an equal contributor to national security in comparison to traditional, secret intelligence disciplines
such IMINT or HUMINT. The widespread and sustained attention to contemporary open source reforms, however, can be traced to three investigatory commissions. Two of these commissions—the Joint Inquiry (2002)
and the 9/11 Commission (2002–2004)—were created in the aftermath of
9/11, while the third—the WMD Commission (2004–2005)—was established in response to the 2003 Iraq WMD intelligence failure. In analyzing

the connections among the final reports of these commissions, as well as the speech and writing of open source stakeholders more broadly, we are able to track how stakeholders have attempted to establish open source as a distinct and legitimate form of intelligence in order to spur its institutionalization within the U.S. intelligence community.

Specifically, following the 9/11 catastrophe, the Joint Inquiry of the House and Senate Intelligence Committees issued its *Report* (2002). In the "Additional Views" section of the *Report*, Senator Mike Dewine (R-OH) stated, "The Intelligence Community needs to pay more attention to the collection and analysis of open-source information. This type of information needs to be examined and needs to be taken more seriously. We must remember that open-source information was used to warn investigators in 1999 that al-Qaeda terrorists might fly a hijacked airliner into American buildings."[21] Dewine continued, "The Intelligence Community is simply not accustomed to assessing the value of open sources nor is it used to integrating them into their work. In fact, the Intelligence Community is more inclined to use open-source material as a last resort, not as a primary source, no matter how compelling the information. This attitude needs to change."[22]

The 9/11 Commission's *Final Report* issued in 2004 echoed many of the Joint Inquiry's conclusions. Significantly, however, the *Final Report* contained a chart depicting a proposed reorganization of the U.S. intelligence community. This chart contained a reference to an "Open Source Agency" residing *outside* the CIA yet reporting to the CIA director.[23] A copy of this chart is provided in Figure 4.1.

Figure 4.1:
Open Source Agency referenced in the 9/11 Commission's *Final Report*

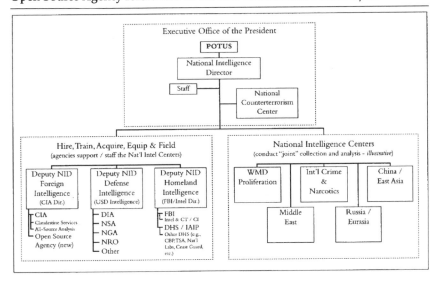

A 9/11 Commission staff member involved in the writing of the *Final Report* claims to not recall where the recommendation for an Open Source Agency originated.[24] However, a stakeholder familiar with the 9/11 Commission claims that Vice Chairman Lee Hamilton was responsible for raising the idea among the commissioners and securing their support for the recommendation.[25] The 9/11 Commission's unattributed and unelaborated reference to an Open Source Agency has subsequently been used by open source stakeholders to assert the legitimacy of open source initiatives and to justify new organizational structures, leadership, and funding. For example, in welcoming participants to the 2007 DNI Open Source Conference, one DNI official declared, "With the recognition of open source in the 9/11 report and the WMD report, with the creation of the position of Assistant Deputy Director for National Intelligence of Open Source . . . we have formal recognition of the importance of open source."[26]

Management scholars have argued that institutionalization is predicated on practices of textual production, dissemination, and consumption; from this perspective, the influence of the 9/11 Commission's fleeting reference to an Open Source Agency is nonetheless profound.[27] Only documents that *endure* and *leave traces* of their influence in other settings are relevant to institutionalization.[28] In other words, "texts must be distributed and interpreted by other actors if they are to have organizing properties and the potential to affect discourse."[29] The principal way the open source–related recommendations of the Joint Inquiry and 9/11 Commission were distributed and interpreted by institutional members was by their codification into law as part of the Intelligence Reform and Terrorism Prevention Act of 2004. IRTPA was based extensively on the findings of the two inquiries. Section 1052 of IRTPA states the following:

(a) SENSE OF CONGRESS.—It is the sense of Congress that—(1) the Director of National Intelligence should establish an intelligence center for the purpose of coordinating the collection, analysis, production, and dissemination of open-source intelligence to elements of the intelligence community; (2) open-source intelligence is a valuable source that must be integrated into the intelligence cycle to ensure that United States policymakers are fully and completely informed; and (3) the intelligence center should ensure that each element of the intelligence community uses open-source intelligence consistent with the mission of such element. . . . The Director of National Intelligence shall ensure that the intelligence community makes efficient and effective use of open-source information and analysis. (c) REPORT.—Not later than June 30, 2005, the Director of National Intelligence shall submit to the congressional intelligence committees a report containing the decision of the Director as to whether an open-source intelligence center will be established. If the Director decides not to establish an open-source intelligence center, such report shall also contain a description of how the intelligence community will use open-source intelligence and effectively integrate open-source intelligence into the national intelligence cycle.[30]

While new laws such as this provide stakeholders a powerful resource for affecting change, other texts may be even more consequential. For example, the WMD Commission's *Report to the President* in 2005 appears to have influenced the shape of open source reforms even more than IRTPA. Specifically, the WMD Commission's *Report to the President* stated the following:

Open Source information has long been viewed by many outside the Intelligence Community as essential to understanding foreign political, economic, social, and even military developments. . . . The Community does not have any broader program [other than the Foreign Broadcast Information Service] to gather and organize the wealth of global information generated each day and increasingly available, if only temporarily, over the Internet. We also believe that the need for exploiting open source material is greater now than ever before. Today, the spread of information technology—and the ever increasing pace at which it advances—is immune to many traditional, clandestine methods of intelligence collection. Whereas advanced technological research once occurred only in large facilities and within enormous government bureaucratic institutions, today it can (and does) occur in nondescript office parks or garages, and with very small clusters of people.[31]

After assessing the lack of institutional support for open source, the *Report to the President*'s authors concluded, "We therefore recommend the creation of an Open Source Directorate at the CIA."[32] The WMD Commission was staffed by institutional insiders who have dominated the U.S. national security establishment since the Cold War—elites including John McCain, Walter Slocombe, and Admiral William O. Studeman. Significantly, the words "Intelligence Professional" were written before many of the biographies of WMD Commission staff members listed on the commission's website. Designation as an "Intelligence Professional" potentially signaled to other national security elites that the WMD Commission abided by traditional institutional norms and values—one being the logic of secrecy. It is unsurprising, then, that the WMD Commission recommended the establishment of an Open Source Center *within* the CIA (which occurred on November 8, 2005). This recommendation contradicted the 9/11 Commission's call for an Open Source Agency residing *outside* the CIA (IRTPA did not indicate where an "open-source intelligence center" should be established). Although the majority of the 9/11 commissioners were clearly long-time Beltway insiders, staff members had fewer public markers of their institutional status. Thus, while the Bush administration endorsed and implemented nearly all 74 recommendations of the WMD Commission, only half of the 9/11 Commission's recommendations had been enacted by 2007—a true measure of relative textual effectiveness.[33] The lack of open congressional or public debate concerning where to situate an open source agency underscores the dominance of the institutional logic of secrecy vis-à-vis open source. The decision to establish the Open Source Center within the CIA appears to have been based not only on maintaining continuity with the agency's existing FBIS, but also on the taken-for-granted premise that persistent institutional secrecy is both necessary and desirable—even for managing an ostensibly public, sharable, and unclassified resource.

Because the final reports of these investigatory commissions do not stand in isolation from earlier documents and wider discussions and debates about open source, it is useful to briefly compare their findings with Steele's writings. As mentioned in chapter 2, from the early 1990s until the establishment of the ADDNI/OS in 2005, Steele's vision of open source dominated the discourse. Specifically, throughout the 1990s and early 2000s, Steele's ideas concerning open source were promoted during annual conferences he hosted in northern Virginia and elsewhere. These conferences brought hundreds of open source stakeholders from government, industry, academe, and nongovernmental organizations [NGOs] together each year to discuss the meanings, uses, and benefits of open source, as well as obstacles to its institutionalization within the U.S. intelligence community. During Steele's open source conference in 2005, journalist Kent Bye summarized Steele's vision of open source:

Steele is advocating for a system that he calls 'Open Source Information System—External' (OSIS-X) that would have educational institutions, NGOs, other governments and possibly even US citizens (i.e. bloggers and citizen journalists) contributing information to this network. He envisions forming symbiotic relationships with these groups making access to this OSIS-X publicly available to the academic institutions and NGOs—and potentially to anyone via the Internet.[34]

After being appointed ADDNI/OS in 2005, Jardines gave a speech at Steele's annual conference and arranged for dozens of intelligence community members to attend. Jardines was initially interested in leveraging Steele's conference, finding it complementary to his own efforts to institutionalize open source. However, it soon became clear that Jardines and Steele held differing assumptions about which logic—openness or secrecy—ought to guide open source's development. Eventually the relationship soured between the two men. For example, in an April 16, 2006, interview with *Military Review*, Steele made these comments:

Young Mr. Jardines, a former Sergeant now working on his PhD, is the Assistant Deputy Director of National Intelligence for Open Source (ADDNI/OS). He has no program authority, no money, and no staff. While I am the virtual 'hub' for 25,000 truly professional individuals worldwide, I am in the same position as Jardines: no program authority, no money, and no staff. While I have the web site and the conference, and the nuclear powered rolodex in this area, what is missing is a serious commitment from the US Government to create a globally-relevant Open Source Agency and a truly global version of the Open Source Information System (OSIS) which is NOT part of the . . . Open Source Center at CIA.[35]

Steele is not alone in calling for an Open Source Agency to be established outside the CIA. Simmons advocated for such an agency during the 2007 and 2008 DNI Open Source conferences.[36] Additionally, in February 2009, Ron Marks, intelligence commentator and senior vice president for Oxford Analytica, Inc. (a prominent open source firm), circulated an op-ed, "Twittering Intelligence," to members of the International Association for Intelligence Education (IAFIE). Marks wrote, "The gathering, provision and analyzing of our new world of total information may need to be moved outside the intelligence community. . . . This could even mean setting up a separate agency based on the Open Source Center to deal with the new information world. . . . An intelligence community wedded to a classified past and encumbered with ancient security rules will only do its level best to strangle open source exploitation."[37] Marks was quickly challenged, however, by IAFIE members who warned him not to view open source as replacing classified materials. Others were brusque and argued that open source is not intelligence. Marks's commentary demonstrates the delicate weaving of the logics of secrecy and openness that open source stakeholders must accomplish in order to avoid inciting reactionary attacks.

It appears that ADDNI/OS Jardines sought to institutionalize the collection and analysis of open source within the U.S. intelligence community in ways that did not overtly challenge the dominant institutional logic of secrecy. Specifically, in July 2006, the ADDNI/OS's office authored "ICD 301: National Open Source Enterprise." This document formally established, through applicable laws and directives, the ADDNI/OS's authority to promulgate preferred descriptions of open source objects, concepts, and roles. In bureaucratic and technical language, ICD 301 described the "roles and responsibilities" of new open source organizations within the intelligence community. For example, ICD 301 stated the following:

The ADDNI/OS shall have the following authorities and responsibilities for the National Open Source Enterprise: (1) Ensuring integrated IC open source collection management strategy and implementation are reflective of Presidential priorities. (2) Oversight, evaluation, policy direction, and tasking of IC open source exploitation organizations. (3) Advisory tasking regarding acquisition of open source information by agencies and departments not within the National Intelligence Program. (4) Development and oversight of the national open source enterprise. (5) Working with the ADDNI/Chief Financial Officer (CFO) and the Deputy Director of National Intelligence for Customer Outcomes (DDNI/CO) to establish program guidance in accordance with Presidential priorities. (6) Oversight of Program Managers' compliance with program guidance in concert with the ADDNI/CFO. (7) Coordination of open source requirements of common concern. (8) Oversight of the procurement of tools and services to support open source exploitation. (9) Oversight of interagency sharing of open source information. (10) Overall guidance, on behalf of the DNI and the DDNI for Collection (DDNI/C) to the

Director, Central Intelligence Agency (D/CIA), in the role as Executive Agent for the DNI.[38]

Significantly, ICD 301 omitted the public and sharable dimensions of open source conceptualizations found within legislation and the final reports of the aforementioned commissions. This omission foreclosed opportunities to bolster these potential dimensions of open source. Management scholars Phillips, Lawrence, and Hardy argue that "texts that are produced by actors who are understood to have a legitimate right to speak, who have resource power or formal authority, or who are centrally located in a field are more likely to become embedded in discourse than texts that are not."[39] By "embedded," the authors mean the extent to which another organization's members incorporate a given text as part of their routine meaning-making processes. As a result of the ADDNI/OS's resource power, formal authority, and a central position in the intelligence community, the ADDNI/OS's preferred depiction of open source has dominated official discourse. Consequently, Steele's influence on the trajectory of open source reforms has waned. Steele has not hosted an open source conference in several years, and he did not attend either the 2007 or 2008 DNI Open Source conferences. Those who share Steele's vision of an independent open source agency find their ability to affect change similarly constrained.

INSTITUTIONALIZATION DEPENDS ON CONTROL OF OFFICIAL DOCUMENTS

The previous discussion described how documents serve as a site of struggle within institutional reform efforts. Intelligence stakeholders use official documents as platforms to advance preferred depictions of open source concepts, objects, roles, and the relationships among these. Once these depictions are established within authoritative documents, stakeholders then point to these documents in their speech and writing as evidence of official sanction. During a roundtable entitled "OSINT 2020: The Future of Open Source Intelligence" held at the National Press Club on July 17, 2010, ADDNI/OS Butler told the audience the following:

I've always found that it's good, if we're going to have a panel and discuss something like OSINT, that we should define right from the outset what we're talking about. So let me offer to you the official definition of OSINT, at least the official IC definition. "Open source intelligence is intelligence produced from publicly available information that is collected, exploited and disseminated in a timely manner to an appropriate audience for the purpose of addressing a specific intelligence requirement." That comes from the Intelligence Community Directive 301 entitled 'National Open Source Enterprise.' And we didn't make it up. It was cribbed, actually, from law—the National Defense Authorization Act for FY 2006.[40]

As noted in chapter 2, it was Simmons who was responsible for the definition of open source contained in the 2006 National Defense Authorization Act. This example illustrates the importance of control over official texts as a key mechanism of institutionalization. In other words, successful institutionalization hinges on the production, circulation, and consumption (embedding) of official texts.[41] It is important to recognize how the trajectory of open source's institutionalization relies on this solipsistic use of language: stakeholders point to official documents to bolster their own authority, credibility, and legitimacy—omitting, of course, discussion of *whose* voice is represented in these official documents. These documents are also ascribed an ability to reconfigure institutional arrangements. Consider the statement of ADDNI/OS Butler during the 2008 DNI Open Source Conference: "In 2006, we published an open source vision for the Intelligence Community. This little red book, which I'd like to call it the little red book to tease my former boss, Eliot Jardines, our first Assistant Deputy DNI for Open Source. And yet, it's had a profound effect on our community. Just 12 pages have driven an awful lot of reform, change, innovation within the Intelligence Community and beyond."[42]

These textual practices are key to transforming the routines, structures, and cultures that characterize the intelligence sector. Specifically, communication scholar François Cooren suggests that the association between humans and texts serves as the origin of institutionalization. Cooren states, "By developing textual agents, organizational members create ways for [organizational] forms to [emerge] and *remain* stable throughout space and time. . . . By *remaining*, these textual agents fabricate relatively fixed spaces and times; they define objectives; they forbid specific behaviors; and they invite or enforce humans to follow specific organizational pathways."[43] Texts are integral to processes of institutionalization in that they perform a function that humans alone cannot. In the case of open source, this function is legitimation. Intelligence officials may speak in ways that legitimate open source within interpersonal settings; however, it is only in tandem with enduring laws, directives, and other widely circulated documents that the legitimacy of open source becomes firmly established within the intelligence community. One official observed the following:

The more paperwork there is on something, the more the bureaucracy will respond. In a bureaucracy, the way you create change, reinforce legitimacy and the notion of change, is to *restate* and *restate* and *restate* your central points. Having one document that says, "I'm in charge of X," is not as good as having ten documents that say, "This individual now has this responsibility," because, typically, someone else will pull out another piece of paper and say, "Well, but you know, my piece of paper says X." So . . . my focus is getting paper out there.[44]

As another participant in this study observed, "What these documents, I think, are doing is saying, 'Hey, you know that open source stuff? That's kinda good. We are going to put more emphasis on it. We are going to put more bodies into it. . . .' If you have the direction saying open source is important, then that sets the whole ball rolling."[45]

While official open source discourse attempts to hold the logics of secrecy and openness in tension, it nevertheless tilts toward the logic of secrecy. Senator Dewine (R-OH) asserted in the 2002 Joint Inquiry *Report* that institutional preferences for secrecy have resulted in analysts and officials' poor attitude toward the use of open source. Jardines also argued that this attitude needed to change, yet a 2008 Defense Science Board report suggests that it endures. The report states, "The Defense Science Board, every commission, and every observer and critic of the Intelligence Community have pointed out the value of open source materials and the relatively efficient, low-risk acquisition attendant on these materials. Notwithstanding, the Intelligence Community retains a propensity to undervalue and shortchange this intelligence collection discipline. . . . Much of what we do not now know and need to know is to be found in open sources. Notwithstanding, acquisition and analysis today is insufficient."[46] Stakeholders have been advancing this argument since World War II; it thus appears that institutional attitudes are indeed slow to change. To help reverse this situation, reformers have engaged in specific practices that aim to rapidly reshape the values, attitudes, and beliefs of institutional members. These practices involve depicting intelligence as a business enterprise.

OPEN SOURCE ADVOCACY: LEVERAGING THE DISCOURSE OF ENTERPRISE

Officials use language and images to create, reproduce, or transform the identities, relationships, and belief systems of institutional members and stakeholders. Management scholars Hardy, Palmer, and Phillips argue that discourses supported by broader discourses (and are not highly contested by competing discourses) are more likely to produce institutions than discourses that are not. Yet "strategic actors cannot simply produce a discourse to suit their immediate needs and, instead, must locate their discursive activities within a meaningful context if they are to shape and construct action. . . . Consequently, if we want to explain how discourses operate, we must examine the broader context in order to ascertain the scope that it provides for action, as well as limits it places on action."[47] To explain how open source stakeholders engage in advocacy, it is necessary to examine how these stakeholders draw on the post-9/11 context and wider cultural discourses to establish *preferred* (rather than consensual) meanings of open source. For example, the *National Open Source Enterprise* brochure (referred to earlier by ADDNI/OS Butler as the "little red book") states, "Increasingly, the answer is out there; we need only be up for the challenge of uncovering it. The task before us is to develop the expertise, tools, and culture of sharing to best harvest the knowledge we need.

Ignoring open sources is no longer an option; they must be viewed as the source of first resort."[48]

Persuading institutional members to be "up for the challenge" of institutionalizing open source as "the source of first resort" involves officials' repeated invocation of what sociologist Paul du Gay calls the neo-liberal discourse of "enterprise."[49] For du Gay, enterprise constitutes a "new rationality of organizational governance" that "blurs traditional distinctions" between government and commercial spheres.[50] Specifically, enterprise discourse asserts that the *commercial firm*, with its associated qualities of employee "initiative, risk-taking, self-reliance and personal responsibility," is the preferred model of organization—whether public, private, or voluntary.[51] Du Gay has studied the forms of knowledge, identity, and agency that enterprise discourse circumscribes within the context of U.K. civil service reform. Similar to the British case, U.S. intelligence officials have attempted to persuade stakeholders of the desirability of their preferred constructions of open source by weaving together at least four distinct-yet-complementary discourses that resemble enterprise; these include culture, entrepreneurialism, evangelism, and Total Quality Management (TQM).

Due to its prominence within post-9/11 reform—especially within the homeland security sector—I describe and critique the discourse of culture separately in chapter 5. The themes of entrepreneurialism, evangelism, and TQM, however, are reflected in the *National Open Source Enterprise* brochure's five goals: (1) make open source the "source of first resort"; (2) establish a "guild of experts who champion the use of open source"; (3) ensure "global input" of sources; (4) develop a "single [technological] architecture" that provides "optimum access to information"; and (5) create an "open source works" capability to capitalize on emerging "tradecraft, analysis, and technology."[52]

In asserting the need for a guild of experts to champion the use of open source, goal #2 invokes the discourse of evangelism, goals #3 and #4 address technical issues yet also link those issues to egalitarian ideals associated with the logic of openness. Goal #5 invokes the discourse of entrepreneurialism. Specifically, in referencing "open source works," goal #5 draws on the image of the famous Lockheed Martin "Skunk Works"—a research and development facility that helped produce innovative Cold War and post–Cold War spy planes and stealth aircraft. Officials strategically deploy these two discourses—entrepreneurialism and evangelism—in conjunction with the vocabulary of TQM, which is characterized by "customer satisfaction," "mission," and "vision," in order to influence the way stakeholders conceptualize open source.[53]

In terms of entrepreneurialism, the 9/11 Commission portrayed the catastrophe as stemming from an institution-wide "failure of imagination."[54] As a result, fostering imagination within the U.S. intelligence community has become a way of ameliorating the perceived effects of bureaucratic stagnation. A principal way officials promote imagination is through the activities of reaching out, collaborating with new partners, and innovating. For example, during the 2008 DNI Open Source Conference, ADDNI/OS Butler stated, "I call your attention to the visionaries, leaders, and talented practitioners who imagined what is possible and challenged us to defy convention, embrace innovation, and fully exploit open sources to achieve decision advantage, and they're all around you in this room today, and they'll be all around you over the next two days during our conference. Please take advantage of that opportunity."[55]

One participant asked DDNI/C Glenn Gaffney, however, "Given how many open source practitioners are out there, how do you determine best of breed?" Gaffney responded, "I'm not a good judge. So what I'm interested in is how do *you* determine best of breed? How will you, in working together, right, discover new avenues, because right now there's a lot of different pockets of open source work going on. . . . It's not a top-down thing. It can't be. It's got to be by the practitioners themselves."[56] Here, responsibility for innovating open source is delegated to practitioners, who, ideally, cultivate entrepreneurial values. These values were vividly illustrated by two stories officials shared with the audience during the 2007 DNI Open Source Conference. Stories interest organizational scholars because they "function ideologically so as to represent the interests of a particular group" and are "integral to sense-making."[57] First, in his opening remarks, ADDNI/OS Jardines featured the story of Bertoldt Jakov:

Seventy-two years ago, Bertoldt Jakov was a German-born journalist who was alarmed by the growing power of the Nazi regime. Mr. Jakov decided to bring his investigative journalist skills to bear to expose the fascist regime's goal of world domination. Bertoldt had uncovered from his sources telltale signs that the Nazis were rearming their military, which obviously was a direct violation of the World War I peace accords. He began by scouring open sources and found a treasure trove of information on Germany's efforts to rebuild its military. This treasure trove resided in a very unlikely place, the social segment of German regional newspapers. By painstakingly cataloging what at first blush appeared to be incidental details regarding name, rank, and unit of assignment, Bertoldt began to construct an exceedingly detailed order of battle for the new German military. . . . Bertoldt set about writing a book to expose Nazi intentions and capabilities to the world. . . . The Gestapo was alerted to his activities, and they became convinced Bertoldt had recruited a highly placed source within the new German military. On March 9, 1935, the Gestapo, posing as literary agents, lured him away from his home in France to Switzerland, where he was drugged and kidnapped. . . . His Gestapo handlers finally conceded to Bertoldt's requests to prove his assertions. They provided him with newspapers from across Germany and much to their amazement, he proved his point.[58]

Second, then DDNI/C Mary Margaret Graham told a similar story during her remarks at the conference:

The story I'd like to tell you, I stole it from somebody who really is passionate about open source, a former ADDI [Assistant Deputy Director of Intelligence] at CIA, Carmen Medina. She came down and sat down with me one day for what was supposed to be a half an hour, and it ended up being two hours. She is completely passionate about the use of open source in the intelligence community and she told me a story that I think captures the breadth of what we can do with what we call open sources. There is a book called *The Hitler Myth*. The author of the myth, of the book, was trying to, in his book, pinpoint when the German people began to turn away from Hitler. And so, the period that he was looking at was 1941 to 1945. The creativity of this way of looking at it struck me and has always stayed with me as a way to use open source. What he did is he went to the obituaries in the two newspapers that at that time served Munich and Bavaria. In 1941, the obituaries of the soldiers who were killed talked about the solders having died for the Fuhrer, the fatherland, and the Volk, the German people. And [from this list] he was able to plot this. By the time 1945 came, the Fuhrer had disappeared, and the German soldiers that were killed, for the most part, died [only] for the Volk. But think about it for a minute. Think about the creativity of understanding that piece of the puzzle. That, for me, describes what we're looking for in the open source arena.[59]

Graham's comment suggested that this story circulates in interpersonal settings where passionate advocates attempt to persuade officials of open source's utility. Both stories constructed open source practitioners as skillful and inventive entrepreneurs.

For Jardines and Graham, the moral of both stories was that conference attendees should use open sources to creatively identify "modern day threats, be [they] terrorism, pandemic flu, or proliferation."[60] Given the context in which they were communicated, both stories seemed to imply that jihadists are analogous to Nazis—an association that has been perpetuated across the federal government.[61] Both stories associated the collection and analysis of open source information with World War II–era national unity, patriotism, excitement, and danger in U.S. society. In other words, the stories created a sense of "organizational drama" whereby the mundane task of analyzing open, free, and public information is elevated to an almost heroic activity.[62] It is worth remembering, however, that "all historical analogies are fallible in one sense or another because they emphasize some aspects of the past while suppressing others to achieve the right fit."[63] In searching for the right representation of the contemporary open source practitioner, for example, Jardines did not emphasize that Bertoldt Jakov—like Joe Turner in *Three Days of the Condor*—used open sources to uncover the objectionable activities of *his own government* and, moreover, was severely punished for doing so.

Jardines's and Graham's use of World War II–era analogies helped foster a patriotic commitment to officials' preferred vision of open source by implying that those who work in academe, the nonprofit sector, and the media could produce vital national intelligence. The stories conveyed the principle, however, that it is still an *individual's* responsibility to recognize the value of open source and adjust his or her beliefs to accommodate this value. Nevertheless, officials also implied that letting individuals decide if and when to embrace entrepreneurial values and practices may be too slow and uneven a process to ensure the timely institutionalization of open source. As a result, officials linked the vocabulary of entrepreneurialism with the vocabulary of evangelism. By evangelism, I mean advocacy characterized by zealousness, based largely on appeals to self-evident moral imperatives rather than evidence. For example, DDNI/C Gaffney evoked evangelism in this statement:

We're not bound to our individual program. We're not bound to this agency, this enterprise, this university, this piece. It doesn't matter. We are bound to truth. Ladies and gentlemen, the name of the game today is the same that it has always been. It is the pursuit of truth. We refer to it as intelligence inside this community circle, but that's why we do it. It is about discovering, discerning truth, and using that truth for its best for our citizenry.[64]

Audience members noted the evangelical tone of officials' open source advocacy. One conference participant asked Gaffney, "Your staff has been quite zealous in promoting the value of open source. Why?" Gaffney responded, "Because they work for a zealot. No, they're zealous in the pursuit because they believe this. It's not just another job in the train of jobs that they have. They're zealous in its pursuit because I sit with them everyday and we talk about what they're doing, and they are excited about what they see going on out there and are looking for how can we use that to improve this intelligence enterprise. And they get more excited by it by the moment."[65] Officials' evangelical vocabulary was presaged by the WMD Commission, which stated, "Because we believe that part of the problem [of the insufficient use of open source] is analyst resistance, not lack of collection, we recommend that some of the new analysts allocated to CIA be specially trained to use open sources and then to act as open source 'evange-analysts' who can jumpstart the open source initiative by showing its value in addressing particular analytic problems. [This] will help improve the Intelligence Community's surprisingly poor 'feel' for cultural and political issues."[66]

The WMD Commission's *Final Report* continued:

In the near term, we believe that without an institutional "champion" and home, open source will never be effectively used by the Intelligence Community. It is our hope that open source will become an integral part of all intelligence activities and that, at some point in the future, there may no longer be a need for a separate directorate. We acknowledge that our recommendation could create one more collection specialty. But, for now, open source is inadequately used and appreciated and is in need of the high-level, focused attention that only a separate directorate can provide.[67]

Both the WMD Commission's recommendation to create an institutional champion for open source and Gaffney's half-joking commitment to zealousness can be interpreted as reflecting the idea that securing legitimacy for open source is less a matter of management than of evangelism.[68] In other words, as management scholar Mark Suchman states, "[Officials] may exert major pressures on the normative order by joining together to actively proselytize for a morality in which their outputs, procedures, structures, and personnel occupy positions of honor and respect. . . . Over time, such collective evangelism helps to build a winning coalition of believers, whose conceptions of socially desirable activity set the terms for subsequent moral debate."[69] Suchman explains that for evangelists to be successful in their efforts to institutionalize new organizational forms and practices, they must eventually build a clear record of success for those forms and practices. This approach is challenging for intelligence officials given that the record of open source's effectiveness remains obscure. For example, during the press conference announcing the establishment of the OSC, DDNI/C Graham "couldn't think of a question that's been answered with open-source information alone, but said she's watched the government's dependence on it increase."[70] Although the number of anecdotes concerning open source's utility are increasing, their actual incidence may still be unknown to many institutional members because secrecy prevents such anecdotes from circulating widely. One official explained, "Part of our effort was to compile the mother listing of all open source success stories; the difficulty is the vast majority of those [stories] are classified."[71] Suchman explains that in absence of a widely known record of success, institutional evangelists can attempt to associate new vocabulary and practices with past vocabulary and practices that institutional members already consider legitimate. In the case of open source, this process occurs, in part, by articulating open source concepts using the vocabulary of TQM.

TQM is characterized by cultivation of customer satisfaction and perceived improvements in employees' well-being. Marcus notes that the CIA's Office of Information Technology adopted TQM in 1991, and by 1994, nearly 90 percent of the staff had received TQM training. Importantly for this discussion, Marcus claims that "no single federal agency has embraced the new managerial ethos [TQM] more passionately than the Defense Department."[72] TQM naturalizes open source evangelism through the use of institutionally sanctioned vocabulary. There are several resemblances between TQM and enterprise discourse. The most prominent of these is a shared emphasis on the *customer*—a term contained in nearly all the speeches and official documents discussed in this chapter. A clear example of open source officials' customer-centric focus is OSC director Doug Naquin's 2008 speech outlining the revamped open source "community action plan." In describing this plan, Naquin stated that his goal was to "tee up and witness a serious conversation among those who

make the actual decisions for the intelligence community about exactly
how open sources could and should play into the overall . . . intelligence
strategy."[73] Attempting to move beyond what he called the "perhaps clichéd" characterizations of open source, Naquin argued for "a serious conversation" to occur among open source "customers" within the areas of
"national policy," "Congress," "intelligence ops," "diplomacy," "military
support," and "law enforcement" (these customers were indicated on
Naquin's presentation slide). Naquin appeared to mock stakeholders who
have argued for an open source agency residing outside the CIA: "I'm
often asked why would an open-source center be in the intelligence community. Well, it's really a question of what do you want to support. If you
wanted to support corn production, you might put it in the Department
of Agriculture."[74]

Naquin claimed, "You'll see that [OSC's] value in the intelligence context gets greater as we move toward the right."[75] On the presentation slide
Naquin was referring to, "the right" was defined by intelligence and its
traditional disciplines (HUMINT, SIGINT, etc.). "The further we can push
that arrow to the right, the more value we have," Naquin stated.[76] In other
words, Naquin implied that the more open source meets customer demands, resembles traditional intelligence disciplines, and conforms to the
institutional logic of secrecy, its value and legitimacy as a form of intelligence increase.

Omitted from Naquin's slide, significantly, was the public—independent
of its elected representatives in Congress—as a customer of open source
intelligence. This omission was in contrast to the *National Open Source Enterprise* brochure's fourth goal, which included sharing open source products "with international partners and the public whenever practical."[77]
One official explained the challenge of including the public as a customer
of intelligence within this text:

The [DNI] leadership was like, "What? With the general public? Are you crazy?"
[The ADDNI/OS's] argument was that there are many incidences like avian flu,
floods, and whatnot that they should be communicating directly with the general
public. The general public is [a] customer. So, [the ADDNI/OS] was able to keep
that mention of making [open source] available to the general public in the document. As far as I know, that's the only intelligence document that says anything
about making intelligence available to the general public.[78]

While there is apparent ambivalence regarding how citizens should be
depicted within open source discourse, the logic of secrecy, wedded to enterprise's managerial vocabulary, excludes citizens from consideration in
the development of open source policy. Here, open source concepts are,
somewhat ironically, constructed within the dominant institutional logic
of secrecy—even as officials nominally declare the importance of public
participation, celebrate open source–related reforms at public conferences,

and assert the desirability of sharing open source products with the public and international partners. Communication scholar Stanley Deetz characterizes this type of communication as mildly duplicitous and paternalistic in that it leads to expression, discussion, and commitment, but generally not to transformation and innovative decisions.[79] For Deetz, the DNI Open Source conferences are a forum for the exchange of viewpoints, but they do little to increase voice. By voice, Deetz means expressions that genuinely influence decisions. While an official at the 2007 conference declared that "it is our hope that you leave here inspired and encouraged to contribute in whatever way each of you can in supporting open source," contributions and support that differed from the ADDNI/OS's preferred vision were never realistically on the table.

SUMMARY

For some stakeholders, the government's TQM-oriented strategy for institutionalizing open source makes sense. One stakeholder remarked, "I think Doug Naquin has done a hell of a job retooling FBIS into an Open Source Center. . . . He's really tried to get people involved throughout the community so that they understand what is available openly."[80] However, others suggest that TQM's culture of the customer potentially complicates the idealized objectivity of intelligence agencies. CIA director Hayden stated in 2008, "Now, given that importance to this discipline, Doug [Naquin, OSC director] sits at my staff meetings each time they occur, and that's three days a week. Open source has a seat at the table, a seat at the table with every other core discipline that comprises the Central Intelligence Agency."[81] Customer-centric discourse may inadvertently encourage the politicization of intelligence in that the value of intelligence becomes derived not necessarily from its fidelity to an underlying material reality, but from its ability to satisfy customers' demands. Enterprise discourse conceptualizes intelligence as a commodity, thus promoting the intense commercialization of this sector. Although the commercialization of intelligence has its advocates,[82] it is worth considering the influence of commercial imperatives in light of rhetorical scholar Robert Newman's observation: "To the extent that an 'intelligence' system is run by an organization whose mission is being evaluated, we no longer have an intelligence system, but a rhetorical system, which functions to reassure, exonerate, and glorify its parent. *Its product is inevitably self-serving.*"[83] Similarly, one stakeholder reacted to the stated connection between CIA director Hayden and OSC director Naquin:

[Doug] Naquin, and Charlie Allen [then the head of Intelligence and Analysis for DHS], and the Director of the CIA at the Open Source Conference—pardon my French—they're all kissing each other's ass. Naquin is saying what a great relationship he has with the Director of the CIA. Why, he's up to his office everyday.

Well, isn't that great? No wonder the academic community, the business community, and others are skeptical [of the OSC]. Who's running whom? Who's the big dog? Naquin's running up to the Director's office everyday. He's having a great time learning all those wonderful secrets, but you won't see the Director running over to Naquin's office, will you? Not likely.[84]

This chapter has explained how officials have constituted post-9/11 open source discourse using the vocabulary of entrepreneurialism, evangelism, and TQM in order to facilitate open source's institutionalization throughout the U.S. intelligence community. In repeatedly describing open source as "the enterprise of enterprises," officials illustrate neo-liberalism's "shift toward a new model of government less involved in direct service provision, and more focused on managing and organizing devolved centers and resources."[85] It remains unclear, however, whether aligning conceptions of open source with dominant institutional logics and vocabularies will ultimately diminish open source's potency as a symbol of institutional reform. One stakeholder explained the issue:

I think Jennifer Sims [an intelligence expert who spoke at the 2008 DNI Open Source Conference] made a very interesting—if not disturbing—argument that more, rather than less, secrecy is actually what is called for [vis-à-vis open source]. It was a remarkable statement to make, because to me, it called into question the whole basis of the conference at which she was speaking. If open source needs to establish itself as an intelligence discipline that is providing confidential "decision advantage," to use her term, then what sense does it make to be hosting a public conference about it?[86]

It is doubtful that such contradictions will become catalysts for wider public debate concerning open source vis-à-vis the reshaping of U.S. intelligence and national security. This is because 9/11 and the 2003 Iraq WMD intelligence failure produced an "epochal" moment, a "periodizing schema in which a logic of dichotomization establishe[d] the available terms of debate in advance, either for or against."[87] In this case, to be against officials' preferred conceptualizations of open source risks being perceived as for bureaucracy and the failure of imagination that bureaucracy ostensibly induces.

2009–2010: THE "ENTERPRISE OF ENTERPRISES" AND THE PROBLEM OF CONTROL

In 2008, open source organizational structures were revised, with Naquin gaining increased authority as the chairman of the National Open Source Committee, which, along with the ADDNI/OS, oversees the institutionalization of open source. In 2009, Naquin and his staff produced the *National Open Source Strategic Action Plan*.[88] In its publicly available form, this plan asserted that open source developments were entering a "new phase," one that required a narrowed "aperture" to focus on maximizing the benefits of the open source enterprise while facilitating other agencies' development of their own open source capabilities. The 2009 plan articulated a different set of mission, vision, and values statements from those specified in the 2006 *National Open Source Enterprise* brochure. In 2006, the goals were to make open source "the source of first resort," develop a guild of open source experts, ensure global input, create a single architecture, and establish an "open source works" capability. In 2009, those goals had slightly shifted to include "universal, cross-domain access" to open source material, integrated mission management, proliferation of open source expertise, and enterprise governance.

Yet, according to the 2009 *Plan,* open source's status as an afterthought persists. For Naquin and his staff, the key to overcoming this challenge is integration while demonstrating impact through decision advantage. The 2009 *Plan* raises the prospect of integration to new heights, the goal being to focus on the "sweet spot" among the overlapping enterprises of homeland, foreign, diplomatic, and defense, while also aligning "with unique mission requirements and policies" of specific organizations.[89] Officials refer to this vision of open source as an "enterprise of enterprises."[90] For Christine McKeown, associate deputy undersecretary of defense for analytic concepts and strategies within the Office of the Under Secretary of Defense for Intelligence, "DNI efforts increasingly are focused on areas where these four different domains [homeland, foreign, diplomatic, and defense] intersect and expand through collaboration and the sharing of people, tradecraft, and technology."[91]

Defining the relationships among people, tradecraft, and technology has been central to recent open source debates. In 2005, testifying before Congress, former chairman of the National Intelligence Council, John Gannon, remarked, "Technology is a major part of the answer to the magnitude of the open source challenge, but it is no substitute for the other essential component: skilled people. The IC must provide the analytic tools needed to assess and exploit the vast amount of information available, and it must invest more in people, whose expertise is crucial for prioritizing, interpreting, and analyzing this information."[92] For Gannon, prioritizing, interpreting, and analyzing open source material involves tradecraft. *Tradecraft* is a term intelligence analysts themselves use to define their work and identity. For example, in his 2005 ethnography of analytical culture within the intelligence community, Rob Johnston notes the widespread use of the term among the hundreds of analysts he interviewed and observed. In using *tradecraft* to describe their work, analysts reproduce their beliefs about the exclusivity and nonscientific nature of their analysis. As one government analyst stated, "What we do is more art and experience than anything else."[93]

Johnston argued that tradecraft corresponded more to analysts' self-perception and professional identity than to the reality of their work. He asserted, "The notion that intelligence operations involve tradecraft, which I define as practiced skill in a trade or art, may be appropriate, but the analytic community's adoption of the concept to describe analysis and analytic methods is not."[94] Instead of exploring tradecraft as a useful metaphor for intelligence analysis, Johnston rejected the term, proposing instead a scientific approach to intelligence analysis. The WMD Commission advocated a similar approach in 2005, stating, "The Intelligence Community has only begun to explore and exploit the power of these emerging technologies. . . . Therefore, we suggest that the DNI establish a program office that can lead the Community effort to obtain advanced information technology for purposes of machine translation, advanced search, knowledge extraction, and similar automated support to analysis."[95]

One potential result of this technological approach is that open source analysts themselves are made to resemble machines. For example, analysts at Intellibridge were paid individual incentive wages as a way to promote output. Management established strict formats, timetables, and minimum word counts for open source products. There was pressure among analysts to not exceed word count standards for fear that the standards would be raised. Production processes were organized along factory lines; often analysts were given narrow, repetitive tasks to complete without understanding the wider context of their work. Analysts used technology to simply keep pace with the unrelenting demands of their job. The pressure to meet strict deadlines for multiple clients required analysts to keep a close eye on the clock and avoid analytical detours and dead ends. It will never be known how many underdeveloped but potentially novel assessments at Intellibridge were jettisoned at the expense of client deadlines. It was simply too time-consuming to explore lines of inquiry that could not be easily included in the day's production in order to make an explicit quota. Such extreme forms of systematization may diminish analysts' commitment to broader organizational goals and values.

To be an open source craftsman implies that analysts themselves shape knowledge, execution, and control over the analytical process. While tradecraft may be fraught with idiosyncrasies, it also promotes novelty—a quality necessary for innovative intelligence assessments. Johnston's assertion that analytical tradecraft is problematic while scientific analysis is ideal demonstrates the familiar pattern of attempting to control organizational processes through improved systematization.[96] Under conditions of uneven and uncertain analytical capabilities, minimal standards of efficiency and effectiveness must be met within intelligence agencies. Johnston's call for a scientific approach is a predictable step in an effort to achieve such standards. My observations at Intellibridge correspond to Johnston's finding that the vast majority of agency analysts have shifted their focus to current production—short-term issues and problem solving. Analytical technologies hold the promise of easing the monotonous grind of current reporting. With technologies to do translation, web search, pattern recognition, and knowledge extraction, analysts may be able to devote more time to strategic assessments. This is still difficult, however, in an environment shot through with commercial imperatives.

At Intellibridge, market pressures often required the adoption of low-cost approaches to collection and analysis. Since most agencies are unable to directly monitor outsourced work processes, they exert control through contract requirements that may similarly compel organizations to adopt automation-like processes. These economic realities force a tradeoff between low-cost tradecraft and high-cost technology. This tradeoff seems counterintuitive—human labor is usually perceived as high cost. But especially in Washington, DC, where master's- and PhD-level analysts are abundant, contractors may find it more economical to hire analysts to mimic automated processes rather than invest in technology that may quickly become obsolete. Information processing speed and access to communication technology create an environment where intelligence analysts have vastly more information more quickly than ever before. Such conditions should be a boon for analysts, but, instead, those conditions create pressures to produce insights at a much faster rate to satisfy intelligence consumers. Outsourcing open source collection and analysis does not solve the problem. The pace of production merely compels private sector organizations to mimic the agencies they support. Without more transparency and oversight, officials will have difficulty discerning the relative value of a particular contractor's open source contributions. Commercial imperatives may stymie officials' attempts to develop open source as an innovative, collaborative, and entrepreneurial intelligence discipline. From this perspective, it is unsurprising that on August 24, 2010, the Department of Defense issued *Instruction No. 3115.12*, which directed officials to "identify OSINT activities and programs within their organizations and unify and streamline OSINT activities by coordinating and collaborating on OSINT collection, acquisition, analysis, operations, production, and dissemination."[97] However, unification and streamlining will not solve the fundamental tension that open source outsourcing creates.

CONCLUSION

At the end of *Three Days of the Condor*, Joe Turner unravels the CIA's Middle Eastern oil plot, disclosing it to the *New York Times* before evading his pursuers and disappearing into the city. Since 9/11, intelligence officials have authored and leveraged a similar image of the entrepreneurial open source practitioner—omitting, of course, any discussion of anti-institutional activities. Officials' ideal open source practitioner is an institutional member (an agency analyst or contractor), or even an ordinary citizen, who overcomes persistent bureaucratic obstacles and secrecy to contribute to defined *external* threats to U.S. national security. This image is invoked in official documents, celebrated at public conferences, and naturalized through institutionally sanctioned vocabulary.

Officials have constructed the concept of open source in ways that protect the authority of the U.S. intelligence community from those who seek to undermine it by extending the moniker of intelligence to the informational activities of noninstitutional actors. Officials' constructions rely on entrepreneurial, evangelical, and TQM-laden vocabulary. However, the perspective used herein suggests that these constructions may be based, at least to some degree, on taken-for-granted assumptions regarding the necessity of secrecy, rather than on calculated reflection. In other words, open source is constructed in accordance with a dominant institutional logic, in part, because few stakeholders are motivated to conceive of viable alternatives.

The events of 9/11 and the 2003 Iraq WMD intelligence failure undermined the legitimacy of the U.S. intelligence community, requiring an unusual level of organizational sense making. This sense making was aided, in part, by the official investigations and final reports of the Joint Inquiry, the 9/11 Commission, and the WMD Commission. The final reports of these investigatory bodies were widely disseminated and incorporated across the U.S. national security apparatus, as subsequent laws, directives, and policies based on their recommendations indicate. Stakeholders have used these recommendations to legitimate preferred open source organizational structures, roles, and practices.

To help rapidly institutionalize preferred meanings of open source, the ADDNI/OS organized and conducted the inaugural 2007 DNI Open Source Conference and a second DNI Open Source Conference in 2008. ICD 301, the *National Open Source Enterprise* brochure, and the keynote and plenary speeches delivered by officials during the conferences drew on authoritative texts and well-established neo-liberal discourses in order to persuade institutional members to adopt preferred beliefs and practices related to open source. However, commercial imperatives may constrain the widespread adoption of these beliefs and practices. The next chapter uses the context of homeland security to further explore the ways officials' vision of open source runs up against persistent institutional obstacles.

CHAPTER 5

Bridging a Cultural Divide: Homeland Security

Goal 1: Effect cultural and business process change throughout the Department to make open source the source of first resort.
> —U.S. Department of Homeland Security, *Open Source Enterprise Strategic Vision*, 2008[1]

The U.S. Department of Homeland Security was established on March 1, 2003. DHS's mission is to "lead the unified national effort to secure the country and preserve our freedoms."[2] In performing this mission, DHS must ensure "that timely, actionable, and complete intelligence and incident-related information reaches the right individuals at the right time to best mitigate threats and risk, while creating a culture of awareness for privacy, civil liberties, and civil rights."[3] Geographers Lauren Martin and Stephanie Simon interpret DHS's mission as involving the "translation of virtual, potential threat[s] into specific, possible outcomes and concrete, material actions."[4] In other words, "homeland security" is constructed from both discourses and practices that describe and enact (via training and simulation) threats and responses. A primary activity of DHS is thus the collection, analysis, and dissemination of information about potential threats to customers (in the lexicon of DHS), including policy makers; federal, state, and local officials in law enforcement; emergency management, public heath, other first-responder communities; private sector personnel; and, at times, the general public. Open source information is vital to homeland security in that it helps officials continuously identify and respond to threats—both actual and potential.

Open source discourse takes on a different vernacular within the context of homeland security, with "open source information sharing" being officials' preferred label for the collection, analysis, and dissemination of open source information. Speakers may also omit the term "open source" from this phrase because the bulk of homeland security–related information sharing occurs at an unclassified or law enforcement sensitive level. Some speakers distinguish between law enforcement sensitive and open source information, while others do not. This chapter indicates that as open source discourse moves toward operational levels within homeland security organizations, the perceived utility of its official depiction within U.S. intelligence community documents tends to diminish—a situation that senior officials attempt to address, in part, through organizing and conducting conferences, training, and education programs. This chapter also indicates that within operational levels of at least some homeland security organizations, open source information sharing appears, at least for now, to be relatively inconsistent, incoherent, and contested. This situation illuminates important theoretical and practical issues regarding the reshaping of intelligence.

DISCOURSE AND OPEN SOURCE CULTURE

Before turning to evidence of open source's uneven and contested institutionalization within the homeland security sector, it is useful to address the distinction between discourse and culture as this distinction has direct bearing on the claims made in this chapter. "Organizational culture" is an overarching term that both organizational members and scholars use to describe a range of organizational phenomena associated with human symbol use. According to organizational theorist Joanne Martin, these phenomena include, but are not limited to, cultural forms (organizational rituals, stories, jargon, humor, architecture, décor, and dress), formal practices (structure, tasks and technology, rules, and controls), and informal practices (unwritten social rules).[5] Martin argues that cultural forms and practices reveal deeper organizational meanings and shared, basic assumptions.

Organizational members may invoke culture in order to further goals related to improved organizational efficiency and effectiveness. This dominant functionalist, or problem-solving, perspective views culture as something the organization *has,* rather than something the organization *is.*[6] Depicting culture as something the organization *has*—a variable, resource, or tool—allows managers to act as though culture can be successfully and consistently shaped and controlled through incentives (or disincentives). Those who study culture as something the organization *is* instead seek to understand how artifacts, practices, values, and beliefs shape and emerge from the communicative interactions of organizational members.[7] This interpretive perspective does not necessarily—or completely—reject the control-oriented impulses of functionalist research; it does, however, offer organizational members and scholars the opportunity to develop a deeper understanding of how people interpret their organizational environments, identities, and work practices.[8]

As the chapter epigraph indicates, DHS officials invoke "cultural change" to encourage members of homeland security–related organizations to make open source "the source of first resort" and perform associated practices efficiently and effectively. These cultural change initiatives are bound up with images of intelligence as a business enterprise and are a primary way officials attempt to institutionalize new forms and practices. Du Gay states that "culture is accorded a privileged positioning in this endeavor because it is seen to structure the way people think, feel and act in organizations."[9] The institutional discourse perspective on culture taken here maintains that "discourses . . . are ordered and integrated by cultures, but also represent a (perhaps even *the* most important) medium in which cultures are constructed, reproduced, contested and changed."[10] Officials assert that cultural change is needed to ensure that intelligence community personnel become attuned to state and local information sharing processes, while simultaneously, state and local personnel become familiar with the conventions of intelligence. As one analyst interviewed for this project explained, "I think it takes a certain type of individual to work at a [homeland security] fusion center. They have to understand the intelligence cycle and information sharing—the importance of both. And they can't have that historical mindset of 'I own the information, and only me and my agency is going to see it.' "[11]

The discourse of cultural change blurs distinctions between "homeland" and "national" security in order to spur cross-agency information sharing and collaboration. In a related example, a 2009 Congressional Research Service report on "Homeland Security Intelligence" stated, "Prior to 9/11, it was possible to make a distinction between 'domestic intelligence'—primarily law enforcement information collected within the United States—and 'foreign intelligence'—primarily military, political, and economic intelligence collected outside the country. Today, threats to the homeland posed by terrorist groups are now [also] national security threats. Intelligence collected outside the United States is often very relevant to the threat environment inside the United States and vice versa."[12]

In the homeland security context, however, officials confront a countervailing discourse of privacy, civil liberties, and civil rights. This discourse is characterized by concerns for constitutional law and the legality of search, seizure, and racial profiling. For example, in establishing the Office for Civil Rights and Civil Liberties in 2004, DHS officials claimed that the office intended to offer DHS employees courses such as: " 'Civil Liberties 101,' a basic introduction to the Department's commitment to the protection of civil rights and civil liberties as described in the new *Strategic Plan;* an introduction to the Department's policy prohibiting unlawful

racial profiling; training on the Fourth Amendment requirements governing searches and seizures; and, various topics to develop awareness of the
cultural issues facing the Department's law enforcement and intelligence
officers, such as an introduction to the Arab and Muslim communities in
the United States."[13] As a context for the activities of contemporary institutional activists, privacy, civil liberties, and civil rights discourse can
be traced to populist reaction to institutional abuses of power performed
during the 1970s. For DHS officials, this discourse must be carefully managed in order to ensure continued mobilization of congressional and public support for preferred open source information sharing policies and
practices. As a result, the discourse of open source information sharing
generates critical tensions that shape its institutionalization.

The government's open source information sharing initiatives will admittedly take time to develop; some might argue, therefore, that evalu-
ating the efficacy of the government's cultural change strategy vis-à-vis
open source is premature. However, the goal of this chapter is to explore,
at a basic level, how stakeholders currently make sense of the interconnections among open source, cultural change, and homeland security.
This case study considers social practice—in other words, the process of
textual *interpretation*. Social practice engages questions regarding the extent to which audiences accept and respond to a text's *preferred* reading.[14]
In the following sections, I first address the logic of open source information sharing within U.S. homeland security affairs. I subsequently discuss
the vocabulary of cultural change produced by intelligence community officials for audiences within intelligence and homeland security–related organizations. Drawing on interview data, I then discuss how institutional
members respond to the interrelated discourses of open source and cultural change and what these responses indicate about the limits of officials' efforts to institutionalize open source.

THE LOGIC OF OPEN SOURCE
INFORMATION SHARING

Intelligence scholar Calvert Jones states that "the logic of information
sharing" is based on the assumption that "the free flow of information
[will] stimulate a robust marketplace of ideas, encouraging diverse, innovative analysis appropriate for dealing with more complex, rapidly
evolving threats."[15] Jones notes that this logic developed in the aftermath
of the Japanese attack on Pearl Harbor in 1941 and the U.S. military's need
to prevent future surprise attacks. For government officials, the post-9/11
institutional environment requires a "trusted partnership" among federal, state, and local agencies to make information sharing integrated,
interconnected, effective, and automatic.[16] As a result, information sharing initiatives have been a key plank of post-9/11 U.S. intelligence reform
strategy. *Hundreds* of governmental, commercial, and nongovernmental

organizations provide officials with open source alerts, updates, and databases to support preparedness efforts.[17] Recently created fusion centers operated by state agencies—the linchpins of U.S. homeland security strategy—integrate, analyze, and disseminate federal, state, local, and private sector open source information.

Within the homeland security sector, it is axiomatic that increased information sharing improves emergency preparedness, response, and recovery. As a result, few researchers have attempted to critically assess this premise. However, studies have found an ambiguous relationship between information sharing and preparedness.[18] In the wake of these findings, it is unsurprising that a September 2008 report prepared by the majority staff of the House of Representatives Homeland Security Committee entitled "Giving a Voice to Open Source Stakeholders: A Survey of State, Local, and Tribal Law Enforcement" declared, "DHS has not effectively exploited [open source] information to provide essential analytical products. In fact, DHS' efforts have lagged behind the rest of the Federal government. While the Office of the Director of National Intelligence (DNI) and the Central Intelligence Agency (CIA) have each established robust open source programs, DHS . . . has yet to articulate a vision for how it will collect, analyze and disseminate open source information."[19] The report explained that only 50 percent of 350 officials surveyed reported that DHS open source "products" met their needs for situational awareness of "all hazards" threats. Additionally, 60 percent of those surveyed reported that "in order to improve matters, DHS needs to establish a robust training program in addition to producing open source intelligence products with actionable recommendations."[20]

I argue that the committee's findings stem, in part, from the relative "incoherence" of open source discourse and the influence of "competing" discourses at the operational levels of homeland security organizations.[21] As one participant in this project argued, "Domestic intelligence is a wide-open frontier. We don't know what it is yet. . . . Everyone is going to be feeling [his or her] way on this. So, anyone who rejects [open source] out of hand at this point is asking for trouble, and anybody who embraces it wholeheartedly and says, 'Ah, here's our answer,' they're also in trouble."[22] Despite officials' attempts to shape the development of open source logics and vocabularies in ways amenable to homeland security practice, a lack of shared meanings among federal, state, and local organizations may inhibit open source's institutionalization in this sector. Here, it is worth returning to theory: organizational theorist Mats Alvesson argues that "the same discourse (language use) in different cultures (meaning contexts) may lead to different reception and thus meanings."[23] In other words, while officials consistently use cultural change vocabulary to spur uniform information sharing and collaboration process across the intelligence community, the ensuing discussion highlights differences that arise within the homeland security sector.

OPEN SOURCE AND THE VOCABULARIES
OF CULTURAL CHANGE

One participant captured a common sentiment when he declared, "I think we have a real problem, which is there's a generation of people who have an old paradigm [a 'need-to-know culture'] that needs to be broken. I don't know how you do that."[24] A prominent way officials have thus far attempted to break this old paradigm is through promoting cultural change. Importantly for this discussion, the Information Sharing Environment was established in 2006 in order to create a trusted information network and promote the sharing of information and intelligence among government agencies at all levels. Central to the ISE's *Implementation Plan* was the development of what it called a "culture of information sharing." While the ISE's *Implementation Plan* did not specify this culture's characteristics, they may be partly inferred from the description of ways that officials might develop this culture, including the following: (1) monetary and nonmonetary awards; (2) agency-wide recognition for those who develop an improved information sharing practice; (3) inclusion in internal newsletters of information sharing accomplishments and the tangible end benefits that resulted; (4) development of awareness materials; (5) establishment of an annual federal award for fostering information sharing; and (6) sharing of best practices regarding effective ways to educate and motivate personnel.[25] Similar to other organizations within the U.S. intelligence community, the ISE depicts culture as a concrete and objective phenomenon that senior officials can control through incentives in order to reduce the likelihood of intelligence failures stemming from insufficient information sharing.

Similarly, the 2007 *National Strategy for Information Sharing* was based, in part, on "foster[ing] a culture of awareness in which people at all levels of government remain cognizant of the functions and needs of others and use knowledge and information from all sources to support counterterrorism efforts."[26] DHS's *Strategic Plan* declared the need to develop a "culture of preparedness," "leverage culture to implement best practices that benefit from component commonalities and differences," and create "a culture of awareness for privacy, civil liberties, and civil rights."[27] DHS stated in its *Intelligence Enterprise Strategic Plan* the need to "promote a culture that supports and rewards initiative, creativity, diversity, and professionalism."[28] These themes were echoed in the DHS *Open Source Enterprise Strategic Vision*. As noted in the chapter epigraph, the *Strategic Vision* brochure stated that DHS's top goal was to "effect cultural and business process change throughout the Department to make open source 'the source of first resort.'"

References to culture thus pervade institutional discourse concerning open source information sharing. This discourse constructs culture as a variable, distinct from other organizational phenomena—a variable that can be isolated, measured, manipulated, and assessed. Along with this conception of culture is the premise that senior officials can directly, uniformly, and successfully shape organizational culture in order to improve the effectiveness of intelligence, law enforcement, and emergency management agencies. Officials understandably would like to believe that culture can be used as a tool for generating employee commitment to open source initiatives.[29] However, the notion that there exists a stable, causal, and law-like relationship between an abstraction called "organizational culture" and organizational outcomes has been repeatedly called into question.[30] Despite culture's indeterminacy, the appeal of cultural explanations for organizational performance endures.[31]

The documents discussed here provide official representations of both existing and preferred organizational cultures. A discourse-centered perspective maintains that we cannot assume that the overall influence of these documents is significant. In other words, we cannot conflate official representations of culture with how stakeholders actually make sense of and use the term—we have to turn to the stakeholders themselves.

OPEN SOURCE AND CULTURAL CHANGE: AN ASSESSMENT

In assessing officials' efforts to spur cultural change, participants provided an array of interpretations concerning the relationships among open source information sharing and homeland security. Using an institutional discourse perspective as a guide, I assembled these interpretations into two overarching categories with several subcategories to help describe and explain them. The first overarching category relates to tensions stemming from incoherence and a lack of structure within the open source information sharing discourse. The second overarching category relates to tensions among open source privacy, civil liberties, and civil rights and commercial discourses that appear to hinder enactment of officials' cultural change initiatives.

Incoherence and lack of structure within the open source information sharing discourse appears to be the result of the following conditions: (1) the phrase "open source information sharing" lacks a widely shared definition; (2) open source products may contain vague, untimely, or excessive information; and (3) open source information sharing discourse both intensifies and ameliorates subcultural divisions among personnel within a given organization, as well as between members of different organizations.

Ambiguous Definition

Participants offered an array of definitions for open source information sharing. For example, one contractor stated, "To me, open source means largely the Internet, which is the largest database of human information and knowledge that we've ever acquired in history."[32] An analyst stated, "Open source gives you a wealth of information on attitudes, perceptions, just general demographic information such as languages, what people like, what people don't like."[33] Another analyst explained that open source collection involved using tools "like Google, Google Maps, [and] Google Earth. . . . We use a lot of social networking sites like MySpace or Facebook, and we use . . . LexisNexis, public records databases, things like that."[34] Similarly, participants' understandings of "information sharing" varied. One analyst stated, "Information sharing means a centralized area where you can grab stuff."[35] A manager stated, however, "I don't know [what 'information sharing' means], and that's one of the problems I think we have right now."[36] Several participants also defined information sharing as a task state and local officials are expected to do without much in return from the federal level. One manager stated, "Information sharing means a two-way street, but more often it's a one-way street." Another claimed, "It means information going to the JTTF [Joint Terrorism Task Force] and very little coming back."[37]

One analyst speculated about why shared meaning of open source information sharing was difficult to obtain: "I think part of the issue is that because [information] is open source, nobody considers that sharing. [Analysts and officials] just think it's out there, and they can access it anytime they want."[38] This analyst further explained, "In our particular organization, at the fusion center here, I don't think there are criteria, or any kind of outline, on how [analysts and officials] think they're going to use open source material. . . . It seems like most fusion centers use open source, but there's no official protocol as to how it's supposed to be used."[39] Another analyst stated, however, "Open source has been a critical part of what we do on a daily basis—and it has been. Any intelligence unit will tell you that. Especially [when] trying to get current information about people, it's really the only source to get that kind of stuff. . . . I know there's a lot of rhetoric, and a lot of companies are trying to sell open source stuff, and they're trying to make it like open source is so brand new . . . but come on! It's been going on for 20 years. This stuff is a regular part of the job."[40]

Wide-ranging understandings of what constitutes open source information sharing raise the question of what, exactly, stakeholders gain by delimiting certain practices as open source–related. As indicated earlier, one could argue that open source information sharing has, in one sense, *always* been practiced within the homeland security sector, given that access to classified information has traditionally been rare among law enforcement and emergency management personnel. It therefore appears that homeland security officials use the term "open source" mainly to demarcate enhanced exploitation of the Internet through various techniques and technological tools. The term also signals a more structured or systematic approach to information collection, analysis, and dissemination

than might otherwise be the norm for homeland security–related organizations. Finally, the term evokes the logic of information sharing and
officials' desire to see collaboration institutionalized within and across
homeland security and national security organizations.

Nevertheless, blurring distinctions between information and intelligence create problems of interpretation and response (just as in the case of
the broader intelligence community). As one analyst observed, "I think it
boils down to how do you use [information]. . . . How do you make 'open
source information' intelligence? I think that is where the rub comes in for
a lot of intelligence analysts. . . . I think it's a safe argument to make that
information is not in-and-of-itself intelligence. But you certainly can't ex-
clude information if it doesn't come from classified means. And I think
that although it's inaccurate, classified has become synonymous with intelligence. So, in other words, classified data is intelligence, and that is not
always the case."[41]

Varying definitions of open source information sharing suggest that
institutional members may be reacting to official open source discourse
primarily because new rules require a demonstrated organizational response. Invoking open source is a way to sustain institutional legitimacy
in an environment where a great deal of homeland security information
is available to noninstitutional actors. However, the lack of perceived effectiveness of DHS open source initiatives—as indicated in the House
Homeland Security Committee's 2008 report—may also relate to vague,
untimely, and excessive information received via homeland security information sharing systems.

Vague, Untimely, and Excessive Information

Participants in this project commented on the poor quality of the homeland security information that they received from federal-level information sharing systems. One said, "It's all after the fact. There's little value
added."[42] Another stated, "When it first came out, I was pretty active on
LLIS [Lessons Learned Information Sharing, an open source information
sharing system], but then I thought, 'Why am I doing this?' "[43] A third law
enforcement officer declared of the information, "It's mostly useless."[44]
One analyst elaborated how vague information constrains organizational
effectiveness: "We'll get a vague warning about threats to water treatment
facilities, and there are several water treatment facilities in this area. The
warning will be based on 'unconfirmed information.' So, I'm left wonder-
ing whether I should go speak with the water treatment operators. I'll call
the FBI to get more information and they'll say, 'We don't have any more
information.' I can't get any specifics. There is just not enough detail for
me to go to the city and request the money to harden those facilities. If I go
to my chief with that information, he's going to laugh at me."[45]

Timeliness is also an issue. One analyst explained, "I'll tell you, I'm an analyst, and the most valuable resources are the ones that have up-to-date information. There's a lot of people [who] try to sell you databases, try to get you to use certain things, but if the information is not up-to-date, then I'm not going to use it, and I'm not going to report it."[46] Participants explained that the types of information useful for them in conducting their work include the following: "Geographically specific information and intelligence would be helpful instead of broad, general statements about threats";[47] "Specific information about suspects and bad guys";[48] "Actionable intelligence. This is something I need to know because it's something I could or should react to."[49] These responses underscore that officials and analysts face a dilemma in determining an appropriate level of vagueness, or equivocality, in the messages they disseminate via open source information sharing systems. Crisis communication scholars have argued that "unequivocal statements [made by organizational representatives] during a crisis might be less valuable than probabilistic statements, [which reflect] more realistically the lack of precise predictability in many crisis situations and [allow] stakeholders to make their own qualitative assessments."[50] These comments suggest, however, that an overabundance of equivocal information in pre-event emergency contexts can lead information sharing systems users to devalue those systems. This finding affirms the claim that, in the context of open source, "the question of appropriate levels of equivocality in crisis messages remains largely unanswered."[51]

However, participants universally valued *interpersonal* communication with their colleagues, finding it the most useful source of relevant information for their operations. One participant explained, "The best source for information I get is from my contemporaries in other jurisdictions close by that I work with on a regular basis. We meet frequently and email frequently. [My colleagues provide] information that has been vetted and is of value."[52] The value officials placed on interpersonal communication likely stemmed, at least in part, from the opportunity it provided for officials to hold each other accountable, construct shared interpretations, and immediately demonstrate their knowledge and expertise.[53] Nevertheless, the government's open source information sharing strategy emphasizes technological systems rather than interpersonal communication.

Information glut is also a persistent problem within intelligence organizations.[54] Even with the establishment of official homeland security information sharing services and portals, the volume of information analysts receive is potentially debilitating. One stakeholder explained, "One of the biggest issues is that there is so much information there, so much being pushed to the fusion centers to try and digest and find value in, it really becomes a challenge."[55] Another analyst explained, "I have 85 accounts now [with] different log-ins for those kinds of sources. . . . [It is a] major pain in the butt. It's just part of my job, I guess, to keep my accounts up to date. You use them because you have to use them, or lose them."[56] One manager explained, "There are so many different databases that it makes it very difficult for the people who are actually doing the investigations to get useful information in a timely manner."[57] The volume of open source information inundating analysts and officials is likely leading many to delete or ignore much of it. Vague and untimely information, as well as information glut, may make homeland security officials and analysts weary of institutionalizing open source practices that exacerbate those conditions.

Cultural Divisions

Institutional members promote culture when it is in their interest to do so. For example, one analyst explained, "I'm definitely all for information sharing. I like the cultural shift that I've seen at the federal government level from 'need to know' . . . to 'responsibility to share.' I think that's a long time coming, but there definitely is value for law enforcement at times to be segregated from the private [and] public sector because the law enforcement–sensitive world that we deal with in law enforcement is what we need. We need law enforcement–sensitive information to help us go about our day-to-day activities."[58] Yet this analyst interpreted culture as a phenomenon that can be discursively engineered by federal officials, as well as a property of occupational groups that develops as a result of a particular world a group deals with. The question thus arises whether top-down cultural change initiatives are able to overcome entrenched subcultural norms.

Stakeholders generally argued that officials' cultural change initiatives would probably be too weak to overcome subcultural divisions. For example, one contractor explained, "I think culturally, institutionally, and traditionally each division of the community . . . has their own process and protocols, and in my experience, none of them like to share with the others. Now, I understand the rhetorical approach that 'information sharing is good and great, and let's all do it,' but quite frankly, that's still a major obstacle in the people I'm running around with: 'What's mine is mine and what's theirs is theirs' kind of thing . . . even though the rhetoric is 'let's all be one big happy family.' "[59] Other officials indicated a more positive relationship between institutional subcultures. One local official stated, "We've always had excellent working relationships with [federal officials]."[60] Stakeholders nevertheless tended to invoke culture to explain occupational differences, criticize and/or praise top-down change initiatives, and note generational tensions surrounding the use of open source–related technologies. One analyst explained, "I hate to say this because this is probably not going to sound very positive: when DHS tries to promote something, in many cases, it's almost like a lot of people view that as [DHS] telling you what to do. And in some cases, that [produces] a negative reaction, and it doesn't matter that the thing might be great, or the project might be great, or the tool might be wonderful; sometimes it's presented as: 'You have to use it because DHS says so,' and I think that's a problem."[61]

Others noted subcultural differences between sworn law enforcement personnel and civilians: "If you are a sworn law enforcement person, there is a different viewpoint than if you are a civilian, and I think that is part of the cultural [difference]. There's basically two cultures right there, right from the beginning, and I think that's part of why certain things are seen with different eyes. . . . I think that's also going to change because you're going to get both cultures to kind of see the value in the other culture, and then, when we finally figure out how to merge and everybody's on the same page, I think that's going to change the view towards open source as well."[62] One analyst further distinguished between subcultures based on generational differences: "[With older analysts], their degree of expertise with technology is usually far below younger people, and I think older analysts or investigators, in general, aren't used to collecting. Analysts especially—they're not used to collecting information. Usually, information is given to them, you know, I mean, from a collector. So, when you're dealing with open sources, you're the person who is actually collecting the information. So, you know, that's another step in the intelligence cycle that you have to be involved with. That's the difference."[63]

Finally, stakeholders invoked culture or mind-set in order to distinguish between open source advocates and those who continue to privilege classified sources:

> The irony of the open source today is that a person like Charlie Allen [the former head of DHS Intelligence and Analysis] . . . his mind-set is to stay on the dark side. His mind-set is not to develop open source assets or capabilities to any great extent. And if you come up with an analytical product? Classify it. There is so much information available that can be transferred, here and there, to regional centers to inform and educate police, emergency services, and others who are engaged in homeland security activities—but as soon as you classify it, you shut them out. You can't give a clearance to everybody, every cop on the street. Every police officer, every fireman can't get a clearance; but if you have a developing threat to the Brooklyn Bridge, you want to be able to get the information out to as many people as possible—even citizens.[64]

These examples suggest that the meanings of open source information sharing are constructed in relation to varying institutional/subcultural identities, organizational contexts, and strategic interests. While many participants acknowledged that *in principle* information sharing is vital to homeland security, several comments suggest that current information sharing initiatives are also interpreted as a way for federal officials to bridge the government's post-9/11 (and Iraq and Katrina) credibility gap with Congress and the public. The open source information sharing issues identified here are certainly well-known to many government officials.[65] Yet officials have responded to these challenges by simply asserting the need for a culture of information sharing within and among federal, state, and local agencies. This strategy potentially glosses over critical differences that influence stakeholders' perceptions and practices. We see in this case that subcultures are likely to perpetuate contrary views from the overall top-down push from DHS officials. Clearly, "different [subcultural] members may interpret the same information from different frames of mind."[66] The comments presented here indicate likely friction points as the government attempts to align members' beliefs about institutional subcultures in efforts to diffuse open source information sharing concepts and practices.

OPEN SOURCE AND CULTURAL CHANGE DISCOURSE CONFRONTS COMPETING DISCOURSES

In addition to problems stemming from incoherence, homeland security officials seeking to institutionalize open source confront the challenge of competing discourses. Two of these discourses include, specifically, privacy, civil liberties, and civil rights and commercial imperatives. The former is relatively well established, while the second is, admittedly, loosely knit; I describe commercial imperatives here as a discourse for its heuristic value in demarcating a set of concerns that may impede the institutionalization of open source in this sector.

Privacy, Civil Liberties, and Civil Rights Discourse

In response to a question about how DHS's stated concern for privacy, civil liberties, and civil rights could influence the institutionalization of open source within the homeland security sector, one participant stated the following:

We've had those discussions, and I said, "Listen, I'm just as sensitive to that issue as anybody else." But, there are a couple of things to put it in perspective. Number one, the alternative is to have the Open Source Center do it. So, I think if we ask the general public, "Would you prefer DHS or CIA to handle domestic open source exploitation?" I think it would be fairly unanimous, you know? So, that's kind of one part of it, and the other part of it is, you know, we really need to articulate that [the] protection of civil liberties is paramount, and so we've done that in a number of ways. . . . You'll see that that's woven into . . . one of the four major goals . . . and then heaped in things like our training that we're doing. We're going to have specific sections on civil liberties, and implications, and what not. And in many ways, the domestic side is more restricted than the foreign side in terms of what you can do with open source.[67]

One analyst explained, however, that privacy, civil liberties, and civil rights concerns were *already* well integrated within open source practices: "Everything that we put out that has anything to do with a U.S. person, or anything that can be construed as a privacy issue, is vetted, like, six ways to Sunday. In fact, I doubt very much if there is an issue or question [that] something would go out. I think they are very, very cognizant here, and probably because of the state police history. . . . You have to be very, very careful what you say about whom and who you put this out to. So, I think they deal with that very well already."[68]

Within DoD-related organizations that possess a homeland security mandate, however, U.S.-persons issues appear unresolved. One analyst explained it this way: "DoD is prohibited from contacting folks outside of the [intelligence] community and outside of DoD. . . . [DoD's open source information sharing policy] conflicts with other regulations and laws . . . about activities that intelligence officers [are] allowed to participate in. These obviously were prior to the DNI push for collaboration, and before the congressional push for open source use within the [intelligence] community as well. Those regulations are still there and haven't been changed."[69] This analyst elaborated further:

Say we were responsible for protecting defense critical infrastructure, which is, of course, attached to civilian infrastructure—they are intertwined. . . . Current interpretation would be you wouldn't even be able to have [civilian infrastructure] information because it is owned by private companies and private U.S. citizens. And even in that case, where you have a mission to do so, there have been rulings against [collecting open source information]. It becomes difficult to defend military bases in the United States. In the way the Department of Defense does planning, for example, you can't defend a base against a threat that's outside your base because you can't collect on that threat outside your base.[70]

This comment suggests that anxiety and frustration remain within areas of DoD that are involved in configuring open source and privacy discourses and practices. Another open source practitioner stated his frustration:

I believe, in general, that the USG [U.S. government] is adopting a "head in the sand" approach—unduly limiting the use of open source material by USG agencies for fear of accusations of Big Brother–type schemes. . . . While working for the USG, I was limited, due to my position, into following EO [Executive Order] 12333 and DoD Directive 5240.1. . . . Bottom line, I could not use open source information to report on any threat that was considered a "U.S. person" by the guiding directives unless [a U.S. person] posed a clear and direct threat to my organization. While I was free to read or watch anything I chose on my own time, I could not include that information in official papers or briefings on those topics.[71]

Another DoD employee countered, however, with the following:

That's a sham of an excuse. When was the last time you've ever seen any public figure ever, ever prosecuted for making a bad call on a U.S. person? Name one prosecution, name one time the DoD has ever been investigated about that, just one. Never, to my knowledge, or anyone else I know, has anyone ever been investigated for making the wrong call regarding information on the Internet about a U.S. citizen/U.S. person. This is an excuse. This is a reason that these people . . . use time and time again to not do anything about actually making use of the [open source] information out there. It's an excuse.[72]

One stakeholder thus concluded it this way:

I think there are a lot of eager lawyers who like to look for problems in this area. I think that should not be a problem because, you know, if it's open source, it's open source. There are all kinds of privacy issues that come up in every day's copy of the *New York Times,* and that's just the way life is. . . . I realize that the lawyers have a different perspective. I realize that they have to respect the provisions of the National Security Acts and other codes that do not want the foreign intelligence agencies like the CIA and DIA getting involved in anything that focuses on U.S. persons.[73]

This stakeholder's comment, "if it's open source, it's open source," captures officials' desire to institutionalize open source practices without adequately addressing what open source is vis-à-vis the competing discourse of privacy, civil liberties, and civil rights. This situation endures: DHS under secretary Caryn Wagner testified before the House Subcommittee on Homeland Security in 2010, "DHS Open Source collection efforts resulted in reporting on a number of specific terrorist and individual behaviors by organizations and individuals, such as Anwar al Awlaki; this kind of reporting provides advice on potential changes to operational and security procedures that keep communities and the nation safer."[74] Wagner noted that DHS "used mobile training teams to conduct Open Source methodologies and capabilities training at 24 fusion centers and component facilities," but she assured members of congress that training included "a formal block . . . on understanding and respecting the privacy of individual citizens."[75]

Commerce Trumps Culture

Interviews with government employees and contractors suggest that commercial imperatives are perhaps the most significant issue complicating officials' cultural change initiatives. Specifically, several contractors interviewed for this project do not yet see the institutionalization of open source occurring. While ICD 301 requires that intelligence agencies include open source contributions within their intelligence products, one contractor claimed that some agencies are using open source contractors in order to simply "check the box."[76] In other words, this contractor explained that agencies use contractors to *minimally* fulfill their obligations under ICD 301. ICD 301 obligates agencies to demonstrate their use of open source, but the document can do little to ensure that members do the following: (1) deeply inculcate open source values as cultural elements; (2) usefully integrate open source and classified intelligence in their operations; or (3) assess the overall worth of their open source activities. This contractor suspects—but has no concrete evidence—that his company's open source products are being cited within classified intelligence assessments merely in order to meet obligations under ICD 301—the actual contribution of these products being more-or-less irrelevant. This contractor was not unduly concerned with this situation, however. Another contractor used an analogy to explain why he, too, was mostly unconcerned with the end result of his company's open source contributions: "We grow grapes, we collect grapes, and we sell them off. So, whoever wants to buy our grapes, they are welcome to it. For the right price, we'll share or not."[77]

Officials' remarks concerning open source information sharing generally omit consideration of commercial imperatives. Contractors, however, consistently note two critical issues. First, commercial firms may be reluctant or unwilling to provide certain open source analytical products to the OSC or other government organizations that might distribute those products broadly. This is due to fears that competitors will be able to mimic that firm's analytical approach, attempt to seize the firm's contracts, or lure away its personnel. Second, government solicitations calling for substantial open source collection and/or analysis activities are often bundled with sensitive/classified requirements. This situation prevents anyone lacking the requisite security clearance from being aware of the open source requirements, thereby limiting the number and range of approaches that might be brought to bear on the problem. Thus, here is where the dominant institutional logic of secrecy directly contradicts espoused values of openness and participation. However, one contractor dismissed this contradiction, arguing that it was understandable that U.S. agencies would not want adversaries to learn the government's open source requirements.

Nevertheless, for some stakeholders, the gulf between officials' espoused and enacted values is abundantly clear in terms of budget allocations. As one participant noted, "You can give all the guidance you want to. . . . It doesn't do a lot of good to put out policy and direction and guidance when you're not going to fund [open source initiatives]. And if they're going to tell somebody they have to pull [funding for open source initiatives] out of hide, well guess what, they're not going to do it; it's not a priority to do that unless Congress makes it a priority."[78] This participant elaborated, "There's a lot of good ideas out there [on how to use open source effectively], things to do and ways to implement those, and there are a lot of them . . . but they don't go anywhere. They're just voiced. It's kind of like, 'Okay, we are meeting the minimum standard [DNI] said we have to [in order] to improve OSINT.' So, we'll put some lip service to it, and, you know, put something on paper that is not necessarily fully implemented or fully resourced—or even minimally resourced."[79]

These comments suggest that commercial and budgetary imperatives may significantly complicate officials' cultural change initiatives. In other words, developing a culture of information sharing is based on the un-stated premise that open source vendors will supply agencies with infor-mation products—despite knowing that these products may be widely shared across federal, state, and local levels. This situation potentially undermines vendors' opportunities to maximize revenue. A significant portion of intelligence work is now contracted or outsourced to Fortune 500 corporations and boutique intelligence shops.[80] There is little public discussion, however, of how commercial imperatives may impede open source information sharing.

This discussion potentially casts the institutionalization of open source within the homeland security sector in an overly negative light. It must be emphasized that several stakeholders asserted that the institutional-ization of open source is proceeding apace. However, most people with whom I spoke emphasized the challenges confronting open source's in-stitutionalization. This may have been a result of my questions, as well as the types of institutional members who agreed to answer my questions: those with concerns about open source's institutionalization may have been more likely to speak with me than those who were satisfied with cur-rent arrangements. While not generalizable in a traditional sense, these findings nevertheless point to important issues for homeland security officials and stakeholders to consider as the institutionalization of open source unfolds.

THE LIMITS OF CULTURAL CHANGE TEXTS

Organizational scholar Tim Kuhn argues that while "there are cases in which people explicitly draw upon a given policy document in talk, it is far more common, both within firms and in conversations with stakeholder groups, to treat structuring resources as 'background' enablements and constraints rendered invisible by routine practice."[81] Supporting Kuhn's argument, one contractor stated, "[Institutional documents are] a focus of our public relations within the community and customers. . . . ICD 200 or ICD 301 is what we base our relationship with [the customer] on, but we don't really market it, it's more part of the personal dialogue, rather than a focused marketing tool. It's more of an inferred given when we are talk-ing to our folks . . . we use it strictly as subliminal public relations."[82] An analyst similarly stated it this way:

We definitely look at the guidelines . . . the recommendations that are provided by the federal government for our participation in an information sharing environ-ment—in how we can participate—taking into consideration any state-level laws or procedures/processes/policies that may preclude certain things. But I think more often than not, there aren't any state-level policies/laws/procedures that prohibit our participation. . . . The *National Strategy for Information Sharing* . . . may result in us changing our business processes. It may result in us sharing the information that we probably felt no one cared about because intelligence requirements haven't been shared with us.[83]

These issues can also be interpreted as tension between coercive and normative elements within open source discourse. One stakeholder captured this dynamic when he stated, "There are only so many directives [officials] can put out regarding information sharing, so I think they're doing the best that they can do. Whether the industry and the community accept [open source] and utilize it, at the end of the day, is up to them."[84] This theme was echoed by other participants who noted that vision documents are unhelpful in establishing what open source practices should actually entail. For example, one participant observed, "I don't think there is [a policy] on how to do open source intelligence collection, analysis, and research. . . . There is some vision and guidance that has come down though the chain of command. . . . But the only thing it says is that 'the intelligence centers will have an OSINT capability'—not further defined. So, commanders can say, 'Yes, I have an OSINT capability; I have all source analysts who can do research on the unclassified Internet.'"[85] Another analyst stated, "I'm not sure that anybody who really reads [ICD 301] is going to understand how that relates to open source—I think that agencies like the CIA and the FBI and other agencies realize the value of open source much more than local and state, or fusion centers."[86] One analyst concluded the following:

I think the bottom line is that Congress must press [homeland security–related organizations] to [institutionalize open source]. And [organizations] must have congressional oversight, and they must report back to Congress, and Congress is going to have to make them do it. I truly don't think they'll do it on their own. They will to some extent, but it's that minimal thing. Congress tells them minimally, 'You have to do this,' and that's what [organizations] are going to do. So, if Congress raises those stakes and makes them higher, and makes them more specific, then [organizations] will have to raise their standard, and they'll have to comply. I'm worried that Congress is the only one that holds that power. The [DNI open source] leadership doesn't have it—it has to come from Congress.[87]

In terms of this tension between top-down coercion and more normative, bottom-up approaches, one analyst remarked, "I think it takes both. I don't think you can have policy makers forcing things on people because that rarely works, and I think that you can't just have people from below trying to push it up. [Open source] might be recognized as valuable [or] it might not. I think it's a combination of the two."[88] This tension concerning the coercive and normative elements of cultural change was widespread. One analyst stated it this way:

This fusion center is run by a state police organization, which many of them are, and in the police or the law enforcement atmosphere, [analysts] don't really use open source or they never have before. . . . I think a lot of agencies—to them intelligence is information that is either sacred, or "law enforcement–sensitive," or not available through other channels. And they don't necessarily believe that open source is a valuable resource, which is funny because they do use it.[89]

These comments underscore the difficulty of pursuing a change strategy that emphasizes a normative commitment to the value of open source within an institution that has historically relied on regulative, top-down guidance. One official explained how this tension between normative and coercive elements is key to understanding the current state of open source's institutionalization:

I'd make a distinction between "operationalized" and "institutionalized." "Institutionalize" is very easy. Every agency has received a number of open source positions and resources. So, from an institutional standpoint, you can now identify open source officers in every agency in the intelligence community. . . . In terms of structure, I would say that this is the first time in the history of the United States intelligence community that there are dedicated open source positions across the board. . . . But in terms of operationalizing [open source], that's very different. We are still a long way from people looking at their business processes and saying, "Okay, how do we inject open source in here?"[90]

As indicated across the speeches and documents discussed in this book, officials have thus far emphasized training as the best mechanism for developing awareness and appreciation of open source—in other words, for influencing normative practices. However, organizational scholars Alex Kondra and Deborah Hurst offer a warning: "[The] likely success of training and development activities is questionable for altering behaviour governed at the normative level. Perhaps training and development activities should be coupled with coercive forces for success or introduced with enough uncertainty so that new rewarded and mimicked behaviours take root."[91] This case study thus suggests that as a result of discursive incoherence and competing discourses, normative and coercive forces may be pulling in different directions across textual, discursive, and social levels of practice. In other words, while senior intelligence officials and policy makers have stressed the need for *normative* changes, at least some institutional members involved in operations see *coercion* as necessary and desirable in spurring the adequate institutionalization of open source. This situation creates a paradox, however, in that from one perspective monitoring and enforcement are not required for practices that are institutionalized.[92] From this perspective, open source is far from being institutionalized within the homeland security sector. Indeed, many of the comments in this chapter underscore that officials' vision of open source is not widely shared. As organizational scholars Nelson Phillips and Namrata Malhotra state, "If an institution is enduring and stable then it does not need regulatory sanctions or other social controls to support it—it is simply taken-for-granted."[93] This has clearly not yet occurred for open source within the homeland security sector.

CONCLUSION: THE SYMBOLISM OF OPEN SOURCE INFORMATION SHARING

This case study explained how officials leverage the logic of information sharing and cultural change vocabulary in order to spur open source's institutionalization within the homeland security sector. This case study has also described how institutional members in this sector respond to cultural change initiatives. These responses evoked images of progress, technological sophistication, and collaboration, but also images of confusion, turf war, and bureaucratic ineptitude. These responses also demonstrated how institutional members construct culture as an organizational phenomenon that is both shaped by and resistant to officials' textual practices. Thus, the task of relating the use of open source information sharing systems to tangible improvements in preparedness is complex. One stakeholder noted the following:

The prevention business is something that is difficult to measure. There are threat assessments or threat advisories . . . that come out from DHS . . . regarding a potential threat—a potential act of terrorism. . . . It could be a threat to subways, could be a threat to trains, you know, whatever. So, the natural reaction at our state and local level, and our law enforcement level, is to increase presence at whatever critical infrastructure or whatever transportation mechanism that is the subject of the threat. . . . I don't know that we could pull into a singular instance where we said as a result of [open source] we prevented a terrorist attack, but certainly, I can't sit here and say it didn't have a positive impact on preventing one—only because the mere presence alone of a uniformed officer on a train maybe/probably/certainly is, I would assume, a deterrent for a terrorist action.[94]

Given the challenges of assessing open source's tangible influence on homeland security preparedness, as well as the dearth of such assessments, this study suggests the need for comparative and longitudinal research of open source information sharing. Open source information sharing is an ambiguous concept, yet its associated meanings and practices can be pinpointed within different organizational contexts and across time using both qualitative and quantitative methods. A longitudinal approach would help assess how official and stakeholder conceptions of open source information sharing and associated practices are changing over time. Such studies could assist policy makers and practitioners pinpoint the utility of various open source information sharing strategies, as well as the impact of associated organizational change initiatives. Attempting to create a trusted partnership and a culture of information sharing in a discursive environment characterized by considerable incoherence and competing discourses may undermine the government's open source initiatives. Officials need to address these challenges, as well as conduct their own investigations of social practice, in order to assess the results of the institutionalization of their preferred vision of open source.

While this case study has focused on institutional open source discourse and the responses of institutional members, future research could explore the interconnections between institutions and *citizens* in the context of homeland security. As one stakeholder declared, "The first line of defense in homeland security is an informed citizen."[95] However, the majority of those interviewed for this study agreed with the sentiment of one analyst, who said, "I don't think [open source intelligence] should be put on the front page of the *Star-Ledger*, you know what I mean? There's a difference between sharing with the general public and sharing with people who are, for example, with the power company or the electric company, or, you know, some other private industry like a pharmaceutical company."[96] Nevertheless, possibilities exist for exploring how open source discourse could facilitate broader citizen participation in homeland security affairs. In 2010, the DNI acknowledged these possibilities in a report to Congress on the status of the ISE. The report stated, "We recognize that to support the Administration's commitment to openness and transparency, we must extend those efforts to include the American public as well."[97] Demonstrating the discursive flexibility of culture as a tool for spurring organizational change, the report asserted that the Obama administration's Open Government objectives could be met, in part, through "creating and institutionalizing a culture of open government."[98] Yet this impulse appears to only extend only so far: "Most federal, state, local, and tribal ISE participants maintain public websites that provide the public with useful information and include directions about where the public can send comments and suggestions."[99] Comments and suggestions do not generally equate to substantive influence.

One area where citizens are, in fact, able to access DHS open source products is through DHS's OSINT branch. Available products include the following: *Daily Infectious Diseases Report; Daily Drug Trafficking and Smuggling Report; Daily Cyber Report; Daily Human Trafficking and Smuggling; Daily Illicit Commercial Trafficking and Smuggling;* and *Homeland Security Central Digest.* However, these daily reports are largely assembled from press clips from BBC News, Reuters, and the Associated Press. One day's headlines for *Homeland Security Central Digest* on November 18, 2010, included the following: "US Bans Kenyan Officials, Businessman over Drugs;" "Super Bowl: 'Magnet for Sex Trafficking;'" "Woman Returns to Florida from Haiti with Cholera;" "Food Safety Bill Clears Key Hurdle in Senate;" and "U.S. Mounted Border Cop Shoots Entrant from Mexico."

All these reports are prefaced with the following information: "Redistribution is encouraged. Please feel free to forward this email w/ attachment to your co-workers and colleagues that might be interested in this product." Notably, DHS appears to have overcome copyright worries by including this disclaimer:

Full article text and may contain copyrighted material whose use has not been specifically authorized by the copyright owner. This information is available to DHS, in the interest of illuminating incidents and events that may have an impact on national security and critical infrastructure protection. We believe that this constitutes a "fair use" of the copyrighted material as provided for in section 107 of the U.S. Copyright Law. If you wish to use this copyrighted material for purposes of your own that go beyond 'fair use,' you must obtain permission from the copyright owner.[100]

Acknowledging the countervailing discourse of privacy, civil liberties, and civil rights, the reports state, "This product may contain U.S. person information that has been deemed necessary for the intended recipient to understand, assess, or act on the information provided. It should be handled in accordance with the recipient's intelligence oversight and/or information handling procedures."[101] Nevertheless, support for DHS open source initiatives appears uncertain. Subscribers to these reports were told in 2010, "Due to non-appropriation of fiscal year 2011 funding, the Department of Homeland Security, Office of Intelligence and Analysis, will be required to discontinue production and distribution of the DHS Daily Illicit Commercial Trafficking and Smuggling Report along with DHS Daily Infectious Diseases Report effective November 1, 2010. We will resume production and distribution as funding becomes available."[102]

The next chapter explores whether and how more robust attention to open source discourse could serve as a site of struggle among citizens and officials in the development of national security.

CHAPTER 6

Open Source as a Resource for Citizen Participation in National Security Affairs

About eighty percent—eight zero—of the information that one needs is available in open source materials.
—Former CIA analyst Ray McGovern in the 2006 documentary
9/11: Press for Truth[1]

The most personally satisfying accomplishment for me . . . would be to raise the level of discussion around open source, to get beyond the "open source is good" stipulation and the accurate, perhaps clichéd, characterizations like "source of first resort," or quotes like Allen Dulles once said, "Eighty percent of what I need to know comes from open source."
—Doug Naquin, director, Open Source Center, 2008[2]

Chapters 4 and 5 explored the institutionalization of open source within the U.S. intelligence community and the homeland security sector. These chapters illustrated how open source's institutionalization involves contestation over words, logics, and theories of how institutions change. These words, logics, and theories are displayed within documents, speeches, daily conversations, and organizational practices. Officials work to institutionalize preferred meanings of open source through the production, circulation, and embedding of authoritative and influential texts; however, contradictions arise from officials' attempts to hold the logics of secrecy and openness in tension within open source plans and policies. The coherence of open source discourse and the prevalence of competing discourses influence how institutional members—especially within organizations possessing a homeland security mandate—interpret and respond to top-down cultural change initiatives.

This chapter differs from the previous two by exploring open source as a potential resource for citizens seeking to influence U.S. national security deliberations. An institutional discourse perspective suggests that a low level of textual production, dissemination, and consumption has so far impeded the institutionalization of open source vocabulary within the citizen activism arena. Nevertheless, the first chapter epigraph by former CIA analyst Ray McGovern suggests possibilities for reducing the metric distance between U.S. citizens and national security experts and elites. Then DHS under secretary for intelligence and analysis, Charles Allen, noted in 2008 that George Kennan, "the father of our containment policy against the expansionism of the Soviet Union, [once] said that he believed that 95 percent of the information needed for national policy decision-making could be found in the open."[3] Such assertions—perhaps unintentionally— raise questions regarding the appropriate role of citizens in U.S. national security affairs given the ubiquity of open source information. The second epigraph by Doug Naquin, however, underscores how institutional members tend to downplay discussion of open source's democratic potential. This chapter explores these tensions in order to speculate whether and how citizens could develop what I term an *open source discourse community*. Using the case of the 9/11 families, I explain how such a community could potentially overcome persistent barriers to more direct participation in U.S. national security affairs.

COMPETING IMAGES OF THE CITIZEN OPEN SOURCE PRACTITIONER

A citizens' open source discourse community could take a variety of forms. For example, some officials might consider Shannen Rossmiller an ideal citizen open source practitioner. According to her website, "[Rossmiller] is the West's premiere 'cyber-hunter,' trolling for terrorists on the blogosphere. Her daring online stings and subsequent captures have brought international accolades, headlines—and the ire of the world's worst. But to millions of fellow Americans, this Montana mom of three has simply become the home-front face of 9/11 courage."[4] A former municipal judge, Rossmiller gained notoriety for using the Internet to ensnare would-be jihadists, aiding intelligence, law enforcement, and military officials in their efforts to thwart terrorism. For example, based largely on Rossmiller's testimony, Army Specialist Ryan G. Anderson was found guilty in 2004 of five counts of seeking to aid al Qaeda and attempted espionage. Anderson was sentenced to five concurrent life terms in prison. A reporter said of Anderson's trial, "[Rossmiller] identified herself as a member of 7-Seas.net, a global organization that tracks terrorist activity and provides the information to government and military officials. After she saw the posting from 'Rashid,' she posted a phony call to jihad against the United States. Rashid wrote back. 'He was curious if a brother fighting on the wrong side could join or defect,' she said. After a series of e-mails, Rossmiller contacted the Homeland Security Department, which put her in touch with the FBI. Anderson, 26, was arrested . . . after he allegedly tried to pass information to undercover Army investigators."[5] Rossmiller appears to embody officials' preferred image of an entrepreneurial and evangelical open source practitioner: an innovator who uses open sources to confront defined threats to U.S. national security. *Evangelical* may here be interpreted literally: Rossmiller's husband cites the couples' Christian faith as their "ultimate protection" against vengeful adversaries.[6] Rossmiller's website is filled with World War II–era iconography, demonstrating the relevance of open source officials' narratives about World War II open source practitioners described in chapter 4.

Another version of a citizens' open source discourse community might envision citizens as active participants in the broader deliberation of U.S. national security policy. For example, between 2001 and 2004, the 9/11 families gleaned information from the Internet and other sources to help them achieve a remarkable level of direct—albeit temporary—participation in U.S. national security affairs via their work with the 9/11 Commission. While the term "9/11 families" generally refers to the relatives of all those who died during the 9/11 attacks, it increasingly demarcates a select group of victims who pressed government leaders for investigations into the catastrophe and continue to advocate for policy reforms.[7] A 2006 documentary about six 9/11 families, *9/11: Press for Truth*, contains a scene where open source is explicitly mentioned. In this scene, quoted in the chapter epigraph, former CIA analyst and national security activist Ray McGovern states that about 80 percent of the information that one needs is available in open source materials.[8] Here, "one" presumably means an intelligence analyst or citizen. *9/11: Press for Truth* describes these families' information-seeking activities using the vocabulary of open source. This reference to open source works to legitimate the families' participation in U.S. national security affairs. This participation included testifying before Congress; participating in closed-door meetings with lawmakers, White House personnel, and agency officials; and holding routine meetings and conference calls with 9/11 Commission leaders and staff members. The 9/11 families also submitted dozens of questions based on their research to the 9/11 Commission during the course of its 18-month investigation, and representatives of some of the families' groups testified during the commission's first public hearing. The case of the 9/11 families thus warrants reconsideration of the role that citizens might play within U.S. national security affairs in light of open source developments.

My analysis is based on interviews I conducted with members of 9/11 families' groups, 9/11 Commission staff members, and other stakeholders involved in open source advocacy and citizen participation in national security affairs. Again, the objective of this chapter is to pinpoint opportunities and challenges that open source discourse potentially creates for citizens seeking to influence U.S. national security deliberations. The case is intended as a tentative, future-looking possibility for open source discourse rather than a definitive example of how citizens can use publicly available information to transform national security policy. I focus on how open source discourse could potentially counter depictions of citizen participation in national security affairs as inappropriate, naive, or dangerous. This case thus follows others that have explored the role of citizens within national security affairs: Bernard Lown and the International Physicians for the Prevention of Nuclear War; Nobel Peace Prize Laureate Jody Williams' campaign to end landmines; Bryan Taylor and colleagues' work on the legacies of the U.S. nuclear weapons production complex; as well as the examples contained in Margaret Keck and Kathryn Sikkink's *Activists Beyond Borders: Advocacy Networks in International Politics*.[9] Similar to these examples, the case of the 9/11 families points to persistent difficulties confronting citizen participation within national security affairs as well as to possibilities for leveraging discursive resources to partially overcome them.

THE CASE OF THE 9/11 FAMILIES

On the morning of September 11, 2001, 19 men associated with the al Qaeda Islamist movement hijacked four commercial airliners and crashed them into the World Trade Center in New York City; the Pentagon in Washington, DC; and a field near Shanksville, Pennsylvania, killing 2,974 people. It was the deadliest attack against the United States since the Japanese attack on Pearl Harbor in 1941. Commentators have argued that because the terrorists attacked both military and civilian targets, the tragedy provided the victims' families with the "moral authority" necessary to challenge institutional norms that have obstructed citizen participation in U.S. national security deliberations.[10] One group of family members became known as the "9/11 Widows," or "Jersey Girls," as Kristen Breitweiser, Patty Casazza, Lorie Van Auken, and Mindy Kleinberg called themselves. Soon after the 9/11 attacks, these women began "manic major midnight Google cramming sessions that went on for hours, days, and weeks at a time" in order to learn about the events.[11] These women cited this information during their repeated media appearances and visits to Washington to urge congressional leaders to establish a commission to investigate the 9/11 attacks. During meetings with lawmakers, Breitweiser would plunk down five two-inch binders brimming with pages of information related to 9/11 and lawmakers' stated positions on national security issues. She would then use this information in advocating for the establishment of a commission: "When we met with an elected official or staffer who disagreed with our position, we simply went to the binders and pointed out that particular congressman's statement in the press, or that particular agency's public admission that proved our point. . . . Frankly, I think we were able to disarm them so easily because they had such low expectations of us; we were underestimated by all of them."[12] The women's confidence and effectiveness was thus bolstered, in part, by the information they gleaned from the Internet.

One source appears to have been especially influential, according to the *9/11: Press for Truth* website: "The families eventually found an ally in Paul Thompson. Dissatisfied with the incomplete picture of September 11th presented in most news reports, Thompson became a citizen journalist of sorts. He stitched together thousands of rare overlooked news clips, buried stories, and government press conferences into a definitive Complete 9/11 Timeline."[13] Thompson's timeline aggregated more than 7,000 pieces of online information in order to catalog the events surrounding 9/11. The 9/11 families discovered the timeline in 2002, and it became a valuable tool for research by the Family Steering Committee. As Kleinberg states in *9/11: Press for Truth:* "It was all our binders . . . but laid out beautifully online. And you had the ability to connect the dots." The remainder of *9/11: Press for Truth* explores questions raised by Thompson's timeline—the implication being that, as an example of open source, the timeline represents much more than mere information.

However, interviews I conducted with 9/11 family members suggest that the term "open source" did not circulate widely among this group. Therefore, director Ray Nowosielski may have included the reference to open source in *9/11: Press for Truth* in order to help legitimate the 9/11 families' participation in national security affairs, as well as reinforce the credibility of Thompson's timeline. By associating the 9/11 families' online research efforts with a former CIA analyst (McGovern) and open source discourse, Nowosielski resembles officials who have similarly worked to elevate the status of public information to something much more important, worthwhile, and consequential—intelligence.

A second vignette further illustrates how the 9/11 families appear to have used open source information to influence events. Following the establishment of the 9/11 Commission, President Bush appointed former secretary of state Henry Kissinger as chairman. Kissinger's appointment prompted cries of disbelief from commentators who noted that Kissinger had a record of deceiving Congress and had himself been accused of war crimes.[14] Members of the FSC arranged to meet Kissinger at his New York City office to discuss the commission a few days after his appointment. Breitweiser conducted an investigation of Kissinger prior to the meeting, uncovering potential conflicts of interest stemming from Kissinger Associates' roster of international clients.[15] According to family members who were present for this meeting, Kissinger became visibly uncomfortable when Van Auken asked him this question: "Would you have any Saudi-American clients that you would like to tell us about?"[16] According to the *New York Times,* Kissinger stepped down from his chairman position within hours of this meeting. However, Kissinger later asserted that he "decided to step down because resolving potential conflicts of interest would have meant liquidating his consulting firm . . . a step that he said would have unduly delayed the commission's work. He did not say he stepped down to avoid releasing a list of clients of his firm."[17]

Concerning this example, one participant in this project argued, "You're sort of mixing categories [open source and public information]. [The 9/11 families] could have found [information about Kissinger] by going to the index of the *New York Times,* which has been around for a hundred years."[18] This comment speaks to a perceived need to demarcate open source from other types of information—a need discussed in the previous two case studies. These two examples of the families' efforts nevertheless raise two interrelated questions. First, what role did information gleaned from the Internet and other open sources play in helping the 9/11 families influence the deliberation and development of U.S. national security policy? Second, what opportunities and challenges does associating the 9/11 families' activities with open source vocabulary—as occurred in *9/11: Press for Truth*—create for citizens more broadly? To help answer these questions, it is useful to assess the 9/11 families' activities across three distinct time periods: (1) pre–9/11 Commission, (2) the commission's investigation, and (3) post–9/11 Commission.

Pre–9/11 Commission Activities

Most participants and commentators agree that the 9/11 Commission would not have been established in the absence of the 9/11 families' efforts. One 9/11 staff member agreed: "[The families] were the force that actually compelled Congress to set up the Commission."[19] In this effort, some 9/11 families were assisted by members of Victims of Pan Am Flight 103. As one participant explained, "In many ways, the success of the 9/11 families can be directly derived from the success of the Pan Am 103 families. [The 9/11 families] learned from the Pan Am 103 families in that the families were in touch with one another and helping out one another—Pan Am 103 was really the one incident that set everything off that enabled a lobbying movement from victims."[20] Indeed, one member of Victims of Pan Am Flight 103 recalled, "The widows, in particular, just kept saying 'somebody ought to be doing something. We ought to have an investigation. We could do this. Somebody ought to be doing that.' I finally explained to her that the only person who is going to get anything done will be her. . . . [If] the 9/11 families didn't do it, nobody was going to do it. About a month later, we had a rally in a park in Washington, and it was the start of the Jersey Girls' visits to Washington."[21] Key to the 9/11 families' success was their moral authority, derived from their status as victims.

National security commentators can assess how the category of "victim" works to both legitimate and delegitimate citizen participation in policy deliberations and decision making. The label of "victim" is a moral and political category, and it is developed and attributed to individuals and groups in complex—and often contradictory—ways.[22] Victims of violence may skillfully use their symbolic status to assert the legitimacy of their subsequent participation in policy making, yet the connotations surrounding their status as victims may simultaneously mark their speech for audiences as inappropriately subjective and emotional. For example, the 9/11 Commission's leadership generally believed that the families' moral authority was to be acknowledged, but only if the families remained *outside* arenas of official deliberation. As one staff member explained, "Victims and their families have a stake in learning what happened and seeing that justice is done. Whichever agency has the responsibility for the investigations or judgments also has a responsibility to discharge those duties to the victims or their surviving family members."[23] Here, victims have no responsibility for actually participating in investigations or rendering judgments. Another 9/11 Commission staff member observed that the principle benefit of the families' participation was their advocacy, not their substantive input: "The thing that made these guys successful is because [9/11] was like a Pearl Harbor. . . . It was life changing, and because of the impact that event had, I think they were able to garner a lot of support and understanding and move things that otherwise might not have been able to be moved."[24]

Regarding the importance of the Internet to the families' research efforts during this time period, one family member claimed, "[The Internet] was critical, I think. Because not only were there groups like the [9/11 families] listserv [which provided a considerable volume of news and information on a daily basis] . . . there were other things: we e-mailed each other constantly and got information from individuals much more than organizations."[25] A 9/11 Commission staff member was more cautious, however: "I think the collection of information—and again, I don't even know how much they collected, when, or why—but the collection of information probably played—and I am speculating here—probably played a significant role in bringing these people—who were laypeople and not experts—into the policy process and arguing for, perhaps, what the scope of the Commission would be, but again, I would just be speculating."[26]

The 9/11 Commission's Investigation

The 9/11 families worked closely with certain lawmakers to establish a commission to investigate the attacks despite nearly 14 months of opposition from the Bush administration. The administration finally yielded after a 90–8 Senate vote in favor of a commission, and President Bush signed the law establishing the 9/11 Commission on November 27, 2002. Following the resignation of Kissinger, a former Republican governor of New Jersey, Thomas Kean, was appointed chair. Lee Hamilton, a former Democratic congressman from Indiana, was appointed vice chair. The 9/11

Commission was composed of five Republican members and five Democratic members, each appointed by his or her party leadership. Thomas Kean, Fred Fielding, Slade Gorton, John Lehman, and James Thompson were the Republican members of the commission. Lee Hamilton, Richard Ben-Veniste, Jamie Gorelick, Timothy Roemer, and Max Cleland (later replaced by Bob Kerrey) were the Democratic members. Kean and Hamilton appointed Philip Zelikow as executive director. Zelikow was a historian from the University of Virginia and was well-known to Washington insiders. Investigative journalist Philip Shenon describes how Zelikow quickly became a controversial figure due to his various connections with Bush administration officials, especially Condoleezza Rice.[27] Shenon also explains that the commission's staff members were recruited mostly from academic institutions, think tanks, and institutional sites, including the CIA.

The 9/11 families' organizations, by contrast, were comprised of members who did not consider themselves national security experts. Regarding the goals of one 9/11 families' organization, a member recalled, "When we put down our original objectives, one of us raised that we don't want to do much—we just want to change the world. And everybody kind of laughed and said, 'Yeah, we do.' So, you know, we knew that was a tall order, and we were all in a kind of deep depression at that point. But I think in retrospect . . . the moral authority that we somehow acquired . . . helped us stand up and make decisions on things that probably we had no business talking about."[28] This leader of a families group claimed that in addition to national security, the 9/11 families also influenced the commission and other organizations' consideration of policy areas, including airline safety and security; high-rise building design; emergency response planning and resources (including communication between emergency services); organization and oversight of national intelligence services; organization of homeland security and disaster relief services; victims' and emergency respondents' compensation programs; immigration policy; foreign support of charitable causes that may be linked to terrorist organizations; and bank transaction security.

It also appears, however, that during this time period, officials, 9/11 Commission staff members, and some 9/11 family members felt ambivalent about their direct participation in national security deliberations. One 9/11 family member recalled it this way: "In the beginning, there were very few doors that were shut to 9/11 families when they wanted to talk to someone, which was amazing. . . . But at some point when [creating the 9/11 Commission] was done, the 9/11 families continued to want to have those doors opened on every issue they felt like they wanted to have a say about. . . . There are some issues that I don't know that 9/11 families had all that much right to feel like they had to be completely in charge of."[29] It is therefore unsurprising that when asked whether the 9/11 families were meaningfully involved in the 9/11 Commission's deliberations, one staff member asserted, "They were not. The commission's recommendations were basically—they were based on fact, and on what [the staff] discovered. The families were instrumental in getting the commission up and running and finding the truth. The recommendations that the commission made were totally based on what [commissioners and staff] saw through the research that they did. The families didn't really push. I won't say that they had no influence, but not that I saw. The deliberations for the recommendations came from the commissioners looking at what was figured out by the facts. . . . There were no family members in that proceeding. . . . [The commissioners] didn't even offer that option."[30] Another staff member agreed with this assessment, but also noted the families' indirect influence:

The various family groups were very important to the creation of the commission. Their questions also influenced our work, providing a kind of added checklist of issues we wanted to be sure we had examined. Once one gets into the substantive work, it was more difficult to help or influence unless the groups had something to contribute. Steve Push and his group were, for example, quite helpful to us in our understanding of the Hamburg story and the German investigations because they shared their insight into those proceedings and obtained copies for us of some valuable records. Also, some other victims' families were helpful in the investigation of [New York City's] emergency response and suggesting some witnesses for the hearing we held in [New York City]. Unfortunately, by 2003, a number of group members had become deeply and understandably embittered by the Bush administration's opposition to the creation of the commission. This process thus hardened suspicions and beliefs that had already been forming in the weeks after the trauma they suffered.[31]

Another staff member suggested that the families' questions may have played a significant role: "Most of their influence was [in] the questions that they asked us that they wanted answers for. So, in the very beginning, we solicited from the families their list of questions, and every time they called us with another angle, or another thing to investigate, we kept [a list], and we made sure all those questions were answered in the commission's report, and we gave them an annotated version of where to find their answers, so they didn't have to go searching."[32] Another 9/11 Commission staff member stated, however, "But it was not like [the families] were asking questions that hadn't dawned on a lot of people, and at the same time, they asked a lot of questions that really bordered on conspiratorial."[33] Another participant underscored the uncertainty surrounding the families' influence: "I don't know if the questions from the families had anything to do with [the Commission's recommendations]. . . . I just don't know the answer to that. I tend to think not. I don't know."[34] This staff member added, however, the following:

It's not clear to anyone [that] [the families] have any special standing as investigators because they lost anyone that day—or grounding in intelligence work. They had great concern, and that concern was addressed, [and it] should [have been] dealt with. We spent more time with the families than we spent with anybody else. They were part of our day from morning 'till dusk.[35]

It thus appears that the 9/11 families moral authority provided only temporary sanction for their partial involvement, but not necessarily their substantive influence, in arenas dominated by technocratic national security discourse. Regarding the 9/11 families' Internet research activities during this time period, one 9/11 Commission staff member speculated, "The only instance where their collection of information may have made a difference was getting Kissinger . . . to resign. That anecdote works. But that's different, right? You should also think about the type of information they collected. On the one hand, they collected personal information about people in the investigation: Kissinger mostly, not Mitchell as much, and Philip [Zelikow]. That is different than information about the investigation. They were much more effective at bringing to light so-called conflicts of interest than policy."[36]

Post–9/11 Commission Activities

For some 9/11 families, the commission's *Final Report* marked a turning point in their struggle, which now centered on getting the commission's recommendations codified into law. Following the disbandment of the 9/11 Commission, all 10 commissioners formed a 501(c)(3) organization, the 9/11 Public Discourse Project, to "educate the public on the issue of terrorism and what can be done to make the country safer."[37] According to the 9/11 Public Discourse Project's website, the organization undertook "a year-long, nationwide public education campaign . . . in an effort to accomplish the following objectives: [enhance] the understanding of American citizens of the nature of the terrorist threat; [and examine] key policy issues contained in the 9-11 Commission's final report."[38] This effort included organizing "commissioner representation at town hall meetings— providing a public forum for citizens to evaluate how best to safeguard America."[39] The 9/11 Public Discourse Project's final report in December 2005 declared, "Change and reform doesn't happen in this country unless the American people demand it. . . . The 9/11 families are an example for every student of government: Citizen involvement makes a huge and positive difference."[40] The 9/11 Public Discourse Project was eventually successful in meeting its goals in that many of the 9/11 Commission's recommendations were included as part of reform legislation in 2004. The implementation of those recommendations, however, remained uneven as the Project's final report and subsequent legislation makes clear.

Although many families were glad to see some of the 9/11 Commission's recommendations codified into law, others were upset by the lack of concrete, specific accountability assigned to national security officials.

For some families, this disappointment endures. For example, on March 3, 2009, the group September 11 Advocates released the following statement in response to Senator Patrick Leahy's proposal to establish a truth commission to investigate Bush-era abuses of power related to the War on Terror: "A 'Truth Commission' will not fix the real problems that our country faces, nor will it guarantee that we will get to the truth. The 9/11 Commission, which you want to model your commission after, is a perfect example of that flawed process. The 9/11 Commission was mandated to follow the facts surrounding the events of September 11, 2001 to wherever they might lead and make national security recommendations based upon those facts. Sadly, prior to even beginning their investigation . . . the 9/11 Commissioners agreed amongst themselves that their role was to fact find, not fault find. This decision resulted in individuals not being held accountable for their specific failures."[41]

Given their differing perspectives and interests, it is important to remember that the 9/11 families were not a monolithic group. As a one 9/11 Commission staff member observed, "What are we suppose to do, have a primary and ascertain [that] you're a family member, and have a vote as to what accountability means and how it should be implemented? And I said this before—there are different levels of coping with grief."[42] This staff member also stated, however, "These are individuals that turned family grief and personal tragedy into a tremendous public service to the extent that we're safer today because of the pressure they put on [Congress] to set up the commission and to enact the reforms. That would not have happened without them. It is a tremendous example of citizen activism at its best."[43] Activism continues for the members of several 9/11 families' groups. One member of Victims of Pan Am Flight 103 warned, however, "It's an exhausting process. A lot of our changes are taking 20 years to happen, and not all of it has been enacted yet, even though they were written into law years ago. I think that it's a very exhausting and painstaking process, but if you have the support to go at it with people—like I'm sure the 9/11 victims can tell you and Pan Am family members can tell you— that's what it takes."[44] The nature and extent of 9/11 families' influence on national security policy thus remains an open question—the answer to which may change in the future.

Clearly, the families can be said to have influenced policy to the extent that the 9/11 Commission was created—at least in part—as a result of their organizing, lobbying, and media efforts. Additionally, as a 9/11 Commission staff member observed, "The role they played in pressuring government agencies to cooperate with us was appropriate and helpful . . . especially looking back and realizing how much time we wasted negotiating, which was such a huge part of what we had to do."[45] Regarding this public relations role, one 9/11 family member stated, "As a family member, you become a pawn for a cause. There are politicians and staff and everybody who would prefer to stay 50 miles away from you because you represent something that they're fighting against. [But] for politicians and industry leaders who you represent . . . you're an amazing tool for them to kind of advance the cause."[46]

Taylor and colleagues argue that citizen advocacy should ideally lead not only to the shaping of public opinion, but should also influence official decision making.[47] Yet 9/11 Commission staff members generally indicated that the families' influence did not extend to the commission's investigation or deliberations. One staff member stated, "Although the families were instrumental in obtaining the creation of the commission, I don't think their contributions were decisive, one way or another, in determining whether the commission would successfully accomplish its mission."[48] Another staff member stated bluntly, "[The families] would probably like to think they had a significant impact on the recommendations, but I'm not so sure, in fact, you can link being a political activist to being substantively and intellectually knowledgeable on a topic. So, you know, it's a little bit of a leap."[49]

These comments suggest that expertise served as a boundary between the inner and outer spheres of the metaphorical container of national security. While 9/11 Commission staff members were generally quicker to invoke this boundary, some 9/11 family members were equally ambivalent about the extent and appropriateness of their influence. One family member concluded, "I'm not so sure in terms of making policy [the families were influential]. I think that what we did more was we made our voices—we spoke in a loud voice, and we spoke in unison."[50] Another family member stated it this way: "I think the trying to influence policy to avoid these things happening again—that's questionable, because you don't know. I mean, it hasn't happened again. . . . Could you attribute that to our efforts? Probably not. . . . Who's to know? From the outside, you just don't know."[51] Another family member argued, however, "There is no way of proving that some of the legislation that was introduced into Congress by a legislator was not, in fact, the result of something that the families did or said. So, while it cannot be directly attributed or attributable to family members' direct effort . . . it can be indirectly attributed to family efforts. . . . I think that it is really difficult to come to a black and white answer."[52] Most participants agree that the Internet was a vital tool for organizing the 9/11 families and contributing to their research efforts. Commentators have argued that the Internet allowed group leaders to mobilize members, disseminate relevant information, and organize.[53]

LINKING OPEN SOURCE AND CITIZEN ACTIVISM

In their efforts to institutionalize open source, homeland security officials draw on similar discursive resources as officials within the intelligence community. Specifically, we find similarities in officials' referencing of key institutional documents, declarations of the need for cultural change, and use of customer-centric TQM vocabulary. These similarities are unsurprising given that the officials involved in the institutionalization of open source within the intelligence community are often the same officials involved in its institutionalization within the homeland security sector. However, links between institutional open source discourse and citizen activism are exceedingly thin. Nevertheless, one example of the interplay between these discourse communities is the controversy surrounding the Pentagon's Able Danger initiative.

Able Danger was a classified Pentagon program conducted prior to 2001 in which intelligence analysts mined open source information in order to contribute to U.S. counterterrorism efforts. Lt. Col. Anthony Shaffer, a former official associated with Able Danger, claims that the program identified Mohamed Atta, one of the 9/11 attack's perpetrators, as well as other hijackers.[54] These claims were refuted in a 2006 DoD inspector general report, yet they remain intriguing for some 9/11 family members and other national security activists. Breitweiser recounts in her memoir that an official associated with Able Danger briefed some of the families about the initiative, raising provocative questions. Able Danger is often associated with 9/11 conspiracy theories and the 9/11 Truth movement. According to media scholar Jack Bratich, the 9/11 Truth movement contains many variations and is not easily summarized but generally maintains that Bush administration officials were somehow complicit in the attacks or purposefully did not prevent them.[55] The case of the 9/11 families is not entirely different from the 9/11 Truth movement in that both cases involve the following questions: "Who counts as a researcher or investigator? What body is invested with the powers of articulation? How does a noninstitutional or amateur investigation accrue cultural authority?"[56]

9/11: Press for Truth linked the 9/11 families' research activities to open source vocabulary. Clearly, however, "no single text is sufficiently powerful to bring an object into being."[57] Here, then, I conclude that a sufficient number of texts have yet to be produced, disseminated, and consumed to constitute a citizens' open source discourse community. Nevertheless, the case of the 9/11 families hints at possibilities for developing that envisioned community by linking citizen discourse and institutional texts. Through the use of open sources, motivated citizens could become more aware of national security issues. The concept of open source reduces the distance between lay and expert authority, thereby subtly enhancing the legitimacy of citizen participation in national security affairs. Stakeholders in the private, academic, and nonprofit sectors potentially increase their credibility and authority as contributors to national security deliberations by describing their activities using institutional open source vocabulary.

However, intelligence officials have successfully marginalized an open source discourse that potentially undermines the overwhelming authority of U.S. intelligence organizations to delineate the nature of national security threats. By maintaining entrenched institutional logics, official

open source discourse increasingly appears inadequate for critically rethinking intelligence—that is, "what [intelligence] is, what we want its
instrumental role in American society to be, and how we as citizens want
to operate within the broader framework of American laws and values."[58]
Such calls for rethinking intelligence are not new. For example, former director of central intelligence (DCI) William Colby wrote in 1978, "It is essential that the relationship of the people to our intelligence apparatus
be redefined and made appropriate to modern America; the American
people must not be expected to continue to follow an intelligence tradition built for other times, realms and establishments. . . . Intelligence
must accept the end of its special status in the American government, and
take on the task of informing the public of its nature and its activities as
any other department or agency. . . . By far the most effective manner of
accomplishing the task of public education is by letting the public benefit directly from the products of intelligence, its information and assessments, and thus building an appreciation for their excellence and their
importance to decisions about American policy."[59] Nevertheless, the case
studies presented in this book collectively suggest that the possibilities
for letting the public benefit directly from the products of intelligence,
in many ways, remain as remote today as they did in 1978. As a former
senior intelligence official interviewed for this project asserted, "[The intelligence community] does not have any direct obligation to inform the
public. It has a tremendous responsibility to the electorate, to the American citizenry, in what it does for the president, and I think the American
people have to believe and have confidence in their intelligence services
as being competent to serve the president on international security issues, but that doesn't mean you are producing products and services for
that public."[60]

Another official stated, "The difficulty, of course, in terms of making
open source intelligence products available [to the public] is we'll lose access [to sources], many times, if [the intelligence community] highlight[s]
what we're doing. We get a lot of data because people don't know—our
adversaries don't know that they're putting this data out there, or that
we've been able to piece it all together."[61] Similarly, another stakeholder
argued, "If [intelligence] analysts understand the intricacies of U.S. policy, and they focus on [open source] articles and come up with an analysis that really sort of reflects U.S. policy interests, I can understand why
the government might not want to see that spread far and wide. It might
give somebody a better understanding of what our interests are."[62] These
statements underscore the challenges involved in persuading the intelligence community to share open source products with the general public.
Indeed, a report titled "Moving Toward a 21st Century Right-to-Know
Agenda: Recommendations to President-Elect Obama and Congress," by
the Right to Know Community—although addressing numerous intelligence issues—contained no discussion of open source.[63]

The phrase "what our interests are" in the quotation above, however, provides an opportunity for conceptualizing open source discourse as a citizen resource. Specifically, I argue that open source discourse could assist citizens in either resisting or compelling official "securitization." By securitization, I mean the process whereby a given phenomenon is constructed—in other words, selected, nominated, and elected—as an existential and widely perceived security threat.[64] Securitization is generally considered to be the prerogative of elites within the executive branch, Congress, and the intelligence community. For example, the intelligence community is responsible for submitting to Congress each year an "Annual Threat Assessment," which authoritatively defines threats to our nation. Security consultants Alex Martin and Peter Wilson note, however, "Much of the commentary [on open source] has been on how Governments can collate and process information that is available in the public sphere, rather than arguing that non-Governmental bodies and individuals can play a role in the process of setting requirements and priorities for the collection of secret intelligence. Effectively the debate about OSINT has been largely restricted to the question of intelligence collection, rather than assessing the potential non-Governmental contribution to the intelligence cycle as a whole."[65]

A potential nongovernmental contribution to the intelligence cycle can be broadly associated with the concept of grassroots statecraft. Political scientist Pearl-Alice Marsh defines grassroots statecraft as "the organized actions of citizens who are directly challenging the foreign policy of their government through contending discourses and 'speech acts.'"[66] Grassroots statecraft differs from traditional forms of citizen participation such as lobbying or interest group politics in that "practitioners of grassroots statecraft seek to alter the very premises of national security discourse. [Citizen practitioners] do not ask 'whom should we support?' but rather 'is there a threat?' They do not accept as given the adversarial and conflictual nature of international politics but rather ask 'What is in the best interests of the people involved?'"[67]

If institutional members agree that *open source* is superior to mere *information*, then open source discourse could contribute to the legitimacy, credibility, and effectiveness of citizens groups who contest official representations of national security threats. This is because *open source* increasingly connotes *intelligence* within institutional discourse (even if many officials do not treat the terms as exact synonyms). This connotation potentially challenges the state's ability to unilaterally define security threats based on official intelligence. As Marsh notes, a key element of grassroots statecraft is the generation and dissemination of "counter-intelligence." Here, a "grassroots intelligentsia" offers alternative, plausible, and persuasive interpretations of ambiguous evidence auditioning for the status of existential threat. Marsh alludes to how this process was accomplished in the case of citizen involvement in shaping official U.S. policy toward apartheid South Africa in the 1980s. Rhetorical scholar Robert Ivie states in a similar vein, "any prevailing perspective is necessarily delimited in its account or interpretation of reality and therefore is rendered more serviceable in a divided world by spirited critique from various points of view."[68] Grassroots statecraft may shift issues deemed by national security officials as existential threats into problems that might be addressed by nonmilitary means. As Marsh states: "What governments deem a security 'problem' is, more often than not, defined intersubjectively, and not by any objectively defined indicators. We must ask not only 'who threatens?' but also 'who is threatened?' "[69] In this way, grassroots statecraft is linked to Critical Security Studies' emancipatory project of explaining how most threats to human security arise not from external enemies, but from the projections generated by one's own state.[70]

One 9/11 family member, however, was skeptical of citizens' ability to successfully generate counter-intelligence: "When you . . . say, 'Well, okay, the intelligence agencies aren't going to talk to one another. You have to make that information available to us—or some of this information—and we'll connect the dots.' That, to me, is a reach. I don't think that's ever going to happen. I mean unclassified information, sure, but to have citizens in a position where we're analyzing intelligence? I don't ever see that happening."[71] Nevertheless, the case studies in this book collectively suggest that open source discourse blurs (but does not eliminate) distinctions between lay and institutional expertise. As a result, it may be increasingly difficult for officials to persuade stakeholders that information becomes intelligence only when it is gathered, analyzed, and disseminated by institutional personnel. As I have argued throughout this book, the distinction between information and intelligence is rhetorically constructed in ways that often have little to do with the intrinsic qualities of the information itself.

The suggestion to leverage open source in the production of counter-intelligence is not intended to stymie official decision making. Rather, the suggestion is based on Ivie's argument that, "in a condition of uncertainty and ambiguity, a decision to terminate the adversary must be based on a strong and thoroughly vetted case that establishes a clear and imminent threat that cannot be contained, deterred, or otherwise ameliorated by peaceful means."[72] Similarly, Martin and Wilson state, "In the case where fear of an enemy is firmly entrenched in Government and public opinion, it might be particularly valuable to involve external subject matter experts who can generate hypotheses that peace is possible. Indeed an open process which asked the question 'what would each side need to know about the other to confidently seek peace?' would generate a list of 'requirements' which could lead to confidence-building measures, open source research and a re-direction of intelligence collection which could contribute to conflict resolution."[73]

This discussion suggests that the recommendation for an open source agency residing *outside* the intelligence community might be worth reconsidering. As one stakeholder observed, "[The OSC] has made a lot of progress, but they're still considered a part of the intelligence community. And there are people in our academic community, there are people in our business community, who simply will not talk with them openly about information they have that they've acquired through their academic research and their business activities. [These people] will not touch them with a 10-foot pole because they are affiliated with the CIA. As long as that's the case, the Open Source Center will never be successful."[74] Additionally, a 9/11 family member stated, "Congress or somebody should have a citizen's commission that they maintain which is able to make— they can take things and bounce them off of them. And I think that'd be a useful function. You'd get some of the people who've been affected by security policy decisions—personally affected—and then kind of get a wide spread representation of the people. . . . I think there's a useful dialogue that occurs if you have a sort of forum versus just taking it from the normal channel through your congressman, the media, or waiting until something happens and then focusing in on one or two individuals."[75] A citizens' open source discourse community, whether formed through a government agency or an ad hoc commission, would immediately confront two challenging problems: vetting and voice.

THE PROBLEMS OF VETTING AND VOICE

In response to a question about whether the Internet and associated technologies enhanced the ability of citizens to directly participate in national security affairs, one 9/11 Commission staff member stated, "You seem to have more confidence than I do in the quality of information available from the Internet. The Internet's limitations are especially acute in cases calling for 'thick description,' where close examination and comparison of primary source material is indispensable to judgment."[76] Similarly, a former intelligence official explained, "The difficulty there, of course, is whether what [information] the general public has is accurate, because there's certainly plenty of open source information; the question is, is it valid."[77] Access to quality information is not a problem confined to citizens, however. As one CIA veteran observed, "[Citizens] have more power in your analytical capability right now—your ability to talk to people, and maneuver through conferences, etc.—than almost any analyst in the [intelligence] community, with the exception of maybe a few national intelligence officers—and even they get hassled by the security guys."[78]

Regarding voice, participants' comments similarly display a distinction between the *principle* and *practice* of participation. As one 9/11 Commission staff member stated, "I think [participation] was in [the families'] right as citizens, given what they'd gone through. [It's] anybody's right to basically make a difference and put their two cents in. . . . That's why our country is who we are."[79] Another staff member similarly stated,

"Just because I didn't agree with the way everyone pursued [participation] doesn't mean I don't think it was their right to do it."[80] In principle, then, staff members supported the right of citizen participation. In practice, however, participation is difficult due to perceived problems of representing diverse voices. A 9/11 Commission staff member asked a question that highlighted this issue: "What are 'the families?' It's a good question. Some got more press than others. Some were more vocal and organized than others. Some became confident media sources, and some did not. And no one elected a leadership for the families; there were several ad hoc organizations formed."[81] Another stakeholder observed, "There were too many [9/11 families groups], so their objectives are all over the lot. There's probably 12 or 14 different 9/11 organizations. . . . There are different groups with different objectives, so it's really difficult to say if they accomplished their objectives. . . . The more people you have, the more complicated it gets."[82]

Thus, we find in this comment support for the claim that opponents of direct democracy depict that form of governance as too complex and unwieldy for effective policy making. The challenge of expertise also surfaced in this context. Several participants agreed with the sentiment of one stakeholder who stated, "It's always hard to make citizens focus on intelligence matters. It just is. Clearly, they would like to see the 'experts' deal with it."[83] A 9/11 Commission staff member explained, "You know, the people who did the research on this thing, for the most part, were leading world experts on their topic. . . . So, from a substantive standpoint, I mean, these ladies and men who were involved got up to speed on certain topics to a certain extent, but competition was pretty strong from the people on the Commission staff who were literally leading world experts on the topics."[84] Another staff member stated, "It's fantastic to see citizens get involved and learn more about the world . . . and be less ignorant about what's going on. At the same time, there is something to be said for people who do this for a living and have made this their life's work. And that doesn't mean that experts aren't wrong—I mean, I disagree with more than my share of 'experts.' But, when citizens get involved, there needs to be a back and forth to understand that there are people who do this for a living, and they have something to contribute to the process, too. You can't become, necessarily, an expert overnight."[85]

Regarding the institutional sine qua non of expertise, a member of Victims of Pan Am Flight 103 responded tersely, "National security, aviation safety, international relations, all those things should be handled by the 'experts,' and look at the wonderful job they've done so far."[86] One 9/11 family member nevertheless stated, "I think there's a lot that we, as citizens, don't know, or need to know, and that's probably not appropriate for us to know. So maybe I would have a different view than some family members. . . . I have opinions about things, but I recognize [that] I'm not likely fully informed, and I think that there is a danger of . . . putting pressure that may limit options, and that's not something I want to see. I feel like we have some really smart people running our government now that I have confidence in, and they certainly could probably benefit from input from citizens, but I'm not sure that I have the in-depth kind of foreign policy experience or security experience that would be of any assistance."[87]

Some citizens, of course, would be eager to make their voices heard— whether or not they perceived themselves to be well informed. Regarding this situation, one stakeholder wryly remarked, "Clearly, if you allow every kook on the face of the Earth to be emailing and interacting with an open source agency, they're not going to get anything done."[88] Similarly, a 9/11 family member observed the following:

Many 9/11 families had good, constructive efforts. After 9/11 there were also an awful lot of people who were shooting from the hip on stuff, and they were reacting emotionally, or they were reacting because they had bad information and just didn't have a sense of—I think you can create a lot of noise by creating too open a forum of people who just want to bitch about stuff. . . . If you can create a forum where you have well-meaning people who are going to do their own work and try to be as responsive as possible and still represent, hopefully, the public view . . . then I think it can be helpful. But a lot of these public forums just degenerate into [shouting]. If the public officials—who are hopefully trying to put in a lot of time and do their best—if you're subjecting them to this on a regular basis, they are just going to clam up, and they're really not going to share information because they don't want to hear these people's opinions. . . . I got a real education in public discourse through this whole process [the 9/11 Commission]: it doesn't always work as well as you think it should.[89]

POSSIBILITIES FOR CHANGE

Some participants in this project suggested that the impulse toward democratic deliberation in the national security arena may not be suppressed; rather, it may simply be absent. As a 9/11 Commission staff member explained, "The real issue is who cares? What people do you think care about [deliberating national security policy]? The general public doesn't even know where . . . Afghanistan is, let alone want to get involved with national security issues. I wish they would, but I could tell you . . . you're not going to find a whole slew of Americans who don't have a passport caring about national security issues."[90] This staff member continued, "Now, could they? Should they? Would they? Maybe. But most of the people who have studied it and been abroad are involved. I mean, the rest of the people are going about regular life. So, you kind of have to think 'yes, it could be good and maybe it should be good' . . . but who would it be? You have the Public Discourse [Project], and that model worked because those people actually cared. They were interested in the topic. They were educated on it. They weren't just your average Joe."[91]

9/11 Commission staff members tended to argue that citizens (the 9/11 families aside) are generally uninterested in participating directly in national security affairs. We must ask, however, whether it is reasonable for elites to maintain policies and practices that promote citizen apathy and then treat that outcome as if it was not contingent on those policies and practices. In contrast, one member of Victims of Pam Am Flight 103 stated, "I think people in this country, unfortunately, have this 'Well, what can I do?' attitude, and [they] don't think they can affect change in our national security and policy when that couldn't be farther from the truth. I think that they need to be kept informed and pay attention, not just by what the media tells them, [but] by going online and reading what's actually going on in Washington, and keeping abreast of it, and actually being an active participant . . . actually writing [to] and meeting with their congressional leaders."[92]

This comment suggests an opportunity to increase citizen authority and legitimacy by integrating open source discourse within three public "dialogue strategies" advanced by security studies and communication scholars William Keller and Gordon Mitchell.[93] These strategies, the authors argue, should be used by journalists in response to an administration's characterization of intelligence. The authors dub these three strategies (1) "shake the tree for unpicked cherries," (2) "cast a pebble into the pond," and (3) "only fools rush in."[94] The first strategy aims to assess the actual strength of analysis underlying an administration's public characterization of intelligence. For example, a journalist might have asked Vice President Cheney the following question concerning his oft-repeated claim that U.S. forces would be "greeted as liberators" in Iraq: "Have agencies of the US IC conducted any official analyses that assess the strength of intelligence data backing your claim that US forces will be 'greeted as liberators?'"[95] The second strategy aims to determine the level of consensus across the intelligence community on a given issue. For example, in the case of Iraq's purchase of aluminum tubes as an alleged indicator of their nuclear proliferation, a question might have been the following: "Which intelligence agency has the most technical expertise to analyze whether the aluminum tubes are suitable for uranium enrichment, and what is its position on the issue?"[96] The third strategy aims to uncover the level of uncertainty regarding intelligence assessments in order to create more time to consider the risks of certain courses of action. For example, in the case of Iraq's alleged possession of unmanned aerial vehicles (UAVs), a comment might have been, "Before committing to preventative war, we should be sure that Iraqi UAVs pose a grave threat to US security. The greater our uncertainly about this judgment, the more likely our use of force will constitute unprovoked aggression."[97]

To these, I argue for the inclusion of a fourth strategy, which I call "open the lid," that includes three uniquely *open source*–related questions. The first is this: *Will the intelligence community share open source analysis (on a given issue) with the public?* Assuming that such analysis omits sensitive information on sources and methods, if the answer is no, a follow-up question is, "Why not?" Currently, officials assert copyright issues and the need to keep adversaries from knowing the intelligence community's interests in arguing against public disclosure of open source analysis. It is highly dubious, however, to argue that such issues should preclude public disclosure of this information if the situation in question involves the potential use of military force. The government's open source analysis may or may not contradict its classified assessments. Public disclosure of open source analysis, however, could spur officials to further scrutinize classified assessments in order to avoid embarrassing recriminations should those classified assessment later prove faulty. A challenge here is that open source material is often integrated with classified material in official reporting. Redacting classified information from a mostly open source report may be one option in promoting transparency. A more straightforward approach is to have the government release only those reports based entirely on open source material, such as those occasionally produced by the Open Source Works.

A second and related question might be this: *Does the intelligence community possess credible open source reporting that contradicts its official position on this issue?* This question is motivated by the WMD Commission's finding that available open source information occasionally challenged or contradicted the intelligence community's classified assessments on Iraq. This question, like the first, aims to ensure that agencies have adequately accounted for open source information that could influence classified judgments. The question also implicitly asks officials to reflect on what constitutes credible open source reporting. If open source reporting has been dismissed, it should, at some point, be clear to the public why it has been dismissed.

Finally, an admittedly radical question would be the following: *If someone has credible information that supports or contradicts the intelligence community's position, how can that person provide that information to the intelligence community?* Although such information can currently be provided to the CIA though its website, this question tests officials' level of public commitment to open source exploitation. Of course, challenges here include managing counterintelligence, vetting, and voice concerns. Some mechanism for vetting information, discouraging false reporting, and managing information volume would need to be created. Nevertheless, these challenges could be viewed not as insurmountable obstacles, but as difficult problems to be solved in the service of developing and sustaining adequate national security. Of course, such radical change assumes that debate among officials and citizens over the form, content, and role of open source information is both possible and desirable. It is likely that such a conception of democracy "currently exists only on the horizon of America's political imagination."[98]

CITIZENS' OPEN SOURCE:
A COMPLICATED PROSPECT

This chapter has indicated that developing open source discourse as a resource for citizens seeking to influence U.S. national security policy deliberations is a complicated proposition. One could argue that the 9/11 families' binders filled with open source information contributed to their confidence and success in establishing the 9/11 Commission. Yet the establishment of the commission appears to be where the families' substantive influence ended. Above all, however, this case reveals stakeholders' deep ambivalence regarding such participation. During the 9/11 Commission's first public hearing, family members Push, Fetchet, Kleinberg, and Vadhan repeatedly called for accountability yet consistently reinforced the distance between the families and the commission. The families' ambivalence regarding their participation in the commission's proceedings suggests they may have accepted the depiction of themselves as unqualified to participate in national security deliberations.

Along these lines, I speculate that the 9/11 Public Discourse Project represents a missed opportunity to develop a citizens' open source discourse community and a forum for citizen participation in national security affairs. One participant countered, however, "There was no way to institutionalize [the Public Discourse Project] unless the people that were there were going to give up their jobs and do it for free. So that was the problem—people couldn't work for nothing. The only way they could have institutionalized it [is] if someone in the government had picked up on it and paid for it."[99] Additionally, another participant stated, "I think a lot of [people involved in the Project] got burned out. Honestly speaking, knowing the people that could have tried to see it institutionalized, they would have said, 'You know . . . I'm done. I can't do it anymore.'"[100]

It may be worth considering, however, that "democracy asks not for people's unlimited energy and knowledge, but for their creative participation."[101] For rhetorical scholar Robert Asen, the value of citizen participation lies in its qualitative contributions in bolstering public agendas, raising issues and questions, and enhancing the democratic process. Asen states, "Democracy requires a leap of faith. Belief in democracy is like belief in God; either one has faith or one does not. Radical skepticism cannot be met with irrefutable, empirical proof. Democracy . . . constitutes a moral project."[102] The question of how an environment saturated with open source information could facilitate more democratic deliberation of U.S. national security affairs thus remains unanswered. The next and final chapter further explores the challenges of developing a more democratic U.S. intelligence sector based on open source developments, as well as summarizes the contributions of this book for officials, policy makers, scholars, and citizens.

CHAPTER 7

Open Source, Democracy, and the Future of U.S. Intelligence

And god knows what happens now . . . hopefully worldwide discussion, debates, and reforms . . . [I] want people to see the truth . . . regardless of who
they are . . . because without information, you cannot make informed decisions as a public . . . or maybe [I'm] just young, naive, and stupid.
  —U.S. Army intelligence officer Bradley Manning on why he allegedly
  provided classified information to WikiLeaks in 2010[1]

"In 15 years, there will be no more secrets." The CIA's Don Burke made
that assertion in 2008.[2] Burke's provocative claim informed the title of this
book. That title, *No More Secrets*, can be interpreted as a declaration that soon
there will indeed be no more secrets—websites such as WikiLeaks appear
to portend that future. Another interpretation views the title as a question:
is it really the case that there are—or soon will be—no more secrets? The
massive growth in classified intelligence programs in the wake of 9/11,
and the government's enduring pursuit of decision advantage, makes that
scenario unlikely. Finally, the title can be interpreted as a normative question: *should* there be no more secrets? That is the question that WikiLeak's
editor-in-chief, Julian Assange, and other activists want audiences to consider; it is also the question that leaders of the U.S. government's open
source enterprise would rather ignore. This book has illustrated how open
source is generally packaged and sold internally within the intelligence
community as a commodity—with producers hawking products to customers. This entrepreneurial frame partially accounts for the reticence of
officials to widely disseminate open source reports to citizens.

Whether the U.S. government's open source enterprise should, in some way, be more open, one thing is clear: its institutionalization within the U.S. intelligence community and among homeland security organizations has been challenging. In *Spying Blind*, Zegart argues that intelligence agency "adaptation is not impossible, but it is close [to impossible]."[3] The history of open source suggests that U.S. intelligence agencies have long struggled to adapt to the challenges and opportunities wrought by ever-expanding sources of information and new technologies. Despite the government's recent accomplishments in developing open source structures, policies, and practices, it remains to be seen whether stakeholders will ultimately deem the post-9/11 institutionalization of open source a success. Whether or not they do, open source's institutional moorings shape its development in ways that tend to diminish its democratic potential: there have been no major DNI Open Source conferences since 2008, and public discussion of open source's broader role within national security affairs appears to be limited.

Richard Best and Alfred Cumming of the Congressional Research Service note a slim possibility, however, for reconsidering the current path of open source's institutionalization along the lines proposed by Steele: "A more radical approach [to reform] would be to establish an Open Source Agency completely outside the Intelligence Community. . . . The goal would be to provide open source information not just to intelligence analysts but to all elements of the Federal Government including congressional committees. . . . The goal would be to establish a center of expertise for the entire Federal Government and to make available to the public free universal access to all unclassified information acquired through this initiative."[4] Best and Cumming note that this approach "would have to be justified on the basis of a widely perceived need and pervasive support throughout the Federal Government. This support, it seems, is not yet apparent."[5] This book has explained how officials and executives have constructed official open source discourse in ways that suppress support for—much less awareness of—more radical approaches. These dominant constructions are based on 3,000-year-old assumptions concerning the role of citizens within national security affairs. Using examples from the field of rhetoric and so-called public intelligence websites, this chapter explains why those assumptions are unlikely to soon change.

Because of its publicly available dimensions, open source will nevertheless continue to evoke the idealized principles of a democratic society. And the competing logics of secrecy and openness will continue to generate oscillation within the speech and writing of open source commentators. As Hulnick wrote in 2008, "The [Obama] administration ought to be more open about intelligence, rather than more secretive. . . . The American people will never trust a system they learn about only from spy fiction, adventure movies, or distorted histories."[6] Nevertheless, Hulnick simultaneously argued, "The judgments rendered by the intelligence system ought to be kept secret so that they do not become a subject of political debate. . . . [Public] releases have hurt the IC's ability to do what it was designed for—to provide unbiased and honest judgments, based on the best data that can be obtained."[7] Chapters 4 and 6 explained how the competing logics of secrecy and openness are paradoxically configured within institutional discourse. Building on chapter 6, this final chapter explains how public intelligence efforts cannot escape generating similar tensions.

PUBLIC INTELLIGENCE

Established in 2006, WikiLeaks garnered widespread public attention in 2010 when it first released classified video footage of a controversial U.S. Apache helicopter strike in Iraq in 2007 in which two Reuters journalists were killed. Within months, the website had subsequently posted 76,900 documents about the war in Afghanistan (the Afghan War Diary) and nearly 400,000 documents concerning the war in Iraq (the Iraq War Logs). Commentators referred to the Iraq War Logs as "the largest security breach of its kind in U.S. military history."[8] In November 2010, WikiLeaks began releasing more than 250,000 U.S. State Department documents, many containing secret information about political events, figures, and policies. Predictably, some commentators praised WikiLeaks for making the information publicly available, while other commentators denounced the leaks—with some even calling for the execution of Assange.[9]

In contrast to the OSC's tagline, "Information to Intelligence," WikiLeaks' tagline could be "Intelligence to Information." WikiLeaks obtains secret material from anonymous sources, organizes it (but does not typically analyze it), and then offers public access to that material via its website. This process symbolically transforms intelligence into publicly available information. WikiLeaks' motive for doing this is to promote a "stronger democracy." According to its website, "Publishing improves transparency, and this transparency creates a better society for all people. Better scrutiny leads to reduced corruption and stronger democracies in all society's institutions, including government, corporations and other organisations. A healthy, vibrant and inquisitive journalistic media plays a vital role in achieving these goals. We are part of that media. Scrutiny requires information."[10]

Most commentators have accused U.S. Army intelligence officer Bradley Manning of being the source of the 2010 WikiLeaks disclosures. Manning was charged on May 29, 2010, with unlawfully downloading classified information onto a personal computer. The chapter epigraph is drawn from online chat logs that purport to contain conversations between Manning and hacker/journalist Adrian Lamo.[11] In these conversations, Manning explains to Lamo that he felt motivated to leak classified information following an investigation he conducted as part of his intelligence duties in Iraq. According to Manning, 15 Iraqis had been detained by the Iraqi Federal

Police for printing "anti-Iraqi literature." Through an interpreter, Manning
learned that the literature in question was a "benign political critique titled 'Where did the money go?'" that exposed corruption within the Iraqi
prime minster's cabinet. When Manning explained the situation to a senior officer, that officer "told me to shut up and explain how we could assist the [Iraqi Federal Police] in finding *MORE* detainees." For Manning,
"Everything started slipping after that . . . I saw things differently."[12]

Manning's statements are drawn from the only source of the online
chat excerpts available in 2010: *Wired* magazine's June 10, 2010, report.[13]
Despite their partiality, the excerpts suggest that Manning's rationaliza-
tions for his actions parallel the arguments of some open source advocates
discussed in this book. Specifically, Manning writes, "Without information, you cannot make informed decisions as a public." Just what information the pubic needs, exactly, as well as how that public can make those
decisions—and with what effect—are left unexplained. As the previous
chapters suggest, these ambiguities complicate the development of democratic open source initiatives more broadly. Indeed, even Manning acknowledges the unstable foundations of his idealism when he speculates
to Lamo, "Maybe [I'm] just young, naive, and stupid."

Despite similarities, the WikiLeaks case also differs from open source
debates. In contrast to Paul Thompson's 9/11 timeline or the OSC's analytical reports, the Afghan War Diary, Iraq War Logs, and U.S. Embassy
Cables were not assembled from open sources of information; rather, they
were produced from mostly classified material. ICD 301 defines open
source as information that anyone can lawfully obtain. In 2010, no court
had yet determined whether WikiLeaks obtained the information posted
on its website unlawfully. In his comments, Manning appears to struggle
with the distinctions between information and intelligence. He states to
Lamo, "It's [the downloaded classified material] public information . . . it's
public data . . . it belongs in the public domain . . . information should be
free . . . if [it's] out in the open . . . it should be a public good."[14] Manning, of course, does not acknowledge his role in making that information
public, and he seems to ignore that the military's Secret Internet Protocol
Router Network (SIPRNet) is not synonymous with open sources. Just because information is *accessible* does not mean it is ipso facto open source.

Manning asserts that "information should be free," thereby conflating
pubic information and classified intelligence. As illustrated in the proceeding chapters, arguments for and against that conflation are at the core
of open source debates.[15] Just as some institutional personnel continue to
view open sources as inferior to secrets, the status of WikiLeaks' material marks it as symbolically tainted for some audiences. For example, in
November 2010 the journal *Science* reported that Harvard University was
restricting student researchers from using the material.[16] The Library of
Congress also blocked staff and patrons from accessing the site.[17] However,
for Lieutenant Colonel Tony Pfaff, "[Open source] intelligence gathering

is no more objectionable than someone reading a newspaper. . . . Once [information] is 'out there' there is nothing wrong with obtaining it."[18] For Pfaff, once another state's classified information appears in open sources, it is fair game for collection and analysis. Pfaff argues, "Intelligence professionals do nothing wrong by accepting and drawing conclusions based on information gained from open sources."[19] However, the same logic does not appear to hold true for U.S. citizens who are denied access to WikiLeaks. The U.S. government can *make* the case that classified information should not be accessed even when it appears in the public domain, but WikiLeaks demonstrates the unlikelihood of ever *closing* that case.

It is too early to tell whether and how WikiLeaks' disclosures will influence the reshaping of U.S. intelligence. According to the DNI, James Clapper, WikiLeaks is "a big yellow flag. And I think it's going to have a very chilling effect on the need to share."[20] In other words, WikiLeaks' disclosures may spark a reversal of post-9/11 cultural change initiatives that have sought to institutionalize open source information sharing among federal, state, and local officials, as well as with international partners. Along these lines, CIA director Leon Panetta stated on November 8, 2010, "When information about our intelligence, our people, or our operations appears in the media, it does incredible damage to our nation's security and our ability to do our job of protecting the nation. More importantly, it could jeopardize lives. For this reason, such leaks cannot be tolerated."[21] As a result, Panetta declared, "Sharing cannot extend beyond the limits set by law and the 'need to know' principle. The media, the public, even former colleagues, are not entitled to details of our work."[22]

WikiLeaks is the most visible of a group of organizations that seek to advance public intelligence. An anonymous group of activists calling themselves Public Intelligence claims to compile information already available in the public domain but that is often buried in obscure locations on the Internet. Like a game of cat-and-mouse, Public Intelligence administrators claim, "We have already received takedown requests from NATO and the U.S. Army for publishing documents discovered via open source methods available to any member of the public."[23] Examples of posted documents include the following: "FBI Weapons of Mass Destruction Directorate Nuclear/Radiological Outreach Briefing," "U.S. Air Force SKL Wireless & Black Data Distribution System Overview;" and "CIA Report: Lessons of the Soviet War in Afghanistan," the latter prepared by the Open Source Works. Administrators of Public Intelligence state, "It is our hope that by making such information available and demonstrating the power of a public resolved to inform itself, we may engender a more informed and proactive populace."[24] The website Cryptome similarly invites users to send "documents for publication that are prohibited by governments worldwide, in particular material on freedom of expression, privacy, cryptology, dual-use technologies, national security, intelligence, and secret governance—open, secret and classified documents—but not limited to those."[25]

While not as audacious as WikiLeaks, Public Intelligence, or Cryptome in disclosing secret or sensitive information, the Federation of American Scientists' Steven Aftergood and the Project on Government Secrecy have worked since 1989 to make U.S. national security institutions subject to more public scrutiny. According to the FAS website, "The FAS Project on Government Secrecy works to promote public access to government information and to illuminate the apparatus of government secrecy, including national security classification and declassification policies. The Project also publishes previously undisclosed or hard-to-find government documents of public policy interest, as well as resources on intelligence policy."[26] Through its *Secrecy News* service, FAS occasionally obtains and disseminates OSC analytical reports that have not been cleared for public release. Recently obtained reports illustrate the breadth of the OSC's efforts: "Subtitled Clips of China's Declassified Underground Nuclear Facility in Chongqing," "German Left-Wing Crime Increase Adds to Public Security Concerns," "Kremlin Allies' Expanding Control of Runet Provokes Only Limited Opposition," "Cuba—Military's Profile in State Media Limited, Positive," "Venezuela—Chavez Moves to Silence Opposition Media."[27]

Importantly for this discussion, Aftergood reported on February 12, 2009, "In a recent meeting with the Director of CIA Information Management Services, we reiterated our view that all unclassified, noncopyrighted publications of the Open Source Center . . . should be made freely available to the public."[28] Similarly, a stakeholder interviewed for this study was frank regarding the OSC's withholding of its analytical products from the public: "I think it's completely absurd that an open source agency is going to be acquiring publicly available information, producing an analytical product, and then classifying it. That, to me, just beggars belief. That reminds me of . . . the CIA, when phone books were stamped [classified]. I mean, these are phone books produced by the telephone company!"[29] Aftergood, however, is quick to distinguish FAS's *Secrecy News* from WikiLeaks, writing the following on November 29, 2010: "Disabling secrecy in the name of transparency would be a sensible goal—if it were true that all secrecy is wrong. But if there is a legitimate role for secrecy in military operations, in intelligence gathering or in diplomatic negotiations, as seems self-evident, then a different approach is called for."[30]

Other public intelligence organizations focus on using open source materials to empower citizens. Since largely abandoning institutional reform efforts in 2007, Steele has turned to public intelligence concerns, spearheading the Earth Intelligence Network. This group defines itself as "a 501(c3) public charity that strives to create public intelligence in the public interest."[31] According to an organizational brochure, the group's mission is to "help any collective define their public intelligence requirements and then to find volunteers, or tax-deductible funding for commercial solutions, such that we can provide public intelligence to those who need it, at no cost to them. This is how we serve the public interest and contribute to saving the Earth."[32] Much of the information available to Earth Intelligence Network's website visitors is derived from Steele's OSS. net website. Additionally, the Center for Empowered Living and Learning (the CELL) in Denver, Colorado, describes itself as "a non-profit institution dedicated to addressing the most important global issue of our time—terrorism. . . . The CELL exists to educate citizens on the realities of today's global terrorism threats, and seeks to empower both individuals and organizations with the knowledge and the tools to proactively effect change."[33] The CELL "intends to facilitate knowledge-sharing, learning and self-reflection as our society takes on terrorism as the most challenging threat to our way of life today."[34] Finally, the NEFA (Nine Eleven Finding Answers) Foundation "strives to help prevent future tragedies in the U.S. and abroad by exposing those responsible for planning, funding, and executing terrorist activities."[35] The group "plays a role in the fight against terror through cohesive and comprehensive efforts to research, analyze, and disseminate information pertaining to past and current terrorist activities. The Foundation shares its findings with law enforcement agencies and the intelligence community where appropriate, and works with other research organizations to educate the public on the threat of terrorism."[36] The popularity of these and dozens of other public intelligence organizations suggests citizen appetite for detailed national security information.

Other open source groups, however, back exclusively institutional interests. For example, the Open Source Intelligence Forum (OSIF) in Washington, DC, is composed of stakeholders in the government and private sector who come together to discuss "the latest information, trends, and events in the area of Open Source intelligence. All of it is informal and off-the-record. Past guests have included the Director of the DNI Open Source Center, the DNI Open Source Coordinator and other users and 'owners' of open source within the US Government."[37] OSIF's goals in no way resemble the antisecrecy ethic promoted by WikiLeaks, Public Intelligence, Cryptome, or FAS. OSIF states, "Open Source is a crucial intelligence that must be well captured to empower today's analysts and policymaker. . . . Both the IC analyst and the collector must be taught to use and collect this information using today's best practices; Any collection systems must be tailored to the unique needs of the IC focusing on a complete definition of requirements, industry best-practices input, and architectural competition."[38]

Similarly, an open source intelligence round table hosted by LexisNexis on April 26, 2010, underscored the clear separation between institutional open source and public intelligence developments. Attending the round table were Naquin, Lowenthal, and Marks. According to an announcement, "The OSINT Round Table was created to make a public space for discussion about the government's needs for Open Source Intelligence and to facilitate relationships between government officials and private sector leaders; in order to foster an increasingly responsive open source intelligence infrastructure that meets the needs of national security decision makers."[39] Here, open source developments are for national security decision makers—not citizens. To protect elite authority, citizens must remain spectators on the outside of open source deliberations.

OPEN SOURCE RUPTURES THE "CONTAINER" OF NATIONAL SECURITY AFFAIRS

A principal reason that WikiLeaks, Public Intelligence, Cryptome, and FAS are controversial is because they threaten to rupture distinctions between open and secret information and destabilize conventional notions of authority, expertise, and control. Within Western democracies, elite control of national security policy making is legitimated on the following grounds: through elections, citizens cede authority and control to their representatives; national security decision making requires secrecy and must therefore remain outside the public sphere; and national security policy should not be influenced by shifting domestic political winds.[40] The origins of these assumptions can be traced to the governance of ancient Greece. In Athens, the people were significantly "consubstantial" with the government—citizen participation was direct rather than representative.[41] Although citizens were not formally separated from their government, the Athenians did, in fact, distinguish between elites and the common people. Athenian elites were those members of society who possessed specialized knowledge of warfare, economics, or political rhetoric; however, the role of the elite was not to rule, but instead it was to address and advise citizens—the "demos."[42] A tension within the Athenian model was that it empowered citizens to make decisions, yet also cast citizens as both vulnerable to elite manipulation and prone to irrationality. For Robert Ivie, the "orator as political expert" had to learn to "compensate for the disabilities of the demos . . . the limitations of mass deliberation in which prudence and understanding might succumb to flattery and emotional manipulation."[43] Although Ivie argues that such "disabilities" are overblown, we nevertheless find in ancient Greece the origins of the elite-insider/citizen-outsider dichotomy endemic to contemporary national security rhetoric and institutional structure.

This insider/outsider dichotomy was reproduced within U.S. political institutions at the moment of the nation's founding. For example, Ivie demonstrates how in repeatedly invoking the metaphor of disease, James Madison and his supporters helped firmly establish the myth of the "demented demos" within U.S. political culture during the Constitutional Convention of 1787.[44] Rhetorical scholars Stephen Hartnett and Jennifer Mercieca similarly explain how the Federalist/Anti-Federalist debates in the postrevolutionary period from 1798 to 1801 reinforced the notion that "average citizens were particularly susceptible to . . . corruption and that the cure could only be found in controlling who participated in the political process."[45] More recently, President Harry Truman's signing of the National Security Act of 1947, which established the modern U.S. national security apparatus, helped ensure that citizens would remain structurally/ officially excluded from national security deliberations. However, Ivie argues that elite control of national security institutions based on the fear of the demented demos represents a myth. Its persistence is not inevitable. For example, some of Madison's contemporaries did not share his view that the "distempered" hands of ordinary citizens needed to be removed from the reins of government. Indeed, Ivie speculates that if Thomas Jefferson had been present at the Constitutional Convention, "a somewhat different story of the people might have been told"; Jefferson, according to Ivie, consistently evoked a "positive image" of democracy, "a faith in the resilience of the people and the perpetuity of the nation."[46]

Within representative democracies, it is generally understood that citizens exercise their right to participate (indirectly) in the formation of national security policy through voting. This assumption was underscored by former vice president Dick Cheney when he declared that the extent of public participation in national security affairs should be "to go vote every four years on who gets to be president."[47] Given the strength of this assumption within U.S. political discourse, the influence of ordinary citizens on the formation of national security policy has historically stemmed from "protest rhetoric," rather than direct participation.[48] Such rhetoric, however, tends to reinforce the insider/outsider dichotomy that constitutes, in part, the metaphorical basis of national security.[49] Specifically, the famous "container schema," which has dominated U.S. foreign relations since at least the end of World War II, is based on the conceptual opposition of inner and outer spheres. Elites have historically succeeded in appropriating the symbolism of the cherished "inside" of the nation, prescribing the form of the nation's defense and security.[50] This rhetorical formulation has allowed elites to represent the nation, yet also divide it. From the nation's founding, national security has served as a site where rational knowledge and divine virtue has required a muscular defense against the ignorant demands of a peripheral, underinformed, passion-prone, and irrational citizenry. Such "domestic containment" has been a consistent theme throughout American history, beginning with the Constitutional Convention, proceeding though the Jacksonian period from 1824 to 1854, and reaching its zenith during the "Red scares" of the interwar and Cold War periods.[51] The juxtaposition of 9/11 commissioner Fred Fielding's statement that "[The 9/11 families] can't be objective because they're just too full of angst and anxiety and resentment" and 9/11 family member Kristen Breitweiser's statement that "we were random and passionate. . . . And that scared [official] Washington—a lot . . . we were neither containable nor controllable" suggests that both the container schema and "demophobia" remain relevant constructs for interpreting contemporary national security developments.[52]

While this insider/outsider dichotomy may appear remarkably stable throughout American history, another perspective emphasizes consistent ruptures, transformations, and deteriorations in the rhetorical relationship between national security elites and common citizens. For example, Mercieca and James Aune describe "vernacular republicanism" as a response to "the rift between the promise of a republicanism in which the people held power and the reality of a republicanism in which the people held very little power."[53] This postrevolutionary rhetoric was characterized by critique, demands for transparency, rejection of elite leadership, and promotion of the common good. The authors argue that "vernacular republicanism is not restricted . . . to early American republican rhetoric, but that the logic of vernacular republicanism is the cornerstone of American reform rhetoric."[54]

However, for activist Daniel Ellsberg, who leaked the infamous Pentagon Papers in 1971, if vernacular republicanism is to undermine elite authority and control, it must be accompanied by the development of "counterpower." Ellsberg states it this way:

During the Vietnam War a major theme of a Quaker activist group I knew of was telling truth to power, which was exemplified by literally going into the Pentagon or White House and speaking frankly in a dialogue with them. I don't at all want to say that is worthless, but there is a difference in values and priorities there. [National security elites] are not going to be reached by that. There is an expression in Congress—that "They may not see the light, but they'll feel the heat." What people in power need is to have their own power undermined by exposure of their wrongly held secrets and their pretensions to legitimacy and their concealment of what their real politics are. They need to be confronted by generating counterpower through Congress, the courts, the Unions, the universities, and the press.[55]

Can open source help generate counterpower? Marsh explains that in the contemporary era, "theories of international relations and foreign policy do not have much to say about the role of the citizenry in foreign policy: From realism to interdependence, we find either silence or outright hostility to citizen involvement."[56] The relative dearth of academic literature on citizen participation in national security affairs is accompanied by a lack of structural opportunities for that participation. It is therefore unsurprising that when asked to consider what the role of citizens *should* be in the development of open source and/or U.S. national security policy, most institutional members interviewed for this project demurred. For example, one analyst stated, "I really don't have a good answer to that question, because that's not really associated with my job. So, I'm going to pass."[57]

When citizens encroach on institutional turf, however, the situation may become tense. On December 21, 1988, a bomb destroyed Pan American

World Airways flight 103 shortly after it departed London's Heathrow Airport en route to New York's John F. Kennedy Airport. All 243 passengers and 16 crew members were killed, as well as 11 people on the ground in Lockerbie, Scotland. A former Libyan intelligence officer, Abdel Basset Ali al-Megrahi, was convicted of 207 counts of murder on January 31, 2001, and was sentenced to life in prison for his role in the attack (he was released on humanitarian grounds and returned to Libya in 2010). Family members of the victims have been actively involved in the investigation and the development of U.S. policy toward Libya. Evidence of this group's likely influence on U.S. policy is found in a December 10, 2007, letter to then secretary of state Condoleezza Rice from senators Frank R. Lautenberg (D-NJ), Robert Menendez (D-NJ), Chuck Schumer (D-NY), Hillary Clinton (D-NY), Patrick Leahy (D-VT), Barbara Mikulski (D-MD), Norm Coleman (R-MN), and Chris Dodd (D-CT) urging Rice to use an upcoming diplomatic visit to Libya to compel the government of that country to fulfill its obligations to American victims of Libyan terrorism—including the Pan Am 103 families.[58] Additionally, a 2007 RAND report concluded that the families' proposals led to the reinforcement of sanctions on Libya in 1996.[59]

One stakeholder described the hostile response of institutional members to the Pan Am 103 families' participation in national security affairs in the aftermath of the tragedy: "That was the type of attitude [hostility] we were given all the time by the State Department, in that, you know, 'Look, leave foreign policy to us. You don't deal with punishing terrorist states. That's our job.' You know? But they weren't doing it."[60] Indeed, a member of Victims of Pam Am Flight 103 explained their process:

We went in the system. We didn't stay outside and hold up a sign. We actually went in and worked with them, which was different [than other forms of citizen participation]. . . . Early on, the agencies were hospitable to us until they realized we were having some effect. . . . Government agencies are incredibly interesting: As long as they don't think you're a threat to them, they are very nice to you. But if you're influencing what Congress makes them do, or doesn't make them do, or how much money they get, they get really hostile.[61]

Another member of Victims of Pam Am Flight 103 explained, "For the last . . . several years we've had a very contentious relationship with the State Department. We've also worked with the Justice Department, National Security Council; we've had meetings with presidents. And during the Clinton administration, there was much more of a dialogue, and a conversation, and an opportunity to meet face-to-face. A lot of that changed with the Bush administration."[62] Some institutional members who participated in this study, however, expressed support for citizen involvement—at least in principle. One analyst declared, "The end result [of keeping open source information secret] is not greater security, the result is greater fear and distrust of what should be a participatory, democratic form of government."[63] Thus, similar to other stakeholder groups, we cannot characterize institutional members as having consistent perspectives on the role of citizens in national security affairs. Generally, however, citizens are depicted as subordinate to national security elites and experts. In this way, the echoes of the Constitutional Convention are heard in commentators' anxieties regarding how WikiLeaks' disclosures could undermine elite control of national security decision making. Across the arc of history, citizens are typically described as prone to emotion and/or lacking the expertise and motivation needed to usefully shape the national security policies of their nation. This depiction of citizens is generally treated as an objective fact, rather than a historical construction reproduced through social practices.

Thus, public intelligence destabilizes the container metaphor in that it potentially levels the playing field between technocratic elites and ordinary citizens. These sites potentially represent a source of counterpower that Ellsberg describes. However, WikiLeaks and similar whistle-blower websites may prove unsustainable in this regard because their allure is based on disclosure of secret information that is difficult to come by. Additionally, unlike the Pentagon Papers, which provided context, high-level sources, and indicated outright deception on the part of senior U.S. officials, WikiLeaks' disclosures are, as of 2010, mostly comprised of low-level, after-action reports and cables from military and diplomatic personnel. In this way, the Pentagon Papers and WikiLeaks are rhetorically dissimilar. WikiLeaks or other public intelligence groups will need to disclose information on par with the Pentagon Papers in order to adequately undermine the general assumption that citizen challenges to national security elites must be contained, suppressed, or circumvented.

On one hand, constraints on the development of public intelligence appear fixed and unlikely to change. On the other hand, this book points to communication as the mechanism though which indeterminacy is recovered, enabling stakeholders with different-yet-relevant perspectives on open source and public intelligence to collaborate in the service of national security. Stanley Deetz implies that instead of fine-tuning open source practices to better respond to "customer" demands, a more creative line of development may be "the building of processes that develop alternative perspectives, fosters their expression, and gives them equal opportunity to influence decisions."[64] This stronger form of democratic practice would meet the different needs and values of a wider number of intelligence stakeholders. The end result of open source and public intelligence developments should not merely be increased agency budgets, more lucrative open source contracts, or the disclosure of secrets for their own sake—the end result should be better decisions.

CONCLUSION: "WHEN I POINT TO THE MOON, DO NOT STARE AT MY FINGER"

In 2006 the annual meeting of the International Association for Intelligence Education was held in McLean, Virginia. Participants considered whether they, as intelligence teachers, researchers, and practitioners, were pursuing a legitimate profession with associated standards and credentials. At one point during the conference, IAFIE's executive director, Mark Lowenthal, invoked the Buddha's adage: "When I point to the moon, do not stare at my finger." Lowenthal urged the audience to avoid staring at the finger: intelligence education, Lowenthal claimed, was indeed a professional endeavor, and it was necessary to move beyond that question.

The Buddha's adage uniquely captures the complexity of the development of post-9/11 open source plans, policies, and practices. Using this adage as an interpretive guide, this final section summarizes the benefits of examining the open source–related reshaping of U.S. intelligence from 2001 to 2010 through the lens of an institutional discourse perspective. First, one can interpret the adage as a warning to commentators: *Do not stare at the Buddha's finger lest you miss the beauty of the moon.* From this perspective, some readers might argue that this book has narrowly focused on the discourse about open source (i.e., "the finger") to the exclusion of its practical national security applications. Indeed, this investigation was concerned "less about how things are done than about how things are to be thought of."[65] This book followed earlier studies of institutions that have examined "the ways that particular statements come to have truth value; the constraints on the production of discourse about objects of knowledge; the effects of discursive practices on social action; and the uses of discourse to exercise power."[66] By focusing on the production, circulation, and reception of open source discourse, I have explained why certain open source knowledge, structures, cultures, and practices—and not others—have ascended to prominence in the post-9/11 era.

Specifically, I explained in chapter 4 how stakeholders strategically included references to open source within the final reports of three high-profile investigatory commissions that followed the 9/11 and Iraq WMD intelligence failures. It is reasonable to assume that these stakeholders were motivated by improvements in the quality and availability of open source information coinciding with the exponential growth of the Internet in the late 1990s and early 2000s. During this time frame, Robert David Steele was a visible and vocal advocate for the contributions that open source collection and analysis activities could make to the quality, timeliness, and efficiency of intelligence. Influential officials within the U.S. intelligence community, business executives, academics, and members of Congress supported Steele's advocacy for open source. Steele's underlying logic of open source evoked images of egalitarianism, transparency, and public accountability. Despite Steele's efforts, however, officials have tended to privilege a traditional institutional logic that favors secrecy. Whether or not these officials, at some level, share Steele's commitments, those who found themselves responsible for institutionalizing open source collection and analysis determined that post-9/11 initiatives would need to be developed in ways that did not spark reactionary attacks from institutional members quick to assert that "open source" is not "intelligence." Thus, the recommendations of the Joint Inquiry, 9/11 Commission, and WMD Commission resulted in the establishment of open source organizational structures, leadership positions, and funding priorities within the intelligence community that largely perpetuated institutional norms of secrecy.

To support their efforts, these officials produced policy documents and public relations materials that consistently referenced the findings of the Joint Inquiry, 9/11 Commission, and WMD Commission. Additionally, these officials drew upon other institutionally acceptable discourses, including entrepreneurialism, evangelism, TQM, and organizational culture, in order to encourage stakeholders to consent to a preferred vision of open source. To spur the rapid diffusion of this vision and associated practices, these officials organized two open source conferences in 2007 and 2008. During these conferences, officials were able to perform numerous forms of institutional work simultaneously and within a tight time frame. As a result of their institutional legitimacy, formal authority and power, resources, and central position within the intelligence sector, these officials were able to marginalize alternative perspectives on open source that potentially undermined the overwhelming authority, exceptionalism, and elitism of the intelligence community. Thus, contrary to Lowenthal's warning, by tracking the production, circulation, and consumption of discourse about open source, I have demonstrated the benefits of "staring at the finger." Specifically, attached to that finger is an individual whose personal, parochial, and bureaucratic interests are not above critical scrutiny.

Nevertheless, one can also conceptualize these interests themselves as being produced by the contexts in which open source stakeholders find themselves. Thus, another interpretation of the Buddha's adage might be this: *Do not stare at the Buddha's finger because the self represented by that finger is only an illusion.*[67] This perspective aligns with assumptions about how language "bears down" on people, shapes overall societal and institutional conditions, and influences what can and cannot be said about open source phenomena.[68] Here, "knowledge emerges from discourse" because "the authority of the speaker, the authorizing powers, and the mode of expression are mutually defining, and all are part of the larger discursive formation that makes it possible to speak of certain objects at all."[69] I thus explained in chapter 4 the origin and logic of institutional secrecy, as well as how associated norms have shaped the trajectory of open source reforms. Discourses operate at both strategic and unconscious levels, and most intelligence officials do not reflect on their taken-for-granted assumptions that render images of open source as a democratic, *public* resource more-or-less "meaningless, impracticable, inadequate or otherwise disqualified."[70]

Another interpretation of the Buddha's adage could be the following: *Staring at the Buddha's finger will not help one achieve enlightenment. One must actually walk the path.* In other words, the Buddha's power is related, in part, to whether his teachings compel the action of others. In the same way, some open source documents may be "trivial" or "localized" in their effects, while others are more consequential in terms of their broader, institutional impact.[71] Specifically, I explained in chapter 5 how open source discourse intersects the logic of information sharing and cultural change efforts in the context of U.S. homeland security. Here, I examined open source texts in relation to the actions of managers and analysts who are required to demonstrate adequate responsiveness to open source initiatives. The coherence and influence of official open source discourse (i.e., "the moon") appear to weaken as this object moves from the upper echelons of the U.S. intelligence community to operational levels within homeland security organizations. In other words, possibilities for the deferral of what open source is are eliminated as this object is enacted through specific organizational practices. According to many of the participants interviewed for this study, these practices remain largely ad hoc, uneven, and uncoordinated. Again, as one official concluded, "In terms of operationalizing [open source] . . . we are still a long way from people looking at their business processes and saying: 'Ok, how do we inject open source in here?' "[72] The case studies demonstrated that open source discourse takes on a different character in each site: the intelligence community, the homeland security sector, and the citizen activism arena.

A critical interpretation of the Buddha's adage might be this: *Do not stare at the Buddha's finger because you might see that the Buddha is not divine—he is human just like you.* This perspective underscores that the officials responsible for the development of open source policy identified in this volume are no more, or less, enlightened than other citizens (this does not mean that expertise is unimportant; rather, it means that expertise is always circumscribed by social and institutional assumptions). Although some of the documents authored by these speakers may carry the force of law, the vision, or path, they have chosen for open source's development and institutionalization represents only one possibility. It is worth remembering that motivated stakeholders might someday choose an alternative path—should they find sufficient reason to do so. In chapter 6, I outlined some of the criteria stakeholders could use in seeking to develop a citizen open source discourse community. I envisioned a situation where citizens could leverage institutional open source concepts and vocabulary in order to legitimate their own organized, active, and effective participation in U.S. national security affairs. This participation could be accomplished, in part, by generating counter-intelligence and counterpower in order to blunt elites' demophobic impulses, which history has shown can all too easily lead to dubious national security decision making.

The goal of this book is both simple and complex: spur intelligence stakeholders to question their taken-for-granted assumptions regarding the nature of open source phenomena, communication, culture, and institutional change. To the extent that open source policies are developed in accordance with the persistent institutional logic of secrecy, open source's ability to foster democratic practices within the national security arena is limited. Such concern is, admittedly, not widely shared among institutional members. It is telling that participants in this study were generally unable to articulate a response to the question: How can citizens know—if at all—whether recent investments in open source have paid off? Indeed, it is still unclear whether new open source structures and practices have meaningfully enhanced national security, blunted analytical misjudgments, or reined in policy makers' mischaracterization or misuse of intelligence. Citizens, journalists, and scholars cannot know with any certainty whether these changes are worthwhile. Obtaining and assessing information that would illuminate this situation is generally the task of those who have access to classified reports—namely, members of intelligence oversight committees in Congress. Some stakeholders, however, remain skeptical of the effectiveness of congressional oversight. One participant in this study declared the following:

Those committees have failed completely in their role, in my opinion. So if the intelligence committees are not succeeding in their role to oversee, well, maybe then a robust open source capability will allow the American people to see where their dollars are going. That's what [Robert] Steele says. . . . He has a vision of what is needed, and it's not as far off as what you might think. And when he talks about these [envisioned] billion dollar [open source] structures—Well? What do we have on the dark side? Tens of billions of dollars? For what? To fail us on 9/11 and to fail us again on [Iraq] WMD?[73]

This stakeholder suggested that open source could, ideally, become a resource for citizens seeking to hold their government accountable and influence the development of national security policy. So far, however, institutional open source remains overwhelmingly insular despite the two major public conferences officials have conducted. This public discourse has not yet created substantive opportunities for citizen participation. This situation stems, in part, from the persistent legacy of the "elite, expert, insider"/"citizen, layperson, outsider" dichotomy endemic to national security discourse. Changing this situation will be difficult because it requires officials to revise assumptions that have long undergirded U.S. intelligence. These conditions help explain why, in one sense, Wallner's question, "But what, precisely, is the meaning of open source?" can never be unequivocally answered—the answer is contingent upon meanings that can never be totally fixed.[74]

THE FUTURE OF OPEN SOURCE

As with any project, this one is marked by limitations. Institutional secrecy likely hindered the willingness of current intelligence officials to be interviewed for this project. I may have formed different interpretations of events if key intelligence officials involved in the institutionalization of open source during 2009–2010 had agreed to participate. I have tried to account for the perspectives of these officials, however, by examining their public comments during the DNI Open Source conferences, within congressional testimony, and in media reports. News reports have also cast suspicion over the legality and ethicality of the operations of homeland security intelligence fusion centers. This situation may have contributed to officials' refusal to grant me access to those facilities in order to interview personnel on-site. Certainly, immersion within organizational sites where open source activities are practiced at the operational level would have enhanced this study.

Another challenge involved determining the appropriate level of detail needed to adequately animate my critical claims. If anything, I have erred on the side of including too many examples of the discourse under investigation. My goal in doing so, however, was to indicate to readers that the themes and tensions that I identified in each case study were prominent. I attempted to maintain open source discourse as an emergent and dynamic phenomenon; however, my descriptions and explanations, at times, may have inadvertently contributed to naturalizing certain assumptions or perspectives. This tension may have stemmed, in part, from trying to maintain multiple orientations to language within the same study, as well as trying to make the research readable for the groups under investigation. The findings of this book are thus not generalizable in the traditional sense of being predictive and widely applicable irrespective of organizational context. I believe that the findings are reasonable and persuasive, however, when considered in light of governmental and nongovernmental reports that have reached similar conclusions regarding the challenges of open source's institutionalization and associated post-9/11 reforms.

Finally, it is challenging to bring any large project to a close, and this one is no exception. The institutional events and processes depicted in this book display both evolution and repetition. As a result, it is perhaps less useful to create the impression of definitive closure than to assess the character of an ongoing struggle. From 2001 to 2005, I participated in efforts to institutionalize open source within the U.S. intelligence community while working for a private intelligence contractor in Washington, DC. I did this by selling open source collection and analysis services to intelligence organizations within the U.S. government. I have described how efforts to institutionalize open source developed gravity and momentum following the formal establishment of both the ADDNI/OS and the OSC in 2005. A 2008 article in *U.S. News & World Report* notes that Kim

Robson, a senior open source official, claims that "open source is starting to be institutionalized."[75] This endorsement of my claims indicates how, for some stakeholders, the widespread institutionalization of open source is inevitable given the political, economic, and technological changes of a post–Cold War world.

The *U.S. News & World Report* article notes, "Open-source information is both a curse and a blessing to intelligence professionals. On the one hand, it makes information far more accessible, sometimes more timely, and easier to disseminate. . . . On the other hand, it means a loss of power for . . . intelligence agencies."[76] This theme of tradeoffs and paradoxes is by now familiar, and this book has depicted how stakeholders have conceptualized and managed them. As a result, we know more about how the institutionalization of open source has thus far unfolded, the implications of these developments for various groups, and the challenges and opportunities these developments offer citizens seeking to advance the principles of a democratic society. Many of the stakeholders with whom I interacted in Washington, DC, from 2001 to 2005 are still, to this day, actively struggling to institutionalize their preferred meanings of open source via the bruising politics of government bureaucracy and corporate contracting. This book reminds us of the essential, potent role of discourse as both the source and medium of that struggle. Ideally, it will be the implications of this condition—as much as any international or technological developments—that contribute to the reshaping of U.S. intelligence in the 21st century.

APPENDIX

Open Source Contexts and Practices

This appendix describes open source contexts and practices in order to provide a more vivid picture of what open source work often entails. This description is based on my experience working for an open source contractor, supplemented by examples from press reports, government and commercial websites, job boards, and open source vendors' and OSC's promotional materials.[1] The contexts and practices described herein relate mainly to private sector contractors working on behalf of U.S. government clients. I use this perspective because many of the U.S. government's open source initiatives (outside the OSC's efforts and agencies' in-house intelligence units) rely on a growing number of commercial providers whose primary goal is to earn a profit. As a result, insight into the work these providers undertake in pursuit of revenue and market share is useful for understanding the opportunities and challenges of open source exploitation and the future of U.S. intelligence.

The rise of open source contracting parallels the growth of secret intelligence contracting. Shorrock notes that the aggregate value of intelligence contracts rose from $18 billion in 1995 to $42 billion in 2005, with the bulk of that increase occurring after the 9/11 attacks.[2] Institutional secrecy prevents the American public from knowing how these contracts are awarded and performed. By comparison, open source appears to be a good candidate for more transparency. Indeed, companies such as BAE Systems, Eurasia Group, iJET, Jane's Strategic Advisory Services, Oxford Analytica, Radiance Technologies, SILObreaker and Infosphere AB, SOSi, and STRATFOR openly promote their work within the U.S. national security sector. These and other corporations provide their clients with a vast number of information tools, techniques, products, and services. However, similar to the commercialization of secret intelligence, there are no publicly available figures for the overall level of open source contracting and outsourcing.

The expansion of intelligence contracting throughout the 1990s created fertile ground for open source advocates to leverage corporate discourses to institutionalize open source in ways that advanced their interests. During an October 6, 2000, speech before the Washington College of Law, then NIC chairman John Gannon declared, "We . . . need to have close and enduring partnerships in the commercial world to benefit from the private sector's continuing pursuit of new technology and from its best practices in dealing with the open-source challenge."[3] The 9/11 terrorist attacks and the run-up to the 2003 Iraq War momentarily destabilized institutional assumptions, permitting stakeholders to struggle over new arrangements and practices. Commercial open source advocates seized the moment, using corporate-inflected speech and writing to vault open source to the forefront of intelligence reform debates. Open source advocates brought together taken-for-granted institutional and commercial logics in ways that profoundly shaped the course of open source's development.

Mercado wrote in a 2005 *Studies in Intelligence* article, "Policymakers and intelligence executives would . . . do well to resist the siren call of those who argue that we should simply privatize OSINT. Private corporations are an excellent source of dictionaries, software, and contractors for our government. But private companies alone are no substitute for accountable, dedicated OSINT professionals in government offices."[4] The profit motive is a primary reason stakeholders should be concerned with how these developments relate to changing conceptualizations of open source. For example, the open source sector is characterized by an overwhelming emphasis on threat, risk, and uncertainty. As Gibson writes, "Where policy and decision-makers . . . must manage the complexity, uncertainty and ambiguity of the global, postmodern, risk society, OSINT offers a lifeline to intelligence."[5] However, open source providers must both respond to and *sustain* a sense of anxiety within their clients in order to continually demonstrate value and relevance. As former CIA analyst Michael Scheuer said of the open source provider SITE, "An Arabic word can have four or five different meanings in translation."[6] SITE, said Scheuer, always chooses the "most warlike translation."[7]

I am not arguing that threats, risks, and uncertainties are constructed by open source providers in the sense of being made-up fictions; I am suggesting, however, that phenomena that rise to a given level of threat do so, in part, through processes of human communication.[8] In other words, sociologist Lynn Eden argues that "our knowledge of . . . reality is always, and profoundly, mediated by the social: what actors already know, what they want to know, how they think they can go about learning more, and the criteria by which they judge and make new knowledge."[9] For example, every year the U.S. intelligence community presents to Congress an assessment of the major threats to U.S. national security.[10] The intelligence community uses this assessment to persuade Congress and citizens that defense of certain national values is warranted. Similarly, if we want to better understand the reshaping of U.S. intelligence, it is necessary to scrutinize the social realities of open source stakeholders—especially private sector actors who have much to gain or lose in the contestation over the meanings of open source. This appendix provides that scrutiny in a way that is accessible to audiences who may be unfamiliar with open source issues. Open source discourse is characterized by a dizzying array of acronyms, jargon, and buzzwords; therefore, this discussion focuses plainly on *who* is permitted to become an open source analyst, *how* organizations secure open source contracts, *what* work analysts typically perform, *where* they disseminate that work, and *why* organizations typically fail to critically assess the worth of these activities.

BECOMING AN OPEN SOURCE ANALYST

Former CIA assistant DCI for analysis and production Mark Lowenthal states that the basic purpose of intelligence is to "reduce uncertainty."[11] This view of intelligence is intuitive, widespread, and involves at least three related activities: (1) the gathering of information; (2) the application of knowledge and reasoning to that information in order to make judgments concerning its quality, significance, and consequence; and (3) the communicating of those judgments to selected officials in the form of finished intelligence products. Whether one is an open source analyst for a commercial firm or a government agency, the basic purpose of intelligence remains the same. As a result, there are several similarities between commercial open source analysts and their government counterparts. For example, in his article "Intelligence Shop," Harris notes that Eurasia Group's analysts "typically hail from top training grounds, such as the School of Advanced International Studies at Johns Hopkins University or the Fletcher School at Tufts University."[12] Just like some of their institutional cousins, Eurasia Group analysts "assess the likelihood that foreign governments will collapse, whether from coup, natural disaster, economic catastrophe or any other circumstance."[13] However, in contrast to government agencies that focus narrowly on "current intelligence" (short-range issues), Eurasia Group specializes in "things that ought to be on [the client's] radar, but aren't yet."[14]

Becoming a Eurasia Group analyst typically requires "a minimum of five years of relevant professional experience, one year of field experience in [a] region and an advanced degree in political science or other relevant discipline (economics or international relations with an emphasis on economics)."[15] In contrast to Eurasia Group, Jardines, as owner of Open Source Publishing, Inc., told one reporter, "Our employees have no single degree or type of training."[16] Jardines stated, "We prefer candidates to have an advanced degree and speak at least one foreign language. I look for tenacity and creative thinking in a potential employee."[17] A difference between institutional and private sector analysts relates to the issue of U.S. citizenship and the ability to obtain security clearance. Eurasia Group's Maureen Miskovich explained in 2005 that she did not "worry about the government poaching her employees. Many of them aren't U.S. citizens, which reduces their chances of landing a government job."[18] Similarly, the open source provider STRATFOR encourages applicants possessing diverse educational and professional backgrounds in "world affairs, global trade, economics, technological innovation, engineering, military strategy and/or tactical analysis."[19] The company states, "In addition to U.S. applicants, we are also accepting non-U.S. recruits, especially those who would be interested in continuing their relationship with STRATFOR from their country of residence."[20] Successful applicants undertake an unpaid, four-month-long analyst development program at STRATFOR in Austin, Texas. Also in 2010, the open source provider iJET sought intelligence analysts to "support the company's 24/7 mission from its North America Intelligence Operations Center in Annapolis, MD."[21] The company stated, "As an analyst, you will engage in thorough daily monitoring and reporting, handle hotline calls, and write time-sensitive alerts and situation reports. You will liaise with clients, respond to specific inquiries and advise staff deployed abroad under diverse circumstances."[22] A security clearance and U.S. citizenship were not required.

To work for the OSC requires applicants to "successfully complete a thorough medical and psychological exam, a polygraph interview and an extensive background investigation. U.S. citizenship is required."[23] Some open source providers also require analysts to be U.S. citizens and possess an active security clearance. For example, Chenega Federal Systems posted a job announcement in 2010 for an "Open Source Intelligence Analyst." The responsibilities of the position included reading foreign-language newspapers, providing summaries of articles, translations of documents and electronic media, and creating reports. A secret clearance was required in order to "operate directly with Special Operations Forces conducting operations in Hostile Areas and support Sensitive Site Exploitation."[24] Similarly, in 2010, Radiance Technologies was seeking a candidate with "an active Top Secret/SCI [Sensitive Compartmented Information] clearance" to conduct open source searches, collect and analyze information, access databases and libraries, write technical reports, and develop summaries for analysts.[25]

A 2010 interview conducted with a former intern at Jane's Strategic Advisory Services underscored the pressures found in open source work. In response to the question, "What were you working on?" this intern stated, "Well a lot of it is highly confidential. It's really niche. For example detailing the companies who deal in arms and entering them on a database. These are companies who like to keep a low profile—even the big companies. All the information is available through open source research but it takes some digging out."[26] This intern explained, "At times it's repetitive and frustrating. The defence industry isn't very open. Even big companies don't have a lot of material readily available. So it can be tough for example, when you are getting nowhere with your research. This can be compensated by those moments of breakthrough when you suddenly access a layer of information you need."[27]

While many open source analysts focus on international security issues, some examine more multidisciplinary areas. For instance, the Global Intelligence and Forecasting (GIF) Team at the U.S. Department of Agriculture uses open source reporting to identify "emerging animal health issues and animal agriculture issues that have the potential to significantly impact the United States."[28] The multidisciplinary team of 14 analysts maintains expertise in epidemiology, veterinary medicine, policy and industry analysis, agricultural economics, public health, wildlife biology, molecular cell biology, and statistics. The GIF Team scans open source media for animal disease events and other potential hazards to animal health, as well as for "social, technological, environmental, economic, and political factors that may have a significant impact on United States animal agriculture."[29] When the GIF Team finds information of value, it produces a range of alerts, advisories, reports, briefings, and scenarios in order to notify stakeholders.

Internationally, so-called "peacekeeping intelligence"—which is based principally on open source information—has also emerged as a resource for organizations engaged in pre-, active-, and post-conflict missions in the Middle East, Sudan, Uganda, Sri Lanka, Philippines, Columbia, and other conflict zones.[30] Security studies scholars David Carment and Martin Rudner define peacekeeping intelligence as "a new form of intelligence that emphasizes open sources of information, multilateral sharing of intelligence at all levels, the use of intelligence to ensure force protection, and interoperability and commonality with coalition partners and non-governmental organizations."[31] The UN force commander for the Eastern Democratic Republic of the Congo, Major-General Patrick Cammaert, explained his advocacy for the increased use of peacekeeping intelligence using the case of the Rwandan genocide in 1994: "Had there been a more detailed intelligence assessment considering historical tendencies, the political will and military capability of the belligerents, and looking at all the escalation scenarios, we could have [been given a stronger mandate] and prevented the genocide and atrocities that followed."[32] In addition to the UN, ministries of defense and foreign affairs in the Netherlands, Canada, and Switzerland have been at the forefront of developing peacekeeping intelligence approaches.[33]

Even companies established long before the rise of open source discourse in the 2000s have jumped on the open source bandwagon, reframing their services to tap into the growing market. For example, Dun & Bradstreet (D&B) has positioned itself as an open source provider offering "worldwide intelligence to help counteract terrorism and fraud."[34] Analysts are encouraged to sift through the D&B database to find information on businesses, executives, corporate linkages, foreign ownership, and financial information. Some open source work is focused entirely on the private sector under the moniker of "competitive intelligence."[35]

Whether one is engaged in foreign, homeland security, peacekeeping, or competitive intelligence, the physical environment in which open source work occurs is generally similar. When I worked for Intellibridge from 2001 to 2005, analysts spent long hours in front of their desktop computers, scouring the Internet, looking for information that responded to the defined needs of their clients. This on-site work was supplemented by visits to libraries, research in archives, and interviews conducted with subject matter experts. Some commercial open source providers, such as iJET, configure their analysts' desks into a sleek, high-tech "watch-floor" or "trading-floor" layout; private offices are eschewed for rows of desks positioned in sight of large television screens tuned to global news channels such as CNN. However, other providers offer less glamorous surroundings. In a 2006 article for the *New Yorker*, Benjamin Wallace-Wells described his visit to SITE's offices on the seventh floor of a building in an unnamed northeastern city. Wallace-Wells explained, "I half expected to walk into a center full of high-tech equipment, with flashing maps and screens."[36] He discovered instead that the office "looked like a college newspaper's," with a room for SITE's owner, Rita Katz; a room for two translators; and an area called "the pit, where several researchers and interns . . . sat under a long, eye-level row of mug shots of wanted terrorists."[37]

SECURING CONTRACTS

Maintaining gainful employment as an open source analyst requires that one's company secure contracts with government, nongovernmental, or corporate clients. Supporting U.S. government agencies generally requires participating in a formalized procurement process. But before procurement activities can take place, an open source provider's managers must convince an agency's administrators to purchase their products and services. For U.S. intelligence agencies, the problem is usually not a lack of information; rather, it is making sense of what is collected in ways that support that agency's mission. The challenge for contractors is to distinguish the value of their organization's open source information and analysis from other sources that a government agency receives. Convincing administrators to purchase products and services is usually accomplished by providing compelling examples, divulging the names of other potentially impressive clients (and asserting that these clients pay a far greater amount for similar types of information services), and appealing to administrators' fears that their agency is overlooking valuable material.

Illustrating the latter tactic, D&B Government Solutions wrote the following in a 2008 open source intelligence marketing flier: "All 15 Cabinet-level departments, most federal agencies and over 60% of state agencies rely on D&B as a trusted partner to make confident decisions."[38] By comparison, SOSi focuses on the value provided by its personnel, stating on its website, "Whether they are supporting you as integrated staff or program managers, our senior team—*your* senior team—comes from both the private sector and the United States government, with backgrounds ranging from former senior officers to FORTUNE 500/NYSE corporate consultants. The diverse qualifications of the SOSi staff combine to become a single, trusted entity for your most important initiatives."[39]

If sales efforts are successful, a government contract may follow. Publicly available solicitations posted on the Federal Business Opportunities website, as well as information from vendors' websites, reveal a range of desired open source activities. For example, agencies look to open sources to construct biographical sketches for high-level officials, executives, and commentators within a given country in order to assess their relative influence on that country's foreign policies.[40] On the homeland security front, tasks can include creating databases from openly available information on gangs, drug cartels, and organized crime syndicates.[41] Media monitoring can involve examining how media organizations within a country are framing issues and developments; as OSC director Naquin stated in 2005, "There's a lot of interest in 'Is Osama bin Laden losing market share?' if you will. How is he playing vis-a-vis Zarqawi?"[42] Naquin added, "Osama bin Laden hasn't said anything for months and so Zarqawi seems to be really taking up the mantle" (Zarqawi was killed in a U.S airstrike in 2006).[43]

Solicitation # MDA908–02–Q–0055 outlined the DIA's need for "Global Coverage Knowledge Baselines."[44] The solicitation states that "the contractor shall use appropriate data-mining software and acquisition strategies to search the world-wide web (Internet) and other open sources for the best and most useful unclassified information pertaining to the governments of one-hundred-and-fifty-three (153) countries. . . . Each Government Overview shall consist of quickly digested, summarily formatted, factual data, map-overlays, images, charts, and statistics that provide in general detail a description of the government in each Global Coverage country."[45] Another solicitation, W74V8H-05-T-0253, explained that the Office of the Secretary of Defense sought "to develop a repeatable capability for capturing relevant Open Source information about hard-target adversary elite structure and elite decision-making processes, and exploiting such information for the purpose of increasing Combatant Commanders unambiguous warning, as well as positively affecting their operational options."[46] In 2010, solicitation # GS05T11BMC0002RFP outlined a proposal to develop "Open Source Research Centers" in Ohio.[47] These centers were to "provide a trained open source intelligence (OSINT) workforce skilled in supporting both state and federal government agencies already over-burdened with classified research requirements with the resources they need to meet their open source intelligence requirements."[48] The proposal was originally a legislative earmark sponsored by Rep. Michael Turner (R-OH). As a result of new earmark guidelines, the solicitation was made available under full and open competition rules.[49]

Solicitation # FA4600–05–R-0013 outlined support to the "joint/combined operational planning related to intelligence, DoD Information Operations (IO), Global Strike, and Strategic Communications in support of the Global War on Terrorism (GWOT), STRATCOM missions and assigned tasks."[50] The solicitation stated the following:

The objective of this effort is to access, analyze, coordinate, and disseminate FMA [foreign media analysis] in a multi-layered approach to media analysis for joint/combined operational planning and command/services/agencies (C/S/A) decision-maker situational awareness. FMA is particularly critical to achieving and measuring the effects of assurance, deterrence, and dissuasion in the modern battlespace. . . . The contractor must have demonstrated experience in foreign media analysis, open source media collection and processing, robust statistical pattern/trend analysis, foreign language translation, international public information, DoD joint/combined planning, strategic communications planning, research and database development, designing/constructing/and hosting web sites and email list activities. Contractor must have planning and implementation experience with respect to asymmetric threats, as well as an understanding of the international non-English language media. Contractor must have the ability to assess all media sources, including broadcast, print, and electronic providers. Contractor must have detailed experience in translating content from and into Arabic, Urdu, Pashtu, and additional languages that do not use Latin character sets, and the ability to draw analytical conclusions based on statistical trends/patterns and content analyses. The contractor must also have cultural knowledge of major countries in each area of responsibility (AOR) involved in the GWOT.[51]

SOSi elaborates the details of this contract on its website: "The Foreign Media Analysis (FMA) program is one of SOSi's most critical and challenging endeavors. It provides ongoing critical analysis of real-time events and major stories as reported by media sources around the world. These analysis products are delivered to leaders, decision-makers, and action officers, as well as Information Operations (IO) and Strategic Communication (SC) planners worldwide."[52] SOSi lists the products it provides in support of the FMA program, including these publications: *News Alerts, Overnight News Report, Core Analysis Reports, Daily Media Synthesis Reports, Weekly Foreign Print Media Summary, Global Weekly / Monthly Topical Reports, Influential Communicators Report, Al Qaida Brutality Report, STRATCOM Focus*

Calendar Briefing (a four-month view of significant upcoming dates related to national holidays, anniversaries, elections and events), *Detainee Analysis Report, CENTCOM Broadcast Media, Daily Briefs, Special Reports,* and *AdHoc Reporting.*

Similarly to STRATCOM, organizations across the U.S. government both generate and consume open source products and services to support their missions. Private sector analysts could find themselves working on behalf of these organizations: (1) the branches of the U.S. armed services: Marine Corps, Army, Navy, Air Force, and Coast Guard, as well as specialized intelligence centers within and across these services; (2) Unified Combatant Commands, including Africa Command, Central Command, European Command, Joint Forces Command, Northern Command, Pacific Command, Southern Command, Special Operations Command, Strategic, and Transportation Command; and (3) U.S. government departments, including Justice, Drug Enforcement Administration, Energy, Homeland Security, State, and Treasury. Additionally, governmental and quasi-governmental think tanks such as RAND and the Foreign Military Studies Office (FMSO) bring together military specialists and civilian academics to "focus on military and security topics derived from unclassified, foreign media."[53]

The cost of open source support varies widely, and for outsiders, the price tag for open source products and services can seem staggering. The five-year contract awarded to SOSi in 2006 for media monitoring was estimated at nearly $68 million.[54] At Intellibridge, one specialized report on a country's defense sector could have cost $15,000 or more. The open source provider IntelCenter lists the prices of some of its services on its website. IntelCenter describes itself as "studying terrorist groups and other threat actors and disseminating that information in a timely manner to those who can act on it. We look at capabilities and intentions, warnings and indicators, operational characteristics and a wide variety of other points in order to better understand how to interdict terrorist operations and reduce the likelihood of future attacks."[55] IntelCenter services range from a $195 per year subscription to the *FlashNet-Terrorism Alert Service* that provides "near instant notification to your pager, cell phone or personal digital assistant (PDA) of significant terrorist incidents and developments around the world" to a $150,000–$500,000+ per year *Hostage/Kidnapping Profiling and Incident Monitor* that includes "24/7 monitoring and support during ongoing hostage incidents with heavy focus on release of statements and video materials from group holding hostages. Focus on developing analysis to assist in identifying identity of kidnappers, location of hostage(s) and other actionable intelligence to support operations."[56] IntelCenter's descriptions underscore how open source tends to be understood and marketed as a commodity. The challenge for open source providers is to gain clients while not entering into agreements to produce specialized products and services that cannot be reconfigured and sold to other clients. An open source–as-commodity strategy enables providers to leverage work for multiple clients in order to recoup costs.

CONDUCTING OPEN SOURCE EXPLOITATION

Once open source providers have secured contracts and hired, trained, and assigned analysts, the process of conducting open source exploitation begins. James Major notes in *Communicating with Intelligence* that, traditionally, the steps involved in exploitation are often distributed among different personnel: "Collectors of information—whether it is human intelligence, signals intelligence, or imagery intelligence—rely on their ability to capture and transform information into intelligence for the analysts. It is the analysts who rely on their ability to communicate effectively, to translate ideas and actions into 'finished' intelligence products for the commander or policy maker."[57] Within the open source sector, the line between collection and analysis blurs.[58] Nevertheless, the government establishes the topics for open source collection ("requirements" in the lexicon of the intelligence community) within the OSC's collection plans, which are reviewed and approved annually, according to an OSC pamphlet.[59] OSC urges customers to "familiarize themselves with the collection plans and standing requirements related to their areas of interest in order to gain maximum benefit from their participation in the collection tasking process."[60] However, this may be difficult for many OSC users because viewing the plans requires having access to a Top Secret intelligence community intranet.

Once topics and requirements for open source exploitation are established, analysts identify their collection and analysis strategies and tactics. Open source providers generally assert that their work is "not the cut and paste and Googlification that we see in so many places."[61] For example, the OSC's Open Source Academy (OSA) offers training to analysts on topics including "basic tradecraft, Internet exploitation, and reviewing finished intelligence products."[62] OSA Provost Dave Kraus commented, "Our analytic tradecraft courses teach how to analyze the media, including ownership of media organizations and their political leanings. The courses on Internet exploitation go beyond the casual search skills that we've developed at home and in school. There are very precise search and research strategies, that are not intuitive, to cull valuable information from the Internet."[63]

Companies also offer specialized training in open source exploitation methods and tools.[64] Handbooks such as *Intelligence Exploitation of the Internet* and the U.S. Army's *Field Manual for Open Source Intelligence* are freely available online (the latter is marked "FOR OFFICIAL USE ONLY").[65] Training seminars and handbooks provide extensive technical information regarding how to plan for open source exploitation, conduct that exploitation via online and offline search strategies and techniques, assess the quality of sources, and disseminate finished intelligence products. Increasingly, this work involves obtaining information called "gray literature," which is "comprised of research and technical reports, trip reports, working or discussion papers, market surveys, newsletters and other unclassified sources," along with "maps, building diagrams, biographies, ship manifests and commercial imagery."[66] Sources of information can include government, commercial, nonprofit, and activist websites; email lists; videos; blogs; chat rooms; and social media sites such as Facebook, Myspace, and YouTube, as well as statements, news stories, online imagery, résumé services, libraries, and subject matter experts. Speaking of the need to tap experts outside the intelligence community, then DDNI/ A Fingar stated the following during a 2008 conference:

We have to make [outreach to experts] a part of the way we do our business because I would hazard to say it is a part of the way every person in this room does their job now. You are in contact with colleagues and competitors, foreign folk working a problem at all stages of the process. We have to do the same because when we need that expertise—I mean, really need it—it is too late to begin the search. You have to have developed the ties, the relationship, the evaluative criteria. And my vision on this is to have a chunk of the vetting located in the [OSC]. . . . We are on the way there. But this is a change of culture for the community, where if it ain't secret, it ain't real. If somebody is not cleared, they are not worthy. That is yesterday's thinking. We have got to get to tomorrow, where not just our own people, but our customers live.[67]

In addition to offering rosters of subject matter experts, some open source providers market tools and techniques to access information found in the "deep web"—an immense trove of unindexed online material unavailable via standard search engines (some analysts, both inside and outside U.S. intelligence agencies, have access to highly specialized open source tools that I am not privy to because those tools are protected by both government and commercial secrecy). Tools and techniques for searching online resources are diverse: single search engines, meta search engines, vertical search engines, federated search engines, social search engines, and multimedia search engines are all used to locate nuggets of information otherwise buried online. However, analysts who spend their days searching websites for their clients must be careful to protect their anonymity. Administrators of websites can review the IP (internet protocol) addresses of computers visiting their sites, potentially revealing the organizations associated with those IP addresses—for instance, defense and intelligence agencies or their contractors.[68] Software such as Tor prevents "somebody watching your Internet connection from learning what sites you visit, and it prevents the sites you visit from learning your physical location."[69] The company notes, "A branch of the U.S. Navy uses Tor for open source intelligence gathering, and one of its teams used Tor while deployed in the Middle East recently. Law enforcement uses Tor for visiting or surveilling web sites without leaving government IP addresses in their web logs, and for security during sting operations."[70]

Once online anonymity has been established, collection can proceed. For example, Wallace-Wells' article on SITE notes, "Each day, Katz finds about a half-dozen items on Arabic message boards that are worth distributing. Her researchers, who monitor English-language jihadist Web sites, often find a few more. Some are propaganda: videos taking responsibility for attacks, statements of intent to attack, announcements of allegiances or splits. Others involve tactics and weapons."[71] Wallace-Wells explains, "SITE tries to have the items translated and sent to subscribers within an hour and a half of their first appearance online."[72] Open source practitioners may falsely pose as members of nefarious groups or their sympathizers to gain access to additional information. For example, the *Washington Post* reported that in 2008, "U.S. military officials had become convinced that extremists planning attacks on American forces in Iraq were making use of a Web site set up by the Saudi government and the CIA to uncover terrorist plots in the kingdom."[73] The article noted, "Elite U.S. military computer specialists, over the objections of the CIA, mounted a cyberattack that dismantled the online forum."[74] This forum was a "honey pot"—in other words, "an online forum covertly monitored by intelligence agencies to identify attackers and gain information."[75]

The analytical techniques that can be applied to open source material are as varied as the types of material that can be collected. Processing may precede analysis: "Processing may include tasks such as spoken language or machine language translation, running data visualization software, or employing image-processing algorithms before analysis can start."[76] The level of formalization of these techniques differs across open source providers. Within the intelligence community, new analysts are exposed to a range of techniques, especially the "structured analytical techniques" outlined in Richards J. Heuer Jr.'s *Psychology of Intelligence Analysis.*[77] These techniques are designed to overcome cognitive limitations and pitfalls by helping analysts externalize their thinking in ways that can be reviewed and assessed by others. Such formalized analytical approaches were rare at Intellibridge, which typically relied on the reputation and track record of its analysts during the exploitation process.

Once open source information has been collected and analyzed, it must be assembled and disseminated to an audience. Lowenthal states, "The intelligence community has a set product line to cover the types of reports and customers with which it must deal."[78] The "generic format" of intelligence products within the intelligence community is straightforward: a beginning, middle, and end.[79] The beginning usually contains a stand-alone summary of the document. The middle elaborates the author's use of sources and his or her judgments, supporting evidence, and assumptions. The end provides the author's conclusions and a discussion of implications for the future. Annexes and appendixes may include detailed facts, figures, charts, and explanations of methodologies.[80] The generic format is more or less followed in the two gems of the U.S. intelligence community: the PDB (President's Daily Brief) and the National Intelligence Estimate.[81] Of the hundreds of intelligence products that the intelligence community generates and distributes to policy makers each year, the PDB and NIE are consistently cited as the most consequential.[82] Intelligence analysts strive to have their analytical judgments included as part of these products; Zegart states, "Your career as an analyst is determined by . . . how many items you have in the PDB."[83] Indeed, officials cite open source contributions to the PDB as evidence of open source's utility.[84]

Intelligence scholar Loch Johnson explains that PDBs provide current intelligence (similar to a newspaper, but one containing classified material), while NIEs provide comprehensive, long-range research intelligence.[85] PDBs are assembled primarily by the CIA and distributed to perhaps no more than a dozen senior officials. During the Ford administration, PDBs were nearly 20 pages in length. The length has consistently shrunk, and during the second Bush administration the document was only 1–2 pages long.[86] NIEs, by contrast, are extensively researched by relevant agencies throughout the intelligence community, coordinated by the NIC, and distributed more widely than PDBs. NIEs are considered the most authoritative analytical product produced by the intelligence community, and since 1950, the intelligence community has produced an average of 23 NIEs per year.[87]

Private open source providers, of course, have more flexibility in the types of information products they produce. DHS's *Open Source Enterprise Daily Cyber Report* organizes its content topically and contains sections on "Critical Infrastructure Protection," "Information Systems Breaches," "Cyberterrorism & Cyberwarfare," "Vulnerabilities," and "General Cyber/ Electronic Crime." iJET offers a *Daily Intelligence Briefing, Monthly Intelligence Forecast,* and a *World Pandemic Monitor,* among other services. Each business morning, subscribers to the iJET's *Daily Intelligence Briefing* receive a report on terrorist activities, political developments, social unrest, labor strikes, disease outbreaks, crime trends, and other threats. Products may also be organized geographically, by country or region. The presentation of material may be in the form of short summaries that include media reports, official statements, or commentary. Longer analyses may speculate on behind-the-scenes developments in explaining public events. For example, a meeting between world leaders may be abruptly cancelled, and an analysis might discuss media speculation, political and economic drivers, the likely consequences, and future courses of action.

ASSESSING OPEN SOURCE

The OSC's Naquin has acknowledged that in the open source arena, "Rarely is there the 'aha!' The 'oh-you-solved-this or you-prevented-this' moment."[88] This situation is due, in part, to the probabilistic nature of intelligence assessments and the use of equivocal statements—*likely, probably, maybe, possibly,* and so on—within analysts' reports. While equivocal statements are needed to ensure that ambiguity is adequately acknowledged, they make the overall accuracy of open source intelligence products difficult to assess. This situation creates a double-edged sword for open source providers. On one hand, providers demonstrate their value through timely, accurate, and actionable information. On the other hand, measuring one's accuracy potentially undermines claims of expertise should that level of accuracy be less than exceptional. When open source providers that market predictive intelligence fail in that effort, it can create the need for damage control with clients. SITE's Katz acknowledged that her group "doesn't check the scientific accuracy of each manual, or the legitimacy of every threat."[89]

However, there is no agreed-upon threshold for determining an appropriate level of accuracy of intelligence. In a 2008 speech before the New America Foundation, it was DDNI/A Fingar's "guesstimate" that the intelligence community is "right" roughly 85 percent of the time.[90] Fingar, however, wanted to see that percentage shrink to 35 percent. The reason, Fingar said, is that a high percentage of accurate assessments indicates that the intelligence community is answering questions that "are too damn easy."[91] For Fingar, the goal of the intelligence community should be to answer extremely difficult questions, as well as to be allowed to answer those questions incorrectly. I am aware of no studies or guesstimates regarding the degree of accuracy of commercial open source providers' predictions, forecasts, or analysis.

In addition to accuracy, use is another area of underassessment. For example, a 2008 CENTRA Technology report submitted to the DHS's chief intelligence officer (posted on California's Office of Homeland Security website) supports the findings presented in chapter 5 regarding the use of open source within the homeland security sector.[92] Specifically, CENTRA conducted interviews with members of six state and local homeland security fusion centers. According the report, five of those fusion centers reported having received no open source training from federal agencies: "Most analysts learned open source techniques by doing and utilized commercial search engines and online databases."[93] Additionally, each of the fusion centers "struggles with the large number of open source products it receives from DHS, other state and local sources, and the private sector" because these largely contained "redundant information and little analysis."[94] CENTRA found, "In at least one case, this glut of open source products has caused local analysts to ignore such products."[95] The report indicated ways to improve this situation through increased training and tailored support but noted that some of these would take time and be contingent on funding. CENTRA's report, along with the findings of this book, suggests that open source stakeholders at all levels would do well to critically assess how analysts and officials actually use the open source products they receive. These assessments, however, are less likely in an environment dominated by profit-seeking companies that benefit from a fragmented and competitive market—a market where agency administrators remain unaware of their colleagues' open source inputs and outputs and purchase duplicative products and services.

To its credit, the OSC undertook self-assessment in 2009. Specifically, OSC officials sent a survey to a random sample of subscribers.[96] Participants were asked to rank on a scale whether the OSC provided users trustworthy sources, credible content, and unique information, among other variables. Participants were also asked how often they used various types of government-provided open source information services from their own agencies and the OSC, the value of these services, and how they learned of them. Questions asked whether participants believed that the OSC had become their "one-stop shop" for open source products and services, as well as what participants thought the OSC needed to do the enhance its ability to become this one-stop shop. Participants were also asked whether they were aware of and valued a partnership program whereby OSC personnel were available for on-site support.

Finally, participants were asked to rank their level of agreement or disagreement with the statement that "the effective use of open source information is essential in supporting US national security interests." That the OSC even asked that question undercuts the strength of its assertion that open source is "one of the 21st Century's most important sources of intelligence."[97] Given the sensitive nature of the questions asked, as well as the increasing level of secrecy surrounding open source, it is unlikely that stakeholders outside the intelligence community will ever learn the results of the OSC's survey. Nevertheless, we see from the OSC's survey that institutional insecurity regarding the worth of open source and its status as a legitimate form of intelligence endures.

Notes

CHAPTER 1

1. Herman L. Croom, "The Exploitation of Foreign Open Sources," *Studies in Intelligence* 13 (Summer 1969): 135.

2. Alex Kingsbury, "Spy Agencies Turn to Newspapers, NPR, and Wikipedia for Information: The Intelligence Community is Learning to Value 'Open-Source' Information," *U.S. News & World Report*, September 12, 2008, http://www.usnews.com/articles/news/national/2008/09/12/spy-agencies-turn-to-newspapers-npr-and-wikipedia-for-information.html (accessed April 23, 2009).

3. "Open source," "open source information," "open source intelligence," and "OSINT" are often treated as synonyms. See Richard A. Best Jr. and Alfred Cumming, "Open Source Intelligence (OSINT): Issues for Congress," Congressional Research Service, December 5, 2007, 2, http://fas.org/sgp/crs/intel/RL34270.pdf (accessed November 21, 2010). Additionally, this definition should not be confused with "open source software," which refers to freely accessible source code. However, Creative Commons licensing relates to open source information in that both encourage transparency.

4. Remarks and Q&A by the assistant deputy director of national intelligence for open source, Eliot A. Jardines (DNI Open Source Conference, Washington, DC, July 16, 2007), 1, http://www.dni.gov/speeches/20070716_speech_3.pdf (accessed August 15, 2007); for photos and presentations from this conference, and a second DNI Open Source Conference held in 2008, see Office of the Director of National Intelligence, "Open Source Conference Blog," http://dniopensourceblog2007.wordpress.com, Office of the Director of National Intelligence, "DNI Open Source Conference 2008," http://www.dniopensource.org, and Cryptome, "DNI Open Source Conference," http://cryptome.org/eyeball/dni-openeye/dni-openeye.htm.

5. Remarks and Q&A by the assistant deputy director of national intelligence for open source, Eliot A. Jardines (DNI Open Source Conference, Washington, DC, July 16, 2007), 1, http://www.dni.gov/speeches/20070716_speech_3.pdf (accessed August 15, 2007);

6. Ibid., 2–3.

7. Burke is an originator of Intellipedia, the intelligence community's version of the online, collaborative encyclopedia Wikipedia. See Suzanne E. Spaulding, "No More Secrets: Then What?" *Huffington Post,* June 24, 2010, http://www.huffingtonpost.com/suzanne-e-spaulding/no-more-secrets-then-what_b_623997.html (accessed November 21, 2010); Bob Brewin, "No More Secrets?" *Government Executive,* September 15, 2008, http://www.govexec.com/dailyfed/0908/091508wb.htm (accessed November 21, 2010).

8. Dana Priest and William M. Arkin, "Top Secret America," *Washington Post,* July 19, 2010, http://projects.washingtonpost.com/top-secret-america/ (accessed November 21, 2010).

9. Ronald Marks, "Twittering Intelligence," Open Source Intelligence Forum, February 2009, http://www.osif.us/articlesofinterest.html (accessed November 21, 2010).

10. National Intelligence Council, *National Intelligence Estimate, Iran: Nuclear Intentions and Capabilities,* 2007, 6, http://www.dni.gov/press_releases/20071203_release.pdf.

11. "Inside the Iran NIE," MSNBC, December 6, 2007, http://www.msnbc.msn.com/id/22117095 (accessed November 21, 2010).

12. Wyn Q. Bowen, "Open Source Intelligence and Nuclear Safeguards," in *Spinning Intelligence: Why Intelligence Needs the Media, Why the Media Needs Intelligence,* ed. Robert Dover and Michael S. Goodman (New York: Columbia University Press, 2009), 91–104.

13. Ibid.

14. Remarks by the assistant to the president for homeland security and counterterrorism, Frances Fragos Townsend (DNI Open Source Conference, Washington, DC, July 16, 2007), 2, www.dni.gov/speeches/20070716_speech_2.pdf (accessed August 3, 2008).

15. Remarks and Q&A by the director of the CIA, Michael V. Hayden (DNI Open Source Conference, Washington, DC, September 12, 2008), 1, http://cryptome.org/cia-openspy.pdf (accessed March 1, 2009).

16. Gaetano Joe Ilardia, "The 9/11 Attacks—A Study of Al Qaeda's Use of Intelligence and Counterintelligence," *Studies in Conflict & Terrorism* 32, no. 3 (2009): 176.

17. Commission on the Intelligence Capabilities of the United States Regarding Weapons of Mass Destruction, *Report to the President,* March 31, 2005, 23, http://govinfo.library.unt.edu/wmd/about.html (accessed November 21, 2010).

18. Best and Cumming, "Open Source Intelligence," 2.

19. Tony Campbell, "Bedmates or Sparring Partners? Canadian Perspectives on the Media-Intelligence Relationship in 'The New Propaganda Age,'" in Dover and Goodman, *Spinning Intelligence,* 175.

20. Open Source Center, https://www.opensource.gov (accessed November 21, 2010).

21. Ibid.

22. Office of the Director of National Intelligence, *National Intelligence: A Consumer's Guide,* 2009, 29, http://www.dni.gov/reports/IC_Consumers_Guide_2009.pdf (accessed November 21, 2010).

23. Open Source Center, https://www.opensource.gov (accessed November 21, 2010).

24. A representative from World News Connection stated in 2008 that only "about half" of the OSC's content is publicly released (copyright laws often prevent disclosure). Additionally, the information provided to the public generally excludes OSC's analytical products. The World News Connection website states, "The information is obtained from full text and summaries of newspaper articles, conference proceedings, television and radio broadcasts, periodicals, and non-classified technical reports." See National Technical Information Service, U.S. Department of Commerce, "About World News Connection," http://wnc.fedworld.gov/description.html (accessed November 21, 2010).

25. Steven Aftergood, "Secrecy and Error Correction in Open Source Intel," *Secrecy News*, August 31, 2009, http://www.fas.org/sgp/news/secrecy/2009/08/083109.html (accessed November 21, 2010).

26. Open Source Center, *Briefing for the UCGIS Winter Meeting 2008*, February 7, 2008, http://www.ucgis.org/winter2008/presentations/Robson.pdf (accessed November 21, 2010).

27. Open Source Center, https://www.opensource.gov (accessed November 21, 2010).

28. Consider a job announcement for an intelligence community Open Source Officer listed on the CIA website in 2010: "Open Source Officers (OSOs) are the Intelligence Community's foreign media experts. They use foreign language and area knowledge to review and assess foreign open media sources, including Internet sites, newspapers, press agencies, television, radio and specialized publications, collecting intelligence from these media to deliver high-impact products to the US foreign affairs community. OSOs develop and apply in-depth knowledge of a broad range of foreign media to identify trends and patterns, and to write analytical products. They may also translate text, audio and video information and select materials from the media for translation by independent contract translators. OSOs research and analyze the media environment in a particular country or region and prepare media analyses that inform customers of subtle relationships and trends in the media. The candidates we seek are creative, with a keen interest in foreign affairs, strong writing and analytical skills, a well-developed facility for reading and translating one or more of a broad range of foreign languages, and working knowledge of the Internet. Many OSOs have lived in their region of interest and/or have formally studied the politics and history of a particular country or region. Positions are in the metropolitan Washington, D.C. area, with limited opportunities for overseas travel and assignments. In addition to salary and benefits, these Officers are eligible to earn annual language 'bonus' pay based on in-house language proficiency testing. OSOs may also have the opportunity to take courses in additional languages and area studies as well as other relevant training. As a part of the screening process, selected applicants will be sent a language proficiency test and asked to provide an analytic writing sample. The following languages, or language combinations, with relevant area knowledge are sought: Arabic; Bulgarian; Central Asian and Russian; Chinese; Czech; Dari/Pashtu; Farsi/Persian; French and Arabic; French or Portuguese and African Studies; Greek; Hebrew and Arabic; Hindi; Hungarian and Romanian; Indonesian; Korean; Polish; Russian and Ukrainian; Serbo-Croatian; Turkish; and Urdu." See CIA, "Open Source Officer (Foreign Media Analyst)," https://www.cia.gov/careers/opportunities/analytical/open-source-officer-foreign-media-analyst.html (accessed November 21, 2010).

29. The author worked for Intellibridge Corporation from 2001 to 2005; see Preface.

30. ProMED, *The 2003 ProMED-Mail Award for Excellence in Outbreak Reporting on the Internet,* http://apex.oracle.com/pls/otn/wwv_flow.accept (accessed August 3, 2008).

31. Kimberly Saunders, "Open Source Information: A True Collection Discipline" (master's thesis, Royal Military College of Canada, 2000).

32. House Committee on Homeland Security, Subcommittee on Intelligence, Information Sharing, and Terrorism Risk Assessment, *Using Open-Source Information Effectively,* 109th Cong., 1st sess., June 21, 2005, http://www.fas.org/irp/congress/2005_hr/opensource.pdf (accessed November 21, 2010).

33. Elaine Sciolino, "C.I.A. Casting About for New Missions," *New York Times,* February 4, 1992, A1.

34. For a review of officials' tentative steps toward improving open source capabilities throughout the Cold War and pre-9/11 period, see Robert David Steele, "The Open Source Program: Missing in Action," *International Journal of Intelligence and CounterIntelligence* 21, no. 3 (2008): 609–19.

35. John C. Gannon, "Intelligence Challenges for the Next Generation" (remarks, World Affairs Council, Washington, DC, June 4, 1998), http://www.fas.org/irp/cia/product/ddi_speech_060598.html (accessed November 26, 2010).

36. Tim Shorrock, *Spies for Hire: The Secret World of Intelligence Outsourcing* (New York: Simon & Schuster, 2008).

37. J. F. Holden-Rhodes, *Sharing the Secrets: Open Source Intelligence and the War on Drugs* (Albuquerque: University of New Mexico Printing Services, 1994), v.

38. House Committee on Homeland Security, *Using Open-Source Information Effectively,* 31.

39. See William J. Lahneman, "Outsourcing the IC's Stovepipes," *International Journal of Intelligence and CounterIntelligence* 16, no. 4 (2003): 573.

40. A technical discussion of open source discovery tools is beyond the scope of this book. These tools have relevance for multiple fields struggling to overcome the problems of information glut and are a needed focus for future communication research.

41. Quarterback Consulting provided an overview of the private intelligence market in their 2003 *Private Intelligence Industry Report.*

42. The scope and scale of the open source sector relates to how associated practices are defined. For example, commentator Benjamin Wallace-Wells asserts, "The world of private, open-source counterterrorism operations is tiny— a few dozen people, if you're counting liberally." Open source provider SOSi, however, states on its website (http://www.sosiltd.com/about_us/default.htm), "Through careful cultivation, our strategic partnerships with a number of private-sector companies, government-services providers, academic institutions and think tanks keep us well ahead of the curve, regardless of the task or challenge. Our team of more than 1,200 professionals supports operations on nearly every continent and spans the widest spectrum of professional, linguistic and cultural backgrounds." See Benjamin Wallace-Wells, "Private Jihad: How Rita Katz Got into the Spying Business," *New Yorker,* May 29, 2006, http://www.newyorker.com/archive/2006/05/29/060529fa_fact (accessed December 9, 2010).

43. Timothy J. Burger, "Opening Up the CIA," *Time*, August 7, 2005, http://www.time.com/time/magazine/article/0,9171,1090889,00.html (accessed February 23, 2011).

44. Shorrock, *Spies For Hire*, 13.

45. Shane Harris, "Intelligence Incorporated," *Government Executive*, May 15, 2005, 40–47; Shane Harris, "Intelligence Shop," *Government Executive*, May 1, 2005, http://www.govexec.com/features/0505-01/0505-01na3.htm (accessed August 4, 2008).

46. Joby Warrick, "Leak Severed a Link to Al-Qaeda's Secrets: Firm Says Administration's Handling of Video Ruined its Spying Efforts," *Washington Post*, October 9, 2007, A1.

47. Total Intelligence Solutions, "Former CIA and Counterterrorism Experts Respond to Security and Intelligence Demands of the Private Sector," news release, February 20, 2006, http://www.prnewswire.com/news-releases/former-cia-and-counterterrorism-experts-respond-to-security-and-intelligence-demands-of-the-private-sector-58023627.html (accessed August 4, 2008).

48. Ibid.

49. Office of the Director of National Intelligence, "Key Facts about Contractors," 2010, http://www.dni.gov/content/Truth_About_Contractors.pdf (accessed November 21, 2010).

50. Ibid.

51. Paul F. Wallner, "Open Sources and the Intelligence Community: Myths and Realities," *American Intelligence Journal* (Spring/Summer 1993): 19.

52. Edward Schiappa, *Defining Reality: Definitions and the Politics of Meaning* (Carbondale: Southern Illinois University Press, 2003), 3.

53. Open Source Center, https://www.opensource.gov (accessed November 21, 2010).

54. Patience Wait, "Intelligence Units Mine the Benefits of Public Sources: Open Source Center Draws, Analyzes Info from a Variety of Public Databases," *Government Computer News*, March 20, 2006, http://www.gcn.com/print/25_6/40152-1.html (accessed November 21, 2010).

55. "CIA Mines 'Rich' Content from Blogs," *Washington Times*, April 18, 2006, http://www.washingtontimes.com/news/2006/apr/18/20060418-110124-3694r/ (accessed November 21, 2010).

56. Arthur S. Hulnick, "The Downside of Open Source Intelligence," *International Journal of Intelligence and CounterIntelligence* 15, no. 4 (2002): 565.

57. Best and Cumming, "Open Source Intelligence," 2.

58. William Nolte, "Thinking about Rethinking: Reform in Other Professions," *Studies in Intelligence* 52, no. 2 (2008): 19.

59. Executive Order 12333, *United States Intelligence Activities*, December 4, 1981, http://www.fas.org/irp/offdocs/eo12333.htm (accessed November 21, 2010).

60. Karl E. Weick, Kathleen E. Sutcliffe, and David Obstfeld, "Organizing and the Process of Sensemaking," *Organization Science* 16, no. 4 (2005): 409.

61. Markus Perkmann and André Spicer, "How Are Management Fashions Institutionalized? The Role of Institutional Work," *Human Relations* 61, no. 6 (2008): 812.

62. This figure does not include many intelligence-related activities conducted by the U.S. Department of Defense, whose budget totaled $515.4 billion in FY 2009.

63. Hamilton Bean and Lisa B. Keränen, "The Role of Homeland Security Information Bulletins within Emergency Management Organizations: A Case Study of Enactment," *Journal of Homeland Security and Emergency Management* 4, no. 2 (2007): Article 6.

64. John Rollins, "Fusion Centers: Issues and Options for Congress," Congressional Research Service, January 18, 2008, 2, http://www.csmweb.com/Library%20Documents/RL34070.pdf (accessed August 4, 2008).

65. House Committee on Homeland Security, Subcommittee on Intelligence, Information Sharing, and Terrorism Risk Assessment, *Moving Beyond the First Five Years: Evolving the Office of Intelligence and Analysis to Better Serve State, Local, and Tribal Needs*, 110th Cong., 2nd sess., April 24, 2008, 48.

66. Ibid.

67. Office of the Director of National Intelligence, *United States Intelligence Community 500 Day Plan Integration and Collaboration*, 2007, http://www.dni.gov/500-day-plan.pdf (accessed November 26, 2010).

68. Gregory F. Treverton, *The Next Steps in Reshaping Intelligence* (Santa Monica, CA: RAND, 2005).

69. Joanne Martin, Peter Frost, and Olivia O'Neill, "Organizational Culture: Beyond Struggles for Intellectual Dominance," in *The Sage Handbook of Organization Studies*, 2nd ed., ed. Stewart R. Clegg, Cynthia Hardy, Thomas B. Lawrence, and Walter R. Nord (London: Sage, 2006), 725–53.

70. Nolte, "Thinking about Rethinking," 22.

71. Kristen Breitweiser, *Wake-Up Call: The Political Education of a 9/11 Widow* (New York: Warner Books, 2006); Thomas Kean and Lee Hamilton, *Without Precedent: The Inside Story of the 9/11 Commission* (New York: Alfred A. Knopf, 2006); Philip Shenon, *The Commission: The Uncensored History of the 9/11 Investigation* (New York: Twelve, 2008).

72. Kean and Hamilton, *Without Precedent*.

73. Breitweiser, *Wake-Up Call*, 87.

74. Pearl-Alice Marsh, "Grassroots Statecraft and Citizens' Challenges to U.S. National Security Policy," in *On Security*, ed. Ronnie D. Lipschutz (New York: Columbia University Press, 1995), 124–48.

75. Commission on the Intelligence Capabilities of the United States, *Report to the President*, 378.

76. James J. Wirtz, "The American Approach to Intelligence Studies," in *Handbook of Intelligence Studies*, ed. Loch. K. Johnson (New York: Routledge, 2007), 29.

77. The process of institutionalization involves the contextualized production and reception of meaning. I therefore used interpretive methods to explore the complexities of post-9/11 open source discourses, their enactment, and the responses of institutional members and stakeholders. I introduced a critical element to this analysis by exploring the implications of open source in relation to democratic deliberation of U.S. national security policy.

78. Mary Simpson and George Cheney, "Marketization, Participation, and Communication within New Zealand Retirement Villages: A Critical-Rhetorical and Discursive Analysis," *Discourse and Communication* 1, no. 2 (2007): 191–222.

79. Norman Fairclough, *Discourse and Social Change* (Cambridge: Polity Press, 1992).

80. Simpson and Cheney, "Marketization, Participation, and Communication." On the need for rhetorical scholars to investigate their claims regarding audience conjectures, see Jennifer Stromer-Galley and Edward Schiappa, "The Argumentative Burdens of Audience Conjectures: Audience Research in Popular Culture Criticism," *Communication Theory* 8, no. 1 (1998): 27–62.

81. Cynthia Hardy, Ian Palmer, and Nelson Phillips, "Discourse as a Strategic Resource," *Human Relations* 53, no. 9 (2000): 1227–48; Nelson Phillips and Cynthia Hardy, *Discourse Analysis: Investigating Processes of Social Construction* (Thousand Oaks, CA: Sage, 2002); Nelson Phillips, Thomas B. Lawrence, and Cynthia Hardy, "Discourse and Institutions," *Academy of Management Review* 29, no. 4 (2004): 635–52.

82. Cynthia Hardy, "How Institutions Communicate; or How Does Communicating Institutionalize?" *Management Communication Quarterly* 25, no. 1 (2011): 191–99.

83. George Cheney, Lars Thøger Christensen, Charles Conrad, and Daniel J. Lair, "Corporate Rhetoric as Organizational Discourse," in *The Sage Handbook of Organizational Discourse,* ed. David Grant, Cynthia Hardy, Cliff Oswick, and Linda Putnam (London: Sage, 2004): 79–104.

84. Christopher Grey, "Security Studies and Organization Studies: Parallels and Possibilities," *Organization* 16, no. 2 (2009): 311.

85. Ibid., 314.

86. Bryan C. Taylor, Book review of *The Boundaries of the New Frontier: Rhetoric and Communication at Fermi National Accelerator Laboratory,* by Joanna S. Ploeger. *Rhetoric & Public Affairs* 41, no. 1 (2011): 14–16.

87. Phillips, Lawrence, and Hardy, "Discourse and Institutions."

CHAPTER 2

1. Joseph E. Roop, "Foreign Broadcast Information Service History Part 1: 1941–1947," Central Intelligence Agency, April 1969, 9, http://www.foia.cia.gov/txt/FBIS_history_part1.pdf (accessed November 30, 2010).

2. Croom, "The Exploitation of Foreign Open Sources," 129.

3. Commission on the Roles and Capabilities of the United States Intelligence Community, *Preparing for the 21st Century: An Appraisal of U.S. Intelligence,* March 1, 1996, 88, http://www.gpoaccess.gov/int/index.html (accessed November 30, 2010) (hereafter "Aspin-Brown Commission").

4. Michael Andregg, "Intelligence Ethics: Laying the Foundation for the Second Oldest Profession," in Johnson, *Handbook of Intelligence Studies,* 52–63.

5. Charles E. Lathrop, *The Literary Spy: The Ultimate Source for Quotations on Espionage and Intelligence* (New Haven, CT: Yale University Press, 2004).

6. Michael Goodman, "British Intelligence and the British Broadcasting Corporation: A Snapshot of a Happy Marriage," in Dover and Goodman, *Spinning Intelligence,* 118.

7. Stephen C. Mercado, "FBIS against the Axis, 1941–1945: Open-Source Intelligence from the Airwaves," *Studies in Intelligence* 11 (Fall/Winter 2001), https://www.cia.gov/library/center-for-the-study-of-intelligence/sci-publications/csi-studies/fall_winter-2001/article04.html (accessed November 29, 2010).

8. FBMS was renamed the Foreign Broadcast Information Service in 1947, and in 2005, FBIS, in turn, was renamed the OSC and given expanded capabilities and authorities.

9. See Mercado, "FBIS against the Axis"; Kalev Leetaru, "The Scope of FBIS and BBC Open-Source Media Coverage, 1979–2008," *Studies in Intelligence* 54, no. 1 (2010): 17–37.

10. House Committee on Homeland Security, *Using Open-Source Information Effectively*, 6.

11. Waldo Drake, "*Times'* Man, Gets Assignment with Fleet," *Los Angeles Times*, August 1941.

12. Kathy Peiss, "Cultural Policy in a Time of War: The American Response to Endangered Books in World War II," *Library Trends* 55, no. 3 (2007): 377.

13. Patsy Wagstaff, interview with the author, Sun Sites, Arizona, September 2, 1995.

14. Pedro A. Loureiro, "U.S. Counterintelligence against Japan in Southern California, 1933–1941" (PhD dissertation, San Diego State University, 1987).

15. Drake, "*Times'* Man, Gets Assignment."

16. Lee Van Atta, "L.A. Ship News Reporter Now Official Eyes, Ears of U.S. Fleet," *Los Angeles Times*, August 1, 1941.

17. Joseph C. Harsch, *At the Hinge of History: A Reporter's Story* (Athens: University of Georgia Press, 1993).

18. William W. Drake, "I Don't Think They'd Be Such Damned Fools," in *Air Raid, Pearl Harbor! Recollections of a Day of Infamy*, ed. Paul Stillwell (Annapolis, MD: U.S. Naval Institute Press, 1981), 269–70.

19. Quoted in Mercado, "FBIS against the Axis."

20. Roop, "Foreign Broadcast Information Service History."

21. Ibid.

22. Ibid.

23. Ibid., 23.

24. Ibid.

25. Ibid.

26. Patsy Wagstaff, interview.

27. E. B. Potter, *Nimitz* (Annapolis, MD: U.S. Naval Institute Press, 1976).

28. Ibid.

29. Ibid.

30. Larry J. Frank, "The United States Navy v. the *Chicago Tribune*," *Historian* 42, no. 2 (1980): 284–303.

31. Ibid.

32. Hulnick, "The Downside of Open Source Intelligence."

33. Mercado, "FBIS against the Axis."

34. Peiss, "Cultural Policy in a Time of War," 378–79.

35. Ibid., 379.

36. Ibid.

37. Croom, "The Exploitation of Foreign Open Sources."

38. Ibid., 131.

39. Ibid., 133.

40. Ibid., 135.

41. Ibid., 136.

42. Best and Cumming, "Open Source Intelligence."

43. Croom, "The Exploitation of Foreign Open Sources."

Zegart, *Spying Blind: The CIA, the FBI, and the Origins of 9/11* (Princeton University Press, 2007); Johnson, *Handbook of Intelligence Studies*.
wever, Michael Warner, "Reading the Riot Act: The Schlesinger
Intelligence and National Security 24, no. 3 (2009): 387–417.
Spying Blind.

"The Open Source Program."
Spying Blind, 60.
rks and Q&A by the deputy director, 8.

thy Kuhn, "A Communicative Theory of the Firm: Developing an
Perspective on Intra-Organizational Power and Stakeholder Relation-
nization Studies 29, no. 8–9 (2008): 1235.
thy Kuhn, "A 'Demented Work Ethic' and a 'Lifestyle Firm': Discourse,
d Workplace Time Commitments," *Organization Studies* 27, no. 9 (2006):

milton Bean, "Communication and Intelligence: Allies or Enemies?,"
l Journal of Intelligence and CounterIntelligence 22, no. 2 (2009): 360–65;
etz, *Democracy in an Age of Corporate Colonization: Developments in Com-
 and the Politics of Everyday Life* (Albany: State University of New York
2).
ul J. DiMaggio and Walter W. Powell, "The Iron Cage Revisited: Institu-
morphism and Collective Rationality in Organizational Fields," *American
al Review* 48, no. 2 (1983): 147–60.
. Richard Scott, *Institutions and Organizations* (Thousand Oaks, CA: Sage,

bid.
ohn W. Meyer and Brian Rowan, "Institutional Organizations: Formal
re as Myth and Ceremony," *American Journal of Sociology* 83, no. 2 (1977).

Stevyn Gibson, "Open Source Intelligence: An Intelligence Lifeline," *RUSI
 149, no. 1 (2004): 19.
John C. Lammers and Joshua B. Barbour, "An Institutional Theory of Orga-
nal Communication," *Communication Theory* 16, no. 3 (2006): 1–22.
David Grant, Cynthia Hardy, Cliff Oswick, and Linda Putnam, ed., *The Sage
ook of Organizational Discourse* (London: Sage, 2004), 3.
. Andrew Feenberg, *Transforming Technology: A Critical Theory Revisited* (Ox-
Oxford University Press, 2002).
. Kuhn, "A 'Demented Work Ethic,'" 1235.
. Grant et al., *The Sage Handbook of Organizational Discourse*, 25.
. Hardy, "Scaling Up and Bearing Down."
4. Maguire, Hardy, and Lawrence, for example, define institutional entrepre-
rship as the "activities of actors who have an interest in particular institutional
ngements and who leverage resources to create new institutions or transform
sting ones." Similarly, Lawrence and Suddaby define institutional entrepre-
rship as the "purposeful action of individuals and organizations aimed at
ating, maintaining, and disrupting institutions." See Steve Maguire, Cynthia
rdy, and Thomas B. Lawrence, "Institutional Entrepreneurship in Emerging
elds: HIV/AIDS Treatment Advocacy in Canada," *Academy of Management Jour-

44. Glenn Hastedt, "Intelligence Estimates: NIEs vs. the Open Press in the 1958
China Straits Crisis," *International Journal of Intelligence and CounterIntelligence* 23,
no. 1 (2010): 104–32.

45. Ibid., 126.

46. Ibid., 127.

47. Ibid.

48. Robert W. Pringle, "The Limits of OSINT: Diagnosing the Soviet Media,
1985–1989," *International Journal of Intelligence and CounterIntelligence* 16, no. 2
(2003): 280–89.

49. Ibid., 287.

50. Ibid., 288.

51. Steele, "The Open Source Program."

52. Ibid., 611.

53. Ibid.

54. Wallner, "Open Sources and the Intelligence Community," 19.

55. Ibid., 20.

56. A note about my interactions with Steele is warranted. My article, "The
DNI's Open Source Center: An Organizational Communication Perspective," was
published in 2007 in the *International Journal of Intelligence and CounterIntelligence*.
In 2008, Steele wrote a rejoinder, "The Open Source Program: Missing in Action,"
that praised, critiqued, and extended the article. I had never met nor corresponded
with Steele. On June 6, 2008, Steele contacted me via email to ask whether he could
send me a box of files. He stated, "I am closing down the OSS office as we are
absorbed in a much larger enterprise (Fortune 100) where I will be the director of
collection, processing, and analysis. I have a box of original OSS materials that I
would like to give you exclusive access to and ownership of." My review of the
materials (seven boxes total) indicated that they were OSS business records, briefing materials for potential clients, conference materials and attendee lists, videos,
books, and commentary—all unclassified. Due to their proprietary nature, business records have not been directly cited in the development of this book. I have
instead relied on publicly available materials in my description of Steele's advocacy efforts. This material includes archival documents publicly available from
the OSS.net website. For these, I am deeply indebted to Steele. Readers interested
in the 1990s and early 2000s period of open source should consult the extensive
archive of materials found at Steele's OSS.net website.

57. Steele, "The Open Source Program," 611.

58. House Permanent Select Committee on Intelligence, H.R. 4165, National
Security Act of 1992, 102nd Cong., 2nd sess., March 4 and 11, 1992, 12.

59. Director of Central Intelligence, *Directive 2/12, Community Open Source Program,* March 1, 1994, http://www.fas.org/irp/offdocs/dcid212.htm (accessed
November 30, 2010).

60. Community Open Source Program Office, *Community Open Source Strategic
Plan,* February 1995, 3, http://www.oss.net/dynamaster/file_archive/040320/
bc201247d9056a4f07e6f5e720be9823/OSS1997-02-34.pdf (accessed December 9,
2010).

61. Wallner, "Open Sources and the Intelligence Community," 19.

62. National Intelligence Council, *Open Source Task Force: A Vision for the Future,* January 13, 1992, http://www.phibetaiota.net/1992/01/1992-national-intelli

gence-council-open-source-task-force-a-vision-for-the-future/ (accessed November 30, 2010).

63. Ibid., 1.

64. Ibid., 3.

65. Ibid., 4.

66. Robert David Steele, "United States Marine Corps Comments on Joint Open Source Task Force Report and Recommendations," January 6, 1992, http://www.oss.net/dynamaster/file_archive/060324/9906ba66ee5fe750bb8fe5712b1e20e7/92 Jan 11 Steele on IC OSINT.pdf (accessed November 30, 2010).

67. Ibid., 1.

68. Noah Shachtman, "How to Restore Spies Credibility: Go Open Source," *Wired*, December 14, 2007, http://www.wired.com/dangerroom/2007/12/how-to-restore/ (accessed November 30, 2010).

69. Ibid.

70. Ibid.

71. See "Open Source Burundi Exercise," September 20, 2000, http://lists101.his.com/pipermail/intelforum/2000-September/002802.html (accessed December 2, 2010).

72. Aspin-Brown Commission, 88.

73. Ibid.

74. Ibid., 89.

75. Robert David Steele, "Fixing the White House and National Intelligence," *International Journal of Intelligence and CounterIntelligence* 23, no. 2 (2010): 353–73.

76. Frederick L. Wettering, "OSINT's Primary Advocate," review of *The New Craft of Intelligence: Personal, Public and Political*, by Robert David Steele, *International Journal of Intelligence and CounterIntelligence* 16, no. 3 (2003): 507.

77. Arthur S. Hulnick, "OSINT: Is It Really Intelligence?" (paper presented at the annual convention of the American Political Science Association, Boston, MA, August 2008), http://www.allacademic.com//meta/p_mla_apa_research_citation/2/8/1/2/1/pages281211/p281211-1.php (accessed November 30, 2010).

78. Mark Tovey, ed., *Collective Intelligence: Creating a Prosperous World at Peace* (Oakton, VA: Earth Intelligence Network, 2008): iii.

79. NNDB, "Rob Simmons," http://www.nndb.com/people/462/000040342 (accessed November 30, 2010).

80. Republican Leadership Council, "Bio—Congressman Rob Simmons," http://www.republican-leadership.com/bios/rob-simmons (accessed November 30, 2010).

81. Robert M. Simmons, "Open Source Intelligence: An Examination of Its Exploitation in the Defense Intelligence Community" (master's thesis, Joint Military Intelligence College, 1995), http://www.phibetaiota.net/1995/08/history-1995-simmons-open-source-intelligence-an-examination-of-its-exploitation-in-the-defense-intelligence-community/ (accessed December 1, 2010).

82. Ibid., 3.

83. Ibid., 4.

84. Robert David Steele, *Information Operations: All Information, All Languages, All the Time* (Oakton, VA: OSS International Press, 2006): 3.

85. Ibid., 5.

86. National Defense Authorization Act for Fiscal Year 2006, Public Law 109–163, http://www.dod.gov/dodgc/olc/docs/PL109-163.pdf (accessed December 2,

2010). Simmons had attempted to incl
lation. See, for example, Simmons's st
hearings regarding the 9/11 Recomm
of Representatives, October 7, 2004),
F?r108:1:./temp/~r108hzdTlb:e1320829

87. Chris Strohm, "Lawmaker Calls
dent Agency," *Government Executive*, Jun
dailyfed/0606/060706tdpm1.htm (accessed

88. Ibid.

89. Kent Bye, "Interview Audio: Congi
Homeland Security Intelligence & Informa
ary 25, 2006, http://www.echochamberproje
ber 2, 2010).

90. Geospatial Intelligence Forum, U.S. C
"Q&A: General Michael V. Hayden," http://w
com/mgt-home/133-mgt-2006-volume-4-issu
hayden.html (accessed December 1, 2010).

91. Wait, "Intelligence Units Mine the Benefi

92. Eliot A. Jardines, Written Testimony, Hou
curity, Subcommittee on Intelligence, Information
sessment, *Using Open-Source Information Effectively*
2005, http://www.fas.org/irp/congress/2005_hr/
December 2, 2010).

93. Wallner, "Open Sources and the Intelligence

94. Kent Bye, "Interview Audio: Eliot Jardines,
National Intelligence for Open Source," January 25, 2
berproject.com/jardines (accessed December 2, 2010).

95. Robert David Steele, "PORTAL: OSINT, ADDI
www.oss.net (accessed March 8, 2006).

96. House Committee on Homeland Security, *Usin
Effectively*, 32–33.

97. Kent Bye, "Interview Audio: Elliot Jardines."

98. Doug Naquin, "Remarks by Doug Naquin, CII
2007," *CIRA Newsletter* 32, no. 4 (2007), http://www.fas.
pdf, 3 (accessed December 2, 2010).

99. Ibid., 5.

100. Ibid., 3.

101. Ibid., 5.

102. Ibid., 3.

103. Ibid., 6.

104. Ibid.

CHAPTER 3

1. Remarks and Q&A by the deputy director of nationa
analysis, Thomas Fingar (DNI Open Source Conference, Washing
2007), http://www.dni.gov/speeches/20070717_speech_3.pdf (ac
2008).

2. Amy B.
ton, NJ: Prince

3. See, ho
Report, 1971,"

4. Zegart

5. Ibid.

6. Steele

7. Zegar

8. Rema

9. Ibid.

10. Timo
Alternative
ships," *Org*

11. Timc
Identity, an
1342.

12. Ha
Internation
Stanley D
munication
Press, 199

13. Pa
tional Iso
Sociologic

14. V
1995).

15. I

16. J
Structu
340–63

17.
Journal

18.
nizatio

19
Hand

20
ford:

nal 47, no. 5 (2004): 657; Thomas B. Lawrence and Roy Suddaby, "Institutions and Institutional Work," in Clegg et al., *The Sage Handbook of Organization Studies*, 2nd ed., 215.

25. Raghu Garud, Cynthia Hardy, and Steve Maguire, "Institutional Entrepreneurship as Embedded Agency: An Introduction to the Special Issue," *Organization Studies* 28, no. 7 (2007): 957–70.

26. Ibid., 962.

27. Lawrence and Suddaby, "Institutions and Institutional Work."

28. Perkmann and Spicer, "How Are Management Fashions Institutionalized?"

29. Ibid., 834–37.

30. Gillian Symon states, "rhetorical analysis is … a kind of discourse analysis that concentrates on analyzing linguistic strategies of argumentation as individuals seek to convince an audience of a construction of reality congruent with their interests (through justification) yet undermining of others (through criticism)" (78). See Gillian Symon, "Developing the Political Perspective on Technological Change through Rhetorical Analysis," *Management Communication Quarterly* 22, no. 1 (2008): 74–98. George Cheney and colleagues note many similarities between rhetoric and discourse but also contrast the terms by referencing each concept's specific intellectual history, associated vocabulary, and lines of inquiry. See George Cheney, Lars Thøger Christensen, Charles Conrad, and Daniel J. Lair, "Corporate Rhetoric as Organizational Discourse," in Grant et al., *The Sage Handbook of Organizational Discourse*, 79–104.

31. Cheney, Christensen, Conrad, and Lair, "Corporate Rhetoric as Organizational Discourse."

32. Robert P. Newman, "Communication Pathologies of Intelligence Systems," *Speech Monographs* 42, (November 1975): 273.

33. Gordon R. Mitchell, "Team B Intelligence Coups," *Quarterly Journal of Speech* 92, no. 2 (2006): 144–73.

34. Stephen J. Hartnett and Laura A. Stengrim, *Globalization and Empire: The U.S. Invasion of Iraq, Free Markets, and the Twilight of Democracy* (Tuscaloosa: University of Alabama Press, 2005).

35. H. L. Goodall, Jr., "Why We Must Win the War on Terror: Communication, Narrative, and the Future of National Security," *Qualitative Inquiry* 12, no. 1 (2006): 30–59.

36. G. Thomas Goodnight, "Strategic Doctrine, Public Debate and the Terror War," in *Hitting First: Preventive Force in U.S. Security Strategy*, ed. W. W. Keller and G. R. Mitchell, 93–114. Pittsburgh, PA: University of Pittsburgh Press, 2006.

37. Zegart, *Spying Blind*.

38. Bryan C. Taylor, William J. Kinsella, Stephen P. Depoe, and Maribeth S. Metzler, ed., *Nuclear Legacies: Communication, Controversy, and the U.S. Nuclear Weapons Complex* (Lanham, MD: Lexington Books, 2007).

39. Ibid., 381.

40. Ibid., 382.

41. Robert L. Ivie, *Democracy and America's War on Terror* (Tuscaloosa: University of Alabama Press, 2005).

42. Bryan C. Taylor, "COMM 6360: The Rhetoric and Culture of U.S. National Security" (lecture, January 23, 2008, University of Colorado at Boulder).

43. Chris Barker, *Making Sense of Cultural Studies: Central Problems and Critical Debates* (London: Sage, 2002).

44. Peter Gill and Mark Phythian, *Intelligence in an Insecure World* (Cambridge: Polity Press, 2006).

45. Eirik G. Furubotn, "The New Institutional Economics and the Theory of the Firm," *Journal of Economic Behavior & Organization* 45, no. 2 (2001): 133–53.

46. Alan I. Marcus, "'Would You Like Fries with That, Sir?' The Evolution of Management Theories and the Rise and Fall of Total Quality Management within the American Federal Government," *Management & Organizational History* 3, no. 3–4 (2008): 319.

47. Perkmann and Spicer, "How Are Management Fashions Institutionalized?," 839.

48. Perkmann and Spicer, "How Are Management Fashions Institutionalized?"

49. Ibid., 836.

50. This is a process that Perkmann and Spicer refer to as "partaking."

51. Interview, intelligence official, 2008.

52. Phillips, Lawrence, and Hardy, "Discourse and Institutions," 644.

53. Ibid., 643.

54. Remarks and Q&A by the deputy director, 3.

55. Kuhn explains that conferences constitute a genre of organizational communication because they can be grouped by similar "situational requirements," "substantive characteristics," and "stylistic characteristics," all of which are coordinated by an "organizing principle." Situational requirements relate to a matter that must be managed or resolved—in other words, a crisis, issue, or need. Substantive characteristics relate to the "social motives, themes, and topics being expressed in the communication," while stylistic characteristics involve the methods by which organizations convey their messages. See Timothy Kuhn, "The Discourse of Issues Management: A Genre of Organizational Communication," *Communication Quarterly* 45, no. 3 (1997): 188–210.

56. Remarks and Q&A by the assistant deputy director, 2.

57. Office of the Director of National Intelligence, "Transcripts from the DNI Open Source Conference 2008" (Washington, DC, September 11 and 12, 2008), http://www.dni.gov/speeches/20080912_speech.pdf, 6 (accessed March 6, 2009) (hereafter "Transcripts").

58. Remarks and Q&A by the deputy director, 1.

59. Remarks and Q&A by the director, 4.

60. Lawrence and Suddaby, "Institutions and Institutional Work," 222.

61. Remarks and Q&A by the deputy director, 2.

62. Remarks and Q&A by the deputy director of national intelligence for collection, Mary Margaret Graham (DNI Open Source Conference, Washington, DC, July 17, 2007), http://www.dni.gov/speeches/20070717_speech_2.pdf, 2 (accessed August 3, 2008).

63. Ibid.

64. "Transcripts," 34.

65. Ibid., 42.

66. Interview, policy maker, 2009.

67. Remarks and Q&A by the assistant deputy director, 2.

68. "Transcripts," 5.

69. Ibid., 27.

70. Remarks and Q&A by the deputy director of national intelligence for collection, 3.

71. "Transcripts," 23–24.

72. Lawrence and Suddaby, "Institutions and Institutional Work," 226.

73. "Transcripts."

74. Lawrence and Suddaby, "Institutions and Institutional Work," 229.

75. Ben Bain, "Officers to Get Guidelines for Open-Source Intell," *Federal Computer Week,* June 18, 2010, http://fcw.com/Articles/2010/06/18/Web-open-source-intell.aspx (accessed December 2, 2010).

77. Lawrence and Suddaby, "Institutions and Institutional Work," 225.

78. Remarks and Q&A by the assistant deputy director, 1.

79. Lawrence and Suddaby, "Institutions and Institutional Work," 224–25.

80. "Transcripts," 22.

81. Ibid., 25.

82. Interview, intelligence contractor, 2009.

83. Phillips, Lawrence, and Hardy, "Discourse and Institutions."

CHAPTER 4

1. Lorenzo Semple Jr., *Three Days of the Condor,* directed by Sydney Pollack (United States: Paramount Pictures, 1975).

2. Remarks and Q&A by the assistant deputy director of national intelligence for open source, Eliot A. Jardines (DNI Open Source Conference, Washington, DC, July 16, 2007), http://www.dni.gov/speeches/20070716_speech_3.pdf (accessed August 15, 2007).

3. Management scholars Roy Suddaby and Royston Greenwood explain that institutional logics are unstated assumptions that guide members' sense making by prescribing and proscribing actions. These logics influence ways of interpreting the world, constraining and enabling action. Scholars interested in institutional change examine the strategic use of language in order to understand how shifts in institutional logics occur. See Roy Suddaby and Royston Greenwood, "Rhetorical Strategies of Legitimacy," *Administrative Science Quarterly* 50, no. 1 (2005): 35–67.

4. Mark Lowenthal, *Intelligence: From Secrets to Policy,* 3rd ed. (Washington, DC: CQ Press, 2006): 4–5.

5. Joseph E. Stiglitz, "On Liberty, the Right to Know, and Public Discourse: The Role of Transparency in Public Life," in *Government Secrecy: Classic and Contemporary Readings,* ed. Susan L. Maret and Jan Goldman (Westport, CT: Libraries Unlimited, 2009), 697.

6. *U.S. News and World Report,* "In Obama White House, New Rules on Day One," January 22, 2009, http://www.usnews.com/articles/news/washington-whispers/2009/01/22/in-obama-white-house-new-rules-on-day-one.html (accessed March 2, 2009).

7. For a discussion of this issue, see Sources and Methods, "Determining Source Reliability on the Internet," October 30, 2008, http://sourcesandmethods.blogspot.com/2008/10/how-to-determining-source-reliability.html (accessed December 2, 2010).

8. Susan B. Glasser, "Probing Galaxies of Data for Nuggets," *Washington Post,* November 25, 2005, A35.

9. David Martin, "Secret Information in Plain Sight," *CBS News,* January 10, 2006, http://www.cbsnews.com/stories/2006/01/10/eveningnews/main1198667.shtml (accessed May 8, 2009).

10. Remarks and Q&A by the assistant deputy director, 7.

11. Office of the Director of National Intelligence, *Intelligence Community Directive 301, National Open Source Enterprise,* July 11, 2006, 8, http://www.fas.org/irp/dni/icd/icd-301.pdf (accessed December 2, 2010).

12. Ibid.

13. This quote comes from Intellibridge managers who were speaking with a U.S. Navy admiral about open source issues in 2004.

14. Interview, intelligence contractor, 2009.

15. National Defense Authorization Act, 3411–2.

16. NATO, *Open Source Intelligence Handbook,* November 2001, V, http://en.wikipedia.org/wiki/NATO_Open_Source_Intelligence_Handbook (accessed December 2, 2010).

17. Remarks and Q&A by the director, 6.

18. Remarks and Q&A by the assistant deputy director, 4.

19. Victor Marchetti and John D. Marks, *The CIA and the Cult of Intelligence* (New York: Dell Publishing, 1974), 273.

20. Interview, intelligence commentator, 2009.

21. House Permanent Select Committee on Intelligence, *Report of the Joint Inquiry,* GPO Access, "Congressional Reports: Joint Inquiry into Intelligence Community Activities before and after the Terrorist Attacks of September 11, 2001," http://www.gpoaccess.gov/serialset/creports/911.html, 636 (accessed December 3, 2010).

22. Ibid.

23. National Commission on Terrorist Attacks upon the United States, *The 9/11 Commission Report,* July 22, 2004, 413, http://www.9-11commission.gov (accessed December 2, 2010).

24. Interview, 9/11 Commission staff member, 2008.

25. Interview, policy maker, 2009.

26. Remarks and Q&A by the assistant deputy director, 1–2.

27. Phillips, Lawrence, and Hardy, "Discourse and Institutions."

28. Ibid.

29. Ibid., 640.

30. The Intelligence Reform and Terrorism Prevention Act of 2004, Public Law 108–458, 3693, http://www.nctc.gov/docs/pl108_458.pdf (accessed December 3, 2010).

31. Commission on the Intelligence Capabilities, *Report to the President,* 377–78.

32. Ibid., 23.

33. Dan Eggen and Spencer S. Hsu, "House Bill Backs Additional Reforms from 9/11 Report," *Washington Post,* January 9, 2007, http://www.washingtonpost.com/wp-dyn/content/article/2007/01/08/AR2007010801623.html (accessed December 3, 2010).

34. Kent Bye, "Can Open Source Intelligence Be a Non-Violent Alternative to War?" December 3, 2005, http://www.echochamberproject.com/node/718 (accessed December 3, 2010).

35. Robert David Steele, "Steele Interview for Military Review," April 16, 2006, 2–3, http://www.oss.net/dynamaster/file_archive/060417/d0a6e5b9746c0c07eddbde662982b66c/Interview on Academics et al with intelligence 1.1.doc (accessed December 3, 2010).

36. Importantly, Simmons was a featured speaker during the 2007 Open Source Conference. In 2008, however, his role was downgraded to panel member. This suggests that officials may have sought to downplay Simmons's perspective.

44. Glenn Hastedt, "Intelligence Estimates: NIEs vs. the Open Press in the 1958 China Straits Crisis," *International Journal of Intelligence and CounterIntelligence* 23, no. 1 (2010): 104–32.

45. Ibid., 126.

46. Ibid., 127.

47. Ibid.

48. Robert W. Pringle, "The Limits of OSINT: Diagnosing the Soviet Media, 1985–1989," *International Journal of Intelligence and CounterIntelligence* 16, no. 2 (2003): 280–89.

49. Ibid., 287.

50. Ibid., 288.

51. Steele, "The Open Source Program."

52. Ibid., 611.

53. Ibid.

54. Wallner, "Open Sources and the Intelligence Community," 19.

55. Ibid., 20.

56. A note about my interactions with Steele is warranted. My article, "The DNI's Open Source Center: An Organizational Communication Perspective," was published in 2007 in the *International Journal of Intelligence and CounterIntelligence*. In 2008, Steele wrote a rejoinder, "The Open Source Program: Missing in Action," that praised, critiqued, and extended the article. I had never met nor corresponded with Steele. On June 6, 2008, Steele contacted me via email to ask whether he could send me a box of files. He stated, "I am closing down the OSS office as we are absorbed in a much larger enterprise (Fortune 100) where I will be the director of collection, processing, and analysis. I have a box of original OSS materials that I would like to give you exclusive access to and ownership of." My review of the materials (seven boxes total) indicated that they were OSS business records, briefing materials for potential clients, conference materials and attendee lists, videos, books, and commentary—all unclassified. Due to their proprietary nature, business records have not been directly cited in the development of this book. I have instead relied on publicly available materials in my description of Steele's advocacy efforts. This material includes archival documents publicly available from the OSS.net website. For these, I am deeply indebted to Steele. Readers interested in the 1990s and early 2000s period of open source should consult the extensive archive of materials found at Steele's OSS.net website.

57. Steele, "The Open Source Program," 611.

58. House Permanent Select Committee on Intelligence, H.R. 4165, National Security Act of 1992, 102nd Cong., 2nd sess., March 4 and 11, 1992, 12.

59. Director of Central Intelligence, *Directive 2/12, Community Open Source Program,* March 1, 1994, http://www.fas.org/irp/offdocs/dcid212.htm (accessed November 30, 2010).

60. Community Open Source Program Office, *Community Open Source Strategic Plan,* February 1995, 3, http://www.oss.net/dynamaster/file_archive/040320/bc201247d9056a4f07e6f5e720be9823/OSS1997-02-34.pdf (accessed December 9, 2010).

61. Wallner, "Open Sources and the Intelligence Community," 19.

62. National Intelligence Council, *Open Source Task Force: A Vision for the Future,* January 13, 1992, http://www.phibetaiota.net/1992/01/1992-national-intelli

gence-council-open-source-task-force-a-vision-for-the-future/ (accessed November 30, 2010).

63. Ibid., 1.

64. Ibid., 3.

65. Ibid., 4.

66. Robert David Steele, "United States Marine Corps Comments on Joint Open Source Task Force Report and Recommendations," January 6, 1992, http://www.oss.net/dynamaster/file_archive/060324/9906ba66ee5fe750bb8fe5712b1e20e7/92 Jan 11 Steele on IC OSINT.pdf (accessed November 30, 2010).

67. Ibid., 1.

68. Noah Shachtman, "How to Restore Spies Credibility: Go Open Source," *Wired*, December 14, 2007, http://www.wired.com/dangerroom/2007/12/how-to-restore/ (accessed November 30, 2010).

69. Ibid.

70. Ibid.

71. See "Open Source Burundi Exercise," September 20, 2000, http://lists101.his.com/pipermail/intelforum/2000-September/002802.html (accessed December 2, 2010).

72. Aspin-Brown Commission, 88.

73. Ibid.

74. Ibid., 89.

75. Robert David Steele, "Fixing the White House and National Intelligence," *International Journal of Intelligence and CounterIntelligence* 23, no. 2 (2010): 353–73.

76. Frederick L. Wettering, "OSINT's Primary Advocate," review of *The New Craft of Intelligence: Personal, Public and Political*, by Robert David Steele, *International Journal of Intelligence and CounterIntelligence* 16, no. 3 (2003): 507.

77. Arthur S. Hulnick, "OSINT: Is It Really Intelligence?" (paper presented at the annual convention of the American Political Science Association, Boston, MA, August 2008), http://www.allacademic.com//meta/p_mla_apa_research_citation/2/8/1/2/1/pages281211/p281211-1.php (accessed November 30, 2010).

78. Mark Tovey, ed., *Collective Intelligence: Creating a Prosperous World at Peace* (Oakton, VA: Earth Intelligence Network, 2008): iii.

79. NNDB, "Rob Simmons," http://www.nndb.com/people/462/000040342 (accessed November 30, 2010).

80. Republican Leadership Council, "Bio—Congressman Rob Simmons," http://www.republican-leadership.com/bios/rob-simmons (accessed November 30, 2010).

81. Robert M. Simmons, "Open Source Intelligence: An Examination of Its Exploitation in the Defense Intelligence Community" (master's thesis, Joint Military Intelligence College, 1995), http://www.phibetaiota.net/1995/08/history-1995-simmons-open-source-intelligence-an-examination-of-its-exploitation-in-the-defense-intelligence-community/ (accessed December 1, 2010).

82. Ibid., 3.

83. Ibid., 4.

84. Robert David Steele, *Information Operations: All Information, All Languages, All the Time* (Oakton, VA: OSS International Press, 2006): 3.

85. Ibid., 5.

86. National Defense Authorization Act for Fiscal Year 2006, Public Law 109–163, http://www.dod.gov/dodgc/olc/docs/PL109-163.pdf (accessed December 2,

2010). Simmons had attempted to include this language in earlier reform legislation. See, for example, Simmons's statements regarding open source during hearings regarding the 9/11 Recommendations Implementation Act (House of Representatives, October 7, 2004), http://thomas.loc.gov/cgi-bin/query/F?r108:1:./temp/~r108hzdTlb:e1320829 (accessed February 25, 2011).

87. Chris Strohm, "Lawmaker Calls for CIA Center to Become Independent Agency," *Government Executive*, June 7, 2006, http://www.govexec.com/dailyfed/0606/060706tdpm1.htm (accessed December 1, 2010).

88. Ibid.

89. Kent Bye, "Interview Audio: Congressman Rob Simmons, Chairman of Homeland Security Intelligence & Information Sharing Subcommittee," January 25, 2006, http://www.echochamberproject.com/simmons (accessed December 2, 2010).

90. Geospatial Intelligence Forum, U.S. Geospatial Intelligence Foundation, "Q&A: General Michael V. Hayden," http://www.geospatial-intelligence-forum.com/mgt-home/133-mgt-2006-volume-4-issue-1/1195-qaa-general-michael-v-hayden.html (accessed December 1, 2010).

91. Wait, "Intelligence Units Mine the Benefits."

92. Eliot A. Jardines, Written Testimony, House Committee on Homeland Security, Subcommittee on Intelligence, Information Sharing, and Terrorism Risk Assessment, *Using Open-Source Information Effectively*, 109th Cong., 1st sess., June 21, 2005, http://www.fas.org/irp/congress/2005_hr/062105jardines.pdf, 2 (accessed December 2, 2010).

93. Wallner, "Open Sources and the Intelligence Community," 23.

94. Kent Bye, "Interview Audio: Eliot Jardines, Assistant Deputy Director of National Intelligence for Open Source," January 25, 2006, http://www.echochamberproject.com/jardines (accessed December 2, 2010).

95. Robert David Steele, "PORTAL: OSINT, ADDNI/OS, BI/CI Etc.," http://www.oss.net (accessed March 8, 2006).

96. House Committee on Homeland Security, *Using Open-Source Information Effectively*, 32–33.

97. Kent Bye, "Interview Audio: Elliot Jardines."

98. Doug Naquin, "Remarks by Doug Naquin, CIRA Luncheon, 3 October 2007," *CIRA Newsletter* 32, no. 4 (2007), http://www.fas.org/irp/eprint/naquin.pdf, 3 (accessed December 2, 2010).

99. Ibid., 5.

100. Ibid., 3.

101. Ibid., 5.

102. Ibid., 3.

103. Ibid., 6.

104. Ibid.

CHAPTER 3

1. Remarks and Q&A by the deputy director of national intelligence for analysis, Thomas Fingar (DNI Open Source Conference, Washington, DC, July 16, 2007), http://www.dni.gov/speeches/20070717_speech_3.pdf (accessed August 1, 2008).

2. Amy B. Zegart, *Spying Blind: The CIA, the FBI, and the Origins of 9/11* (Princeton, NJ: Princeton University Press, 2007); Johnson, *Handbook of Intelligence Studies*.

3. See, however, Michael Warner, "Reading the Riot Act: The Schlesinger Report, 1971," *Intelligence and National Security* 24, no. 3 (2009): 387–417.

4. Zegart, *Spying Blind*.

5. Ibid.

6. Steele, "The Open Source Program."

7. Zegart, *Spying Blind*, 60.

8. Remarks and Q&A by the deputy director, 8.

9. Ibid.

10. Timothy Kuhn, "A Communicative Theory of the Firm: Developing an Alternative Perspective on Intra-Organizational Power and Stakeholder Relationships," *Organization Studies* 29, no. 8–9 (2008): 1235.

11. Timothy Kuhn, "A 'Demented Work Ethic' and a 'Lifestyle Firm': Discourse, Identity, and Workplace Time Commitments," *Organization Studies* 27, no. 9 (2006): 1342.

12. Hamilton Bean, "Communication and Intelligence: Allies or Enemies?," *International Journal of Intelligence and CounterIntelligence* 22, no. 2 (2009): 360–65; Stanley Deetz, *Democracy in an Age of Corporate Colonization: Developments in Communication and the Politics of Everyday Life* (Albany: State University of New York Press, 1992).

13. Paul J. DiMaggio and Walter W. Powell, "The Iron Cage Revisited: Institutional Isomorphism and Collective Rationality in Organizational Fields," *American Sociological Review* 48, no. 2 (1983): 147–60.

14. W. Richard Scott, *Institutions and Organizations* (Thousand Oaks, CA: Sage, 1995).

15. Ibid.

16. John W. Meyer and Brian Rowan, "Institutional Organizations: Formal Structure as Myth and Ceremony," *American Journal of Sociology* 83, no. 2 (1977). 340–63.

17. Stevyn Gibson, "Open Source Intelligence: An Intelligence Lifeline," *RUSI Journal* 149, no. 1 (2004): 19.

18. John C. Lammers and Joshua B. Barbour, "An Institutional Theory of Organizational Communication," *Communication Theory* 16, no. 3 (2006): 1–22.

19. David Grant, Cynthia Hardy, Cliff Oswick, and Linda Putnam, ed., *The Sage Handbook of Organizational Discourse* (London: Sage, 2004), 3.

20. Andrew Feenberg, *Transforming Technology: A Critical Theory Revisited* (Oxford: Oxford University Press, 2002).

21. Kuhn, "A 'Demented Work Ethic,'" 1235.

22. Grant et al., *The Sage Handbook of Organizational Discourse*, 25.

23. Hardy, "Scaling Up and Bearing Down."

24. Maguire, Hardy, and Lawrence, for example, define institutional entrepreneurship as the "activities of actors who have an interest in particular institutional arrangements and who leverage resources to create new institutions or transform existing ones." Similarly, Lawrence and Suddaby define institutional entrepreneurship as the "purposeful action of individuals and organizations aimed at creating, maintaining, and disrupting institutions." See Steve Maguire, Cynthia Hardy, and Thomas B. Lawrence, "Institutional Entrepreneurship in Emerging Fields: HIV/AIDS Treatment Advocacy in Canada," *Academy of Management Jour-*

nal 47, no. 5 (2004): 657; Thomas B. Lawrence and Roy Suddaby, "Institutions and Institutional Work," in Clegg et al., *The Sage Handbook of Organization Studies*, 2nd ed., 215.

25. Raghu Garud, Cynthia Hardy, and Steve Maguire, "Institutional Entrepreneurship as Embedded Agency: An Introduction to the Special Issue," *Organization Studies* 28, no. 7 (2007): 957–70.

26. Ibid., 962.

27. Lawrence and Suddaby, "Institutions and Institutional Work."

28. Perkmann and Spicer, "How Are Management Fashions Institutionalized?"

29. Ibid., 834–37.

30. Gillian Symon states, "rhetorical analysis is … a kind of discourse analysis that concentrates on analyzing linguistic strategies of argumentation as individuals seek to convince an audience of a construction of reality congruent with their interests (through justification) yet undermining of others (through criticism)" (78). See Gillian Symon, "Developing the Political Perspective on Technological Change through Rhetorical Analysis," *Management Communication Quarterly* 22, no. 1 (2008): 74–98. George Cheney and colleagues note many similarities between rhetoric and discourse but also contrast the terms by referencing each concept's specific intellectual history, associated vocabulary, and lines of inquiry. See George Cheney, Lars Thøger Christensen, Charles Conrad, and Daniel J. Lair, "Corporate Rhetoric as Organizational Discourse," in Grant et al., *The Sage Handbook of Organizational Discourse*, 79–104.

31. Cheney, Christensen, Conrad, and Lair, "Corporate Rhetoric as Organizational Discourse."

32. Robert P. Newman, "Communication Pathologies of Intelligence Systems," *Speech Monographs* 42, (November 1975): 273.

33. Gordon R. Mitchell, "Team B Intelligence Coups," *Quarterly Journal of Speech* 92, no. 2 (2006): 144–73.

34. Stephen J. Hartnett and Laura A. Stengrim, *Globalization and Empire: The U.S. Invasion of Iraq, Free Markets, and the Twilight of Democracy* (Tuscaloosa: University of Alabama Press, 2005).

35. H. L. Goodall, Jr., "Why We Must Win the War on Terror: Communication, Narrative, and the Future of National Security," *Qualitative Inquiry* 12, no. 1 (2006): 30–59.

36. G. Thomas Goodnight, "Strategic Doctrine, Public Debate and the Terror War," in *Hitting First: Preventive Force in U.S. Security Strategy*, ed. W. W. Keller and G. R. Mitchell, 93–114. Pittsburgh, PA: University of Pittsburgh Press, 2006.

37. Zegart, *Spying Blind*.

38. Bryan C. Taylor, William J. Kinsella, Stephen P. Depoe, and Maribeth S. Metzler, ed., *Nuclear Legacies: Communication, Controversy, and the U.S. Nuclear Weapons Complex* (Lanham, MD: Lexington Books, 2007).

39. Ibid., 381.

40. Ibid., 382.

41. Robert L. Ivie, *Democracy and America's War on Terror* (Tuscaloosa: University of Alabama Press, 2005).

42. Bryan C. Taylor, "COMM 6360: The Rhetoric and Culture of U.S. National Security" (lecture, January 23, 2008, University of Colorado at Boulder).

43. Chris Barker, *Making Sense of Cultural Studies: Central Problems and Critical Debates* (London: Sage, 2002).

44. Peter Gill and Mark Phythian, *Intelligence in an Insecure World* (Cambridge: Polity Press, 2006).

45. Eirik G. Furubotn, "The New Institutional Economics and the Theory of the Firm," *Journal of Economic Behavior & Organization* 45, no. 2 (2001): 133–53.

46. Alan I. Marcus, "'Would You Like Fries with That, Sir?' The Evolution of Management Theories and the Rise and Fall of Total Quality Management within the American Federal Government," *Management & Organizational History* 3, no. 3–4 (2008): 319.

47. Perkmann and Spicer, "How Are Management Fashions Institutionalized?," 839.

48. Perkmann and Spicer, "How Are Management Fashions Institutionalized?"

49. Ibid., 836.

50. This is a process that Perkmann and Spicer refer to as "partaking."

51. Interview, intelligence official, 2008.

52. Phillips, Lawrence, and Hardy, "Discourse and Institutions," 644.

53. Ibid., 643.

54. Remarks and Q&A by the deputy director, 3.

55. Kuhn explains that conferences constitute a genre of organizational communication because they can be grouped by similar "situational requirements," "substantive characteristics," and "stylistic characteristics," all of which are coordinated by an "organizing principle." Situational requirements relate to a matter that must be managed or resolved—in other words, a crisis, issue, or need. Substantive characteristics relate to the "social motives, themes, and topics being expressed in the communication," while stylistic characteristics involve the methods by which organizations convey their messages. See Timothy Kuhn, "The Discourse of Issues Management: A Genre of Organizational Communication," *Communication Quarterly* 45, no. 3 (1997): 188–210.

56. Remarks and Q&A by the assistant deputy director, 2.

57. Office of the Director of National Intelligence, "Transcripts from the DNI Open Source Conference 2008" (Washington, DC, September 11 and 12, 2008), http://www.dni.gov/speeches/20080912_speech.pdf, 6 (accessed March 6, 2009) (hereafter "Transcripts").

58. Remarks and Q&A by the deputy director, 1.

59. Remarks and Q&A by the director, 4.

60. Lawrence and Suddaby, "Institutions and Institutional Work," 222.

61. Remarks and Q&A by the deputy director, 2.

62. Remarks and Q&A by the deputy director of national intelligence for collection, Mary Margaret Graham (DNI Open Source Conference, Washington, DC, July 17, 2007), http://www.dni.gov/speeches/20070717_speech_2.pdf, 2 (accessed August 3, 2008).

63. Ibid.

64. "Transcripts," 34.

65. Ibid., 42.

66. Interview, policy maker, 2009.

67. Remarks and Q&A by the assistant deputy director, 2.

68. "Transcripts," 5.

69. Ibid., 27.

70. Remarks and Q&A by the deputy director of national intelligence for collection, 3.

71. "Transcripts," 23–24.

72. Lawrence and Suddaby, "Institutions and Institutional Work," 226.

73. "Transcripts."

74. Lawrence and Suddaby, "Institutions and Institutional Work," 229.

75. Ben Bain, "Officers to Get Guidelines for Open-Source Intell," *Federal Computer Week,* June 18, 2010, http://fcw.com/Articles/2010/06/18/Web-open-source-intell.aspx (accessed December 2, 2010).

77. Lawrence and Suddaby, "Institutions and Institutional Work," 225.

78. Remarks and Q&A by the assistant deputy director, 1.

79. Lawrence and Suddaby, "Institutions and Institutional Work," 224–25.

80. "Transcripts," 22.

81. Ibid., 25.

82. Interview, intelligence contractor, 2009.

83. Phillips, Lawrence, and Hardy, "Discourse and Institutions."

CHAPTER 4

1. Lorenzo Semple Jr., *Three Days of the Condor,* directed by Sydney Pollack (United States: Paramount Pictures, 1975).

2. Remarks and Q&A by the assistant deputy director of national intelligence for open source, Eliot A. Jardines (DNI Open Source Conference, Washington, DC, July 16, 2007), http://www.dni.gov/speeches/20070716_speech_3.pdf (accessed August 15, 2007).

3. Management scholars Roy Suddaby and Royston Greenwood explain that institutional logics are unstated assumptions that guide members' sense making by prescribing and proscribing actions. These logics influence ways of interpreting the world, constraining and enabling action. Scholars interested in institutional change examine the strategic use of language in order to understand how shifts in institutional logics occur. See Roy Suddaby and Royston Greenwood, "Rhetorical Strategies of Legitimacy," *Administrative Science Quarterly* 50, no. 1 (2005): 35–67.

4. Mark Lowenthal, *Intelligence: From Secrets to Policy,* 3rd ed. (Washington, DC: CQ Press, 2006): 4–5.

5. Joseph E. Stiglitz, "On Liberty, the Right to Know, and Public Discourse: The Role of Transparency in Public Life," in *Government Secrecy: Classic and Contemporary Readings,* ed. Susan L. Maret and Jan Goldman (Westport, CT: Libraries Unlimited, 2009), 697.

6. *U.S. News and World Report,* "In Obama White House, New Rules on Day One," January 22, 2009, http://www.usnews.com/articles/news/washington-whispers/2009/01/22/in-obama-white-house-new-rules-on-day-one.html (accessed March 2, 2009).

7. For a discussion of this issue, see Sources and Methods, "Determining Source Reliability on the Internet," October 30, 2008, http://sourcesandmethods.blogspot.com/2008/10/how-to-determining-source-reliability.html (accessed December 2, 2010).

8. Susan B. Glasser, "Probing Galaxies of Data for Nuggets," *Washington Post,* November 25, 2005, A35.

9. David Martin, "Secret Information in Plain Sight," *CBS News,* January 10, 2006, http://www.cbsnews.com/stories/2006/01/10/eveningnews/main1198667.shtml (accessed May 8, 2009).

10. Remarks and Q&A by the assistant deputy director, 7.

11. Office of the Director of National Intelligence, *Intelligence Community Directive 301, National Open Source Enterprise,* July 11, 2006, 8, http://www.fas.org/irp/dni/icd/icd-301.pdf (accessed December 2, 2010).

12. Ibid.

13. This quote comes from Intellibridge managers who were speaking with a U.S. Navy admiral about open source issues in 2004.

14. Interview, intelligence contractor, 2009.

15. National Defense Authorization Act, 3411–2.

16. NATO, *Open Source Intelligence Handbook,* November 2001, V, http://en.wikipedia.org/wiki/NATO_Open_Source_Intelligence_Handbook (accessed December 2, 2010).

17. Remarks and Q&A by the director, 6.

18. Remarks and Q&A by the assistant deputy director, 4.

19. Victor Marchetti and John D. Marks, *The CIA and the Cult of Intelligence* (New York: Dell Publishing, 1974), 273.

20. Interview, intelligence commentator, 2009.

21. House Permanent Select Committee on Intelligence, *Report of the Joint Inquiry,* GPO Access, "Congressional Reports: Joint Inquiry into Intelligence Community Activities before and after the Terrorist Attacks of September 11, 2001," http://www.gpoaccess.gov/serialset/creports/911.html, 636 (accessed December 3, 2010).

22. Ibid.

23. National Commission on Terrorist Attacks upon the United States, *The 9/11 Commission Report,* July 22, 2004, 413, http://www.9-11commission.gov (accessed December 2, 2010).

24. Interview, 9/11 Commission staff member, 2008.

25. Interview, policy maker, 2009.

26. Remarks and Q&A by the assistant deputy director, 1–2.

27. Phillips, Lawrence, and Hardy, "Discourse and Institutions."

28. Ibid.

29. Ibid., 640.

30. The Intelligence Reform and Terrorism Prevention Act of 2004, Public Law 108–458, 3693, http://www.nctc.gov/docs/pl108_458.pdf (accessed December 3, 2010).

31. Commission on the Intelligence Capabilities, *Report to the President,* 377–78.

32. Ibid., 23.

33. Dan Eggen and Spencer S. Hsu, "House Bill Backs Additional Reforms from 9/11 Report," *Washington Post,* January 9, 2007, http://www.washingtonpost.com/wp-dyn/content/article/2007/01/08/AR2007010801623.html (accessed December 3, 2010).

34. Kent Bye, "Can Open Source Intelligence Be a Non-Violent Alternative to War?" December 3, 2005, http://www.echochamberproject.com/node/718 (accessed December 3, 2010).

35. Robert David Steele, "Steele Interview for Military Review," April 16, 2006, 2–3, http://www.oss.net/dynamaster/file_archive/060417/d0a6e5b9746c0c07eddbde662982b66c/Interview on Academics et al with intelligence 1.1.doc (accessed December 3, 2010).

36. Importantly, Simmons was a featured speaker during the 2007 Open Source Conference. In 2008, however, his role was downgraded to panel member. This suggests that officials may have sought to downplay Simmons's perspective.

37. Marks, "Twittering Intelligence."

38. Office of the Director of National Intelligence, *Intelligence Community Directive 301*, 3.

39. Phillips, Lawrence, and Hardy, "Discourse and Institutions," 643.

40. LexisNexis Open Source Intelligence Roundtable, "OSINT 2020: The Future of Open Source Intelligence," June 17, 2010, 4, http://www.dni.gov/speeches/Speech_OSINT_Roundtable_20100617.pdf (accessed December 3, 2010).

41. Phillips, Lawrence, and Hardy, "Discourse and Institutions."

42. "Transcripts," 4.

43. François Cooren, "Textual Agency: How Texts Do Things in Organizational Settings," *Organization* 11, no. 3 (2004): 388.

44. Interview, intelligence official, 2009.

45. Interview, intelligence analyst, 2009.

46. Defense Science Board, *Defense Imperatives for the New Administration*, August 2008, 38–39, http://www.acq.osd.mil/dsb/reports/ADA489102.pdf (accessed December 3, 2010).

47. Hardy, Palmer, and Phillips, "Discourse as a Strategic Resource," 1228.

48. Office of the Director of National Intelligence, *National Open Source Enterprise*, 2006, 3, http://en.wikipedia.org/wiki/National_Open_Source_Enterprise (accessed December 10, 2007).

49. Paul du Gay, "Against 'Enterprise' (But Not Against 'Enterprise,' for That Would Make No Sense)," *Organization* 11, no. 1 (2004): 37–58.

50. Paul du Gay, *Production of Culture/Cultures of Production* (London: Sage, 1997): 299–307.

51. Ibid., 299–300.

52. Office of the Director of National Intelligence, *National Open Source Enterprise*, 7–12.

53. Marcus, "'Would You Like Fries with That, Sir?'"

54. Peter Grier and Faye Bowers, "Failure of 'Imagination' Led to 9/11," *Christian Science Monitor*, July 23, 2004, http://www.csmonitor.com/2004/0723/p01s03-uspo.html (accessed December 3, 2010).

55. "Transcripts," 7.

56. Ibid., 13 (emphasis added).

57. Grant et al., *The Sage Handbook of Organizational Discourse*, 6.

58. Jardines explained, "Thankfully for Bertoldt, the Nazis had publicly announced his arrest, which resulted in vehement protests by Swiss authorities, who turned up numerous witnesses to the kidnapping and who objected to the Gestapo having almost struck a Swiss border guard as they rammed their way through the border crossing. As a result, diplomatic and public pressure on the German government, Bertoldt was finally released six months later." Remarks and Q&A by the assistant deputy director, 3–4.

59. Remarks and Q&A by the deputy director of national intelligence for collection, 3–4.

60. Remarks and Q&A by the assistant deputy director, 4.

61. David H. Noon, "Operation Enduring Analogy: World War II, the War on Terror, and the Uses of Historical Memory," *Rhetoric & Public Affairs* 7, no. 3 (2004) 339–64.

62. Nick Trujillo and George Dionisopoulos, "Cop Talk, Police Stories, and the Social Construction of Organizational Drama," *Central States Speech Journal* 38, no. 3–4 (1987): 196–209.

63. Noon, "Operation Enduring Analogy," 340.

64. "Transcripts," 12.

65. Ibid., 14.

66. Commission on the Intelligence Capabilities, *Report to the President*, 23.

67. Ibid., 379–80.

68. Mark C. Suchman, "Managing Legitimacy: Strategic and Institutional Approaches," *Academy of Management Review* 20, no. 3 (1995): 591.

69. Ibid., 592.

70. "CIA Launching 'Open Source' Intel Center," *Fox News*, November 8, 2005, http://www.foxnews.com/story/0,2933,174997,00.html (accessed January 13, 2009).

71. Interview, intelligence official, 2009.

72. Marcus, " 'Would You Like Fries with That, Sir?' " 314.

73. "Transcripts," 83.

74. Ibid., 38.

75. Ibid.

76. Ibid.

77. Office of the Director of National Intelligence, *National Open Source Enterprise*, 11.

78. Interview, intelligence official, 2009.

79. Stanley Deetz, "Reclaiming Indeterminacy and the Deliberative Process" (paper presented at the Practical Theory, Public Participation, and Community Workshop, Baylor University, January 27–30, 2000), http://www3.baylor.edu/communication_conference/deetz.pdf (accessed December 8, 2010).

80. Interview, intelligence commentator, 2009.

81. "Transcripts," 23.

82. See Harris, "Intelligence Incorporated."

83. Newman, "Communication Pathologies," 274.

84. Interview, policy maker, 2009.

85. Rita Abrahamsen and Michael C. Williams, "Security beyond the State: Global Security Assemblages in International Politics," *International Political Sociology* 3, no. 1 (2009): 5.

86. Interview, intelligence commentator, 2009.

87. Paul du Gay, "The Tyranny of the Epochal: Change, Epochalism, and Organizational Reform," *Organization* 10, no. 4 (2003): 664.

88. National Open Source Committee, *National Open Source Strategic Action Plan*, 2009, http://www.fas.org/irp/dni/osc/nossap.pdf (accessed December 3, 2010).

89. Ibid., 5.

90. "Transcripts," 5, 31, 39, 44, 48, 49, 50.

91. Ibid., 31.

92. John C. Gannon, Written Statement, House Committee on Homeland Security, Subcommittee on Intelligence, Information Sharing, and Terrorism Risk Assessment, *Using Open-Source Information Effectively*, 109th Cong., 1st sess., June 21, 2005, http://www.fas.org/irp/congress/2005_hr/062105gannon.pdf (accessed December 2, 2010).

93. Rob Johnston, *Analytical Culture in the U.S. Intelligence Community: An Ethnographic Study* (Washington, DC: Center for the Study of Intelligence, 2004), 20.

94. Ibid., 17.

95. Commission on the Intelligence Capabilities, *Report to the President*, 397.

96. Shoshana Zuboff, *In the Age of the Smart Machine: The Future of Work and Power* (New York: Basic Books, 1988).

97. Department of Defense, *Instruction 3115.12*, August 24, 2010, http://www.dtic.mil/whs/directives/corres/pdf/311512p.pdf (accessed December 3, 2010).

CHAPTER 5

1. Copies of the *Open Source Enterprise Strategic Vision* brochure were distributed to participants at the 2008 DNI Open Source Conference. As of December 3, 2010, no digital copies were publicly available online (it is available to authorized personnel via government information sharing systems).

2. U.S. Department of Homeland Security, *2008 Strategic Plan*, http://www.dhs.gov/xabout/strategicplan/ (accessed December 3, 2010).

3. Ibid.

4. Lauren Martin and Stephanie Simon, "A Formula for Disaster: The Department of Homeland Security's Virtual Ontology," *Space and Polity* 12, no. 3 (2008): 286.

5. Joanne Martin, *Organizational Culture: Mapping the Terrain* (Thousand Oaks, CA: Sage. 2002).

6. Linda Smircich, "Concepts of Culture and Organizational Analysis," *Administrative Science Quarterly* 28, no. 3 (1983): 339–58.

7. Martin, *Organizational Culture*.

8. Linda L. Putnam and Michael E. Pacanowsky, ed., *Communication and Organizations: An Interpretive Approach* (Beverly Hills, CA: Sage, 1983).

9. Du Gay, *Production of Culture*, 286.

10. Mats Alvesson, "Organizational Culture and Discourse," in Grant et al., *The Sage Handbook of Organizational Discourse*, 331.

11. Interview, fusion center analyst, 2009.

12. Mark A. Randol, "Homeland Security Intelligence: Perceptions, Statutory Definitions, and Approaches," January 14, 2009, 2, Congressional Research Service, http://www.fas.org/sgp/crs/intel/RL33616.pdf (accessed December 3, 2010).

13. U.S. Department of Homeland Security, *Report to Congress on Implementation of Section 705 of the Homeland Security Act and the Establishment of the Office for Civil Rights and Civil Liberties*, 2004, 17, http://www.dhs.gov/xlibrary/assets/CRCL-ReportJun04.pdf (accessed December 3, 2010).

14. Simpson and Cheney, "Marketization, Participation, and Communication."

15. Calvert Jones, "Intelligence Reform: The Logic of Information Sharing," *Intelligence & National Security* 22, no. 3 (2007): 396.

16. See the Information Sharing Environment (ISE) at http://www.ise.gov/default.aspx.

17. Bean and Keränen, "The Role of Homeland Security Information Bulletins."

18. See Brian J. Gerber et al., "On the Front Line: American Cities and the Challenge of Homeland Security Preparedness," *Urban Affairs Review* 41, no. 2 (2005): 182–210; Martin J. Zaworski, "Automated Information Sharing: Does It Help Law Enforcement Officers Work Better?" *National Institute of Justice Journal* 253 (2006): 25–26.

19. U.S. House of Representatives, Homeland Security Committee, *Giving a Voice to Open Source Stakeholders: A Survey of State, Local, and Tribal Law Enforcement*, September 2008, 2, http://homeland.house.gov/SiteDocuments/OpenSourceRe port.pdf (accessed December 3, 2010).

20. Ibid.

21. Phillips, Lawrence, and Hardy, "Discourse and Institutions."

22. Interview, intelligence commentator, 2009.

23. Alvesson, "Organizational Culture and Discourse," 331.

24. Interview, intelligence commentator, 2009.

25. Information Sharing Environment, *ISE Implementation Plan*, 2006, http://www.ise.gov (accessed November 12, 2008).

26. The White House, *National Strategy for Information Sharing*, 2007, 3, http://georgewbush-whitehouse.archives.gov/nsc/infosharing/NSIS_book.pdf (accessed December 5, 2010).

27. U.S. Department of Homeland Security, *2008 Strategic Plan*, 4, 23–24.

28. U.S. Department of Homeland Security, *Intelligence Enterprise Strategic Plan*, January 2006, 14, http://www.fas.org/irp/agency/dhs/stratplan.pdf (accessed December 5, 2010).

29. Martin, Frost, and O'Neill, "Organizational Culture."

30. Ibid.

31. Ibid.; Joann Keyton, *Communication and Organizational Culture: A Key to Understanding Work Experiences* (Thousand Oaks, CA: Sage, 2005).

32. Interview, intelligence contractor, 2008.

33. Interview, intelligence analyst, 2008.

34. Interview, fusion center analyst, 2009.

35. Interview, law enforcement analyst, 2007.

36. Interview, emergency management official, 2007.

37. Interview, emergency management official, 2007.

38. Interview, fusion center analyst, 2008.

39. Ibid.

40. Interview, fusion center analyst, 2008.

41. Interview, homeland security analyst, 2009.

42. Interview, emergency management official, 2007.

43. Interview, emergency management official, 2007.

44. Interview, law enforcement official, 2007.

45. Interview, law enforcement official, 2007.

46. Interview, fusion center analyst, 2008.

47. Interview, emergency management official, 2007.

48. Interview, law enforcement official, 2007.

49. Interview, emergency management official, 2007.

50. Timothy L. Sellnow, Mathew W. Seeger, and Robert R. Ulmer, "Chaos Theory, Informational Needs, and Natural Disasters," *Journal of Applied Communication Research* 30, no. 4 (2002): 288.

51. Ibid., 290.

52. Interview, emergency management official, 2007.

53. David Constant, Sara Kiesler, and Lee Sproull, "What's Mine Is Ours, or Is It? A Study of Attitudes about Information Sharing," *Information Systems Research* 5, no. 4 (1994): 400–21.

54. Johnston, *Analytical Culture.*

55. Interview, intelligence analyst, 2008.

56. Interview, fusion center analyst, 2008.

57. Interview, law enforcement official, 2007.

58. Interview, fusion center analyst, 2009.

59. Interview, intelligence contractor, 2008.

60. Interview, law enforcement official, 2007.

61. Interview, homeland security analyst, 2009.

62. Interview, fusion center analyst, 2009.

63. Interview, intelligence analyst, 2009.

64. Interview, policy maker, 2009.

65. Additional issues noted by participants that are not discussed in-depth here include these concerns: (1) the lack of a shared approach to open source collection and analysis; (2) the absence of shared quality assurance and counterintelligence protocols; and (3) turnover in open source personnel who are simply waiting for security clearances in order to work with classified materials.

66. Alex Z. Kondra and Deborah C. Hurst, "Institutional Processes of Organizational Culture," *Culture and Organization* 15, no. 1 (2009): 42.

67. Interview, intelligence official, 2009.

68. Interview, fusion center analyst, 2009.

69. Interview, homeland security analyst, 2009.

70. Ibid.

71. Interview, intelligence analyst, 2008.

72. Interview, intelligence analyst, 2009.

73. Interview, intelligence commentator, 2008

74. U.S. Department of Homeland Security, "Testimony of Under Secretary Caryn Wagner before the House Subcommittee on Homeland Security on the President's Fiscal Year 2011 Budget Request for the Department's Office of Intelligence and Analysis," March 4, 2010, http://www.dhs.gov/ynews/testimony/testimony_1267716038879.shtm (accessed December 5, 2010).

75. Ibid.

76. Interview, intelligence contractor, 2008.

77. Interview, intelligence contractor, 2008.

78. Interview, homeland security analyst, 2009.

79. Ibid.

80. Shorrock, *Spies for Hire*.

81. Kuhn, "A Communicative Theory of the Firm," 1233.

82. Interview, intelligence contractor, 2008.

83. Interview, fusion center analyst, 2009.

84. Interview, intelligence commentator, 2008.

85. Interview, homeland security analyst, 2009.

86. Interview, fusion center analyst, 2009.

87. Interview, homeland security analyst, 2009.

88. Interview, fusion center analyst, 2009.

89. Interview, fusion center analyst, 2009.

90. Interview, intelligence official, 2008.

91. Kondra and Hurst, "Institutional Processes," 53.

92. Nelson Phillips and Namrata Malhotra, "Taking Social Construction Seriously: Extending the Discursive Approach in Institutional Theory," in *The Sage Handbook of Organizational Institutionalism*, ed. Royston Greenwood, Christine Oliver, Kerstin Sahlin, and Roy Suddaby (London: Sage, 2008), 702–20.

93. Ibid., 710.

94. Interview, fusion center analyst, 2009.

95. Interview, policy maker, 2009.

96. Interview, fusion center analyst, 2009.

97. Information Sharing Environment, *Annual Report to the Congress,* July 2010, 57, http://www.ise.gov/docs/ISE_AR-2010_Final_2010-07-29.pdf (accessed December 5, 2010).

98. Ibid., 58.

99. Ibid., 60.

100. Open Source Content Management, Department of Homeland Security, "DHS-OSE Homeland Security Central Digest—2010-11-17."

101. Ibid.

102. Open Source Content Management, Department of Homeland Security, "Your DHS-OSE Subscription Request," November 5, 2010.

CHAPTER 6

1. *9/11: Press for Truth,* directed by Ray Nowosielski (Los Angeles, CA: Banded Artists, 2006), DVD.

2. "Transcripts," 37.

3. Ibid., 60.

4. Shannen Rossmiller, "Shannen Rossmiller," http://www.shannenross miller.com (accessed December 4, 2010).

5. Melanthia Mitchell, " 'Net Sleuth' Tells Court of Hunt That Snared Guardsman," *USA Today,* May 15, 2004, http://www.usatoday.com/tech/webguide/internetlife/2004-05-13-netsleuth_x.htm (accessed December 4, 2010).

6. Robert C. Yeager, "To Catch a Terrorist: One Mother's Crusade," *Family Circle,* July 15, 2005, http://www.shannenrossmiller.com/media/hpsc2168.pdf (accessed December 4, 2010).

7. See "9/11 Families for a Secure America," http://www.911fsa.org; "The September 11th Families' Association," http://www.911families.org; and "Families of September 11," http://www.familiesofseptember11.org.

8. *9/11: Press for Truth.*

9. See Bernard Lown, *Prescription for Survival: A Doctor's Journey to End Nuclear Madness* (San Francisco: Berrett-Koehler Publishers, 2008); Matthew Evangelista, *Unarmed Forces: The Transnational Movement to End the Cold War* (Ithaca, NY: Cornell University Press, 2002); Jody Williams, Stephen D. Goose, and Mary Wareham, *Banning Landmines: Disarmament, Citizen Diplomacy, and Human Security* (Lanham, MD: Rowman & Littlefield, 2008); Taylor, Kinsella, Depoe, and Metzler, *Nuclear Legacies;* Margaret E. Keck and Kathryn Sikkink, *Activists Beyond Borders: Advocacy Networks in International Politics* (Ithaca, NY: Cornell University Press, 1998).

10. Jonathan Simon, "Parrhesiastic Accountability: Investigatory Commissions and Executive Power in an Age of Terror," *Yale Law Journal* 14 (2005): 1419–57.

11. Breitweiser, *Wake-Up Call,* 89.

12. Ibid., 87–88.

13. See "9/11: Press for Truth," http://www.911pressfortruth.com.

14. Christopher Hitchens, *The Trial of Henry Kissinger* (London: Verso, 2001).

15. *9/11: Press for Truth;* Shenon, *The Commission.*

16. *9/11: Press for Truth.*

17. David Firestone, "Kissinger Pulls Out as Chief of Inquiry into 9/11 Attacks," *New York Times,* December 14, 2002, http://query.nytimes.com/gst/fullpage.html?res=9C01E4D91E3AF937A25751C1A9649C8B63 (accessed December 4, 2010).

18. Interview, intelligence commentator, 2009.

19. Interview, 9/11 Commission staff member, 2009.

20. Interview, intelligence commentator, 2009.

21. Interview, Victims of Pan Am Flight 103 member, 2009.

22. Bryan C. Taylor, "'Our Bruised Arms Hung Up as Monuments': Nuclear Iconography in Post–Cold War Culture," *Critical Studies in Media Communication* 20, no. 1 (2003): 1–34.

23. Interview, 9/11 Commission staff member, 2009.

24. Interview, 9/11 Commission staff member, 2009.

25. Interview, 9/11 families member, 2009.

26. Interview, 9/11 Commission staff member, 2009.

27. Shenon, *The Commission.*

28. Interview, 9/11 families member, 2009.

29. Interview, 9/11 families member, 2009.

30. Interview, 9/11 Commission staff member, 2009.

31. Interview, 9/11 Commission staff member, 2009.

32. Interview, 9/11 Commission staff member, 2009.

33. Interview, 9/11 Commission staff member, 2009.

34. Interview, 9/11 Commission staff member, 2009.

35. Ibid.

36. Interview, 9/11 Commission staff member, 2009.

37. 9/11 Public Discourse Project, http://www.9-11pdp.org/press/index.htm.

38. Ibid.

39. Ibid.

40. 9/11 Public Discourse Project, "Final Report of the 9/11 Public Discourse Project," December 12, 2005, 7, http://www.9/11pdp.org/press/2005-12-05_report.pdf (accessed December 4, 2010).

41. September 11th Advocates, "An Open Letter," news release, March 5, 2009, http://www.scoop.co.nz/stories/HL0903/S00072.htm (accessed December 4, 2010).

42. Interview, 9/11 Commission staff member, 2009.

43. Ibid.

44. Interview, Victims of Pan Am Flight 103 member, 2009.

45. Interview, 9/11 Commission staff member, 2009.

46. Interview, 9/11 families member, 2009.

47. Taylor et al., *Nuclear Legacies.*

48. Interview, 9/11 Commission staff member, 2009.

49. Interview, 9/11 Commission staff member, 2009.

50. Interview, 9/11 families member, 2009.

51. Interview, 9/11 families member, 2009.

52. Interview, 9/11 families member, 2009.

53. Bruce Hoffman and Anna-Brit Kasupski, *The Victims of Terrorism: An Assessment of Their Influence and Growing Role in Policy, Legislation, and the Private Sector* (Santa Monica, CA: RAND, 2007).

54. Anthony Shaffer, *Operation Dark Heart: Spycraft and Special Ops on the Frontlines of Afghanistan—and the Path to Victory* (New York: Thomas Dunne Books, 2010).

55. I did not speak with members of 9/11 families' groups who associate themselves with this movement. The connections between 9/11 Truth and open source advocacy lie outside the scope of this study. See Jack Z. Bratich, *Conspiracy Panics: Political Rationality and Popular Culture* (Albany: State University of New York Press, 2008).

56. Ibid., 152.

57. Phillips and Malhotra, "Taking Social Construction Seriously," 713.

58. Nolte, "Thinking about Rethinking," 19.

59. William Colby, *Honorable Men: My Life in the CIA* (New York: Simon & Schuster, 1978): 459–60.

60. Interview, intelligence contractor, 2009.

61. Interview, intelligence official, 2008.

62. Interview, intelligence commentator, 2009.

63. Right to Know Community, *Moving Toward a 21st Century Right-to-Know Agenda: Recommendations to President-Elect Obama and Congress,* November 2008, http://freegovinfo.info/node/2119 (accessed December 4, 2010).

64. Lene Hansen, *Security as Practice: Discourse Analysis and the Bosnian War* (New York: Routledge, 2006).

65. Alex Martin and Peter Wilson, "The Value of Non-Governmental Intelligence: Widening the Field," *Intelligence and National Security* 23, no. 6 (2008): 771.

66. Marsh, "Grassroots Statecraft," 126.

67. Ibid., 128.

68. Ivie, *Democracy and America's War on Terror,* 186.

69. Marsh, "Grassroots Statecraft," 144–45.

70. Ken Booth, ed., *Critical Security Studies and World Politics* (Boulder, CO: Lynne Rienner Publishers, 2005).

71. Interview, 9/11 families member, 2009.

72. Ivie, *Democracy and America's War on Terror,* 178.

73. Martin and Wilson, "The Value of Non-Governmental Intelligence," 774.

74. Interview, policy maker, 2009.

75. Interview, 9/11 families member, 2009.

76. Interview, 9/11 Commission staff member, 2009.

77. Interview, intelligence official, 2008.

78. Interview, intelligence contractor, 2008.

79. Interview, 9/11 Commission staff member, 2009.

80. Interview, 9/11 Commission staff member, 2009.

81. Interview, 9/11 Commission staff member, 2009.

82. Interview, Victims of Pan Am Flight 103 member, 2009.

83. Interview, intelligence commentator, 2009.

84. Interview, 9/11 Commission staff member, 2009.

85. Interview, 9/11 Commission staff member, 2009.

86. Interview, Victims of Pan Am Flight 103 member, 2009.

87. Interview, 9/11 families member, 2009.

88. Interview, policy maker, 2009.

89. Interview, 9/11 families member, 2009.

90. Interview, 9/11 Commission staff member, 2009.

91. Ibid.

92. Interview, Victims of Pan Am Flight 103 member, 2009.

93. William W. Keller and Gordon R. Mitchell, ed., *Hitting First: Preventative Force in U.S. Security Strategy* (Pittsburgh: University of Pittsburgh Press, 2006).

94. Ibid., 251–59.

95. Ibid., 251.

96. Ibid., 254.

97. Ibid., 257.

98. Ivie, *Democracy and America's War on Terror,* 149.

99. Interview, 9/11 Commission staff member, 2009.

100. Interview, 9/11 Commission staff member, 2009.

101. Robert Asen, "A Discourse Theory of Citizenship," *Quarterly Journal of Speech* 90, no. 2 (2004): 196.

102. Ibid., 198.

CHAPTER 7

1. Kevin Poulsen and Kim Zetter, "'I Can't Believe What I'm Confessing to You': The Wikileaks Chats," *Wired,* June 10, 2010, http://www.wired.com/threatlevel/2010/06/wikileaks-chat/ (accessed December 4, 2010).

2. Spaulding, "No More Secrets"; Brewin, "No More Secrets?"

3. Zegart, *Spying Blind,* 170.

4. Best and Cumming, "Open Source Intelligence," 20–21.

5. Ibid., 21.

6. Arthur S. Hulnick, "Intelligence Reform 2008: Where to from Here?" *International Journal of Intelligence and CounterIntelligence* 21, no. 4 (2008): 631.

7. Ibid., 632.

8. "Pentagon Prepares for Largest Security Breach in U.S Military History as Wikileaks Set to Release 500,000 Iraq Documents," *Mail Online,* October 18, 2010, http://www.dailymail.co.uk/news/article-1321398/WikiLeaks-release-500k-Iraq-documents-US-militarys-largest-security-breach.html (accessed December 4, 2010).

9. Nate Anderson, "Meet the People Who Want Julian Assange 'Whacked,' " *ars technica,* December 3, 2010, http://arstechnica.com/tech-policy/news/2010/12/meet-the-people-who-want-julian-assange-whacked.ars (accessed December 4, 2010).

10. WikiLeaks, "About," http://wikileaks.org/about.html (accessed December 1, 2010).

11. Poulsen and Zetter, "'I Can't Believe What I'm Confessing to You.' "

12. Ibid.

13. Ibid.

14. Ibid.

15. See also Stephen C. Mercado, "Reexamining the Distinction between Open Information and Secrets, *Studies in Intelligence* 49, no. 2 (2005), https://www.cia.gov/library/center-for-the-study-of-intelligence/csi-publications/csi-studies/studies/Vol49no2/reexamining_the_distinction_3.htm (accessed December 8, 2010); Stephen C. Mercado, "Sailing the Sea of OSINT in the Information Age," *Studies in Intelligence* 48, no. 3 (2004), https://www.cia.gov/library/center-for-the-study-of-intelligence/csi-publications/csi-studies/studies/vol48no3/article05.html (accessed December 8, 2010).

16. John Bohannon, "Leaked Documents Provide Bonanza for Researchers," *Science* 330, no. 6004 (2010): 575.

17. Matt Raymond, "Why the Library of Congress Is Blocking WikiLeaks," December 3, 2010, http://blogs.loc.gov/loc/2010/12/why-the-library-of-congress-is-blocking-wikileaks/ (accessed December 4, 2010).

18. Tony Pfaff, "Bungee Jumping Off the Moral Highground: Ethics of Espionage in the Modern Age," in *Ethics of Spying: A Reader for the Intelligence Professional*, ed. Jan Goldman (Lanham, MD: Scarecrow Press, 2006), 77.

19. Ibid., 78.

20. Office of the Director of National Intelligence, "Remarks and Q&A by Director of National Intelligence Mr. James Clapper, Bipartisan Policy Center (BPC)—The State of Domestic Intelligence Reform," October 6, 2010, http://www.dni.gov/speeches/20101006_speech_clapper.pdf (accessed December 4, 2010).

21. Central Intelligence Agency, "Message from the Director: Recent Media Leaks," November 8, 2010, https://www.cia.gov/news-information/press-releases-statements/press-release-2010/message-from-the-director-recent-media-leaks.html (accessed December 4, 2010).

22. Ibid.

23. Public Intelligence, "About," http://publicintelligence.net/about (accessed December 4, 2010).

24. Ibid.

25. Cryptome, http://cryptome.org (accessed December 4, 2010).

26. Federation of American Scientists, FAS Project on Government Secrecy, "About," http://www.fas.org/programs/ssp/govsec/index.html (accessed December 4, 2010).

27. For these and others, consult FAS's website: http://www.fas.org.

28. Steven Aftergood, "Open Source Center Views Iraqi Election," *Secrecy News,* February 12, 2009, http://www.fas.org/sgp/news/secrecy/2009/02/021209.html (accessed December 4, 2010).

29. Interview, policy maker, 2009.

30. Steven Aftergood, "The Race to Fix the Classification System," *Secrecy News,* November 29, 2010, http://www.fas.org/blog/secrecy/2010/11/race_to_fix.html (accessed December 4, 2010).

31. Earth Intelligence Network, http://www.earth-intelligence.net (accessed December 4, 2010).

32. See WiserEarth, "Earth Intelligence Network," http://www.wiserearth.org/organization/view/1cc3f8c7f1a8c0e971731f6d70ed56d4 (accessed December 4, 2010).

33. See the CELL, "About," http://thecell.org/wp/aboutus (accessed December 4, 2010).

34. Ibid.

35. See NEFA Foundation, http://www.nefafoundation.org (accessed December 4, 2010).

36. Ibid.

37. Open Source Intelligence Forum, http://www.osif.us (accessed December 4, 2010).

38. Ibid.

39. LexisNexis, "Open Source Intelligence (OSINT) Round Table Hosted by Lex-isNexis," http://www.lexisnexis.com/trial/uslm136242.asp?access=JCM141077 (accessed December 4, 2010).

40. Marsh, "Grassroots Statecraft."

41. Ivie, *Democracy and America's War on Terror.*

42. Ivie concludes that "this dynamic between a decision-making demos and policy-advocating rhetors was key to the success of the Athenian experience with direct democracy." Ibid., 51–52.

43. Ibid., 58.

44. Ibid., 63.

45. Stephen J. Hartnett and Jennifer R. Mercieca, "'Has Your Courage Rusted?': National Security and the Contested Rhetorical Norms of Republicanism in Post-Revolutionary America, 1798–1801," *Rhetoric & Public Affairs* 9, no. 1 (2006): 83.

46. Ivie, *Democracy and America's War on Terror,* 116.

47. Amanda Terkel, "Cheney Offers False Excuse for His 'So?' Comment: I Meant, 'What's the Question, Martha?'" *Think Progress,* June 2, 2008, http://think progress.org/2008/06/02/cheney-so-revise (accessed December 4, 2010).

48. Ivie, *Democracy and America's War on Terror.*

49. Paul A. Chilton, "The Meaning of Security," in *Post-Realism: The Rhetorical Turn in International Relations,* ed. Francis A. Beer and Robert Hariman (East Lansing: Michigan State University Press, 1996), 193–216.

50. Arnold Wolfers, "'National Security' as an Ambiguous Symbol," *Political Science Quarterly* 67, no. 4 (1952): 481–502.

51. Alan Nadel, *Containment Culture: American Narratives, Postmodernism, and the Atomic Age* (Durham, NC: Duke University Press, 1995); Andrew Ross, "Containing Culture in the Cold War," *Cultural Studies* 1, no. 3 (1987): 328–48.

52. Kristen Lundberg, "Piloting a Bi-Partisan Ship: Strategies and Tactics of the 9/11 Commission" (Kennedy School of Government Case Program, C15–05–1813.0, President and Fellows of Harvard College, Cambridge, MA, 2005), 27; Breitweiser, *Wake-Up Call,* 131.

53. Jennifer R. Mercieca and James A. Aune, "A Vernacular Republican Rhetoric: William Manning's Key of Liberty," *Quarterly Journal of Speech* 91, no. 2 (2005): 120.

54. Ibid., 136.

55. Kurt Jacobsen, "Interview with Daniel Ellsberg," *Logos* 1, no. 4 (2002): 97. Ellsberg has added WikiLeaks to this list of sources of counterpower; he has been a vocal advocate for Assange and Manning.

56. Marsh, "Grassroots Statecraft," 126.

57. Interview, intelligence analyst, 2009.

58. See Victims of Pan Am Flight 103, http://www.victimsofpanamflight103.org.

59. Hoffman and Kasupski, *The Victims of Terrorism,* 19.

60. Interview, Victims of Pan Am Flight 103 member, 2009.

61. Interview, Victims of Pan Am Flight 103 member, 2009.

62. Interview, Victims of Pan Am Flight 103 member, 2009.

63. Interview, intelligence analyst, 2008.

64. Deetz, "Reclaiming Indeterminacy," 10.

65. Marcus, "'Would You Like Fries with That, Sir?,'" 319.

66. Bizzell and Herzberg, *The Rhetorical Tradition*, 1433.

67. Angelina Burch, "When I Point to the Moon, Don't Stare at My Finger," *Axis Mundi*, February 15, 2001, http://library.byzantine-antiquities.org/axismundi05/2000/when_i_point.html (accessed April 5, 2008).

68. Hardy, "Scaling Up and Bearing Down."

69. Bizzell and Herzberg, *The Rhetorical Tradition*, 1433.

70. Jennifer Milliken, "The Study of Discourse in International Relations: A Critique of Research and Methods," *European Journal of International Relations* 5, no. 2 (1999): 229.

71. Hardy, "Scaling Up and Bearing Down."

72. Interview, intelligence official, 2008.

73. Interview, policy maker, 2009.

74. Wallner, "Open Sources and the Intelligence Community," 19.

75. Kingsbury, "Spy Agencies Turn to Newspapers."

76. Ibid.

APPENDIX

1. Material is cited for research, scholarship, teaching, and education purposes and is intended for "fair use" as permitted under Title 17, Section 107 of the United States Code.

2. Shorrock, *Spies for Hire.*

3. John C. Gannon, "NIC Chairman Address to Washington College of Law" (remarks, Washington College of Law, American University, Washington, DC, October 6, 2000), https://www.cia.gov/news-information/speeches-testimony/2000/gannon_speech_10062000.html (accessed December 10, 2010).

4. Mercado, "Reexamining the Distinction."

5. Gibson, "Open Source Intelligence," 21.

6. Wallace-Wells, "Private Jihad."

7. Ibid.

8. This claim is more-or-less congruent with the Copenhagen School of International Relations' conception of "securitization." See Booth, *Critical Security Studies and World Politics.*

9. Lynn Eden, *Whole World on Fire: Organizations, Knowledge, and Nuclear Weapons Devastation* (Ithaca, NY: Cornell University Press, 2004), 50.

10. For example, on February 7, 2008, then DNI J. Michael McConnell articulated the following threats during a hearing before the House Permanent Select Committee on Intelligence: (1) the continuing "global terrorist threat," (2) "the persistent threat of WMD-related proliferation," (3) "vulnerabilities of the U.S. information infrastructure," (4) "growing foreign interest in counterspace programs," (5) "political stability and national and regional conflict in Europe, the Horn of Africa, the Middle East, and Eurasia," (6) "humanitarian concerns stemming from the rise in food and energy prices for poorer states," and (7) "concerns about the financial capabilities of Russia, China, and OPEC countries." See Office of the Director of National Intelligence, *Annual Threat Assessment of the Intelligence Community for the House Permanent Select Committee on Intelligence,* February 7, 2008, http://www.dni.gov/testimonies/20080207_testimony.pdf (accessed December 10, 2010).

11. Mark M. Lowenthal, "Towards a Reasonable Standard for Analysis: How Right, How Often on Which Issues?" *Intelligence and National Security* 23, no. 3 (2008): 313.

12. Harris, "Intelligence Shop."

13. Ibid.

14. Ibid.

15. See Eurasia Group, "Careers at Eurasia Group," http://www.eurasiagroup.net/careers (accessed December 10, 2010).

16. Randolph Fillmore, "Integrating Open Source Intelligence," August 23, 2005, http://drnatsecmgt.blogspot.com/2005/08/mr-eliot-jardines-of-open-source.html (accessed December 10, 2010).

17. Ibid.

18. Harris, "Intelligence Shop."

19. See STRATFOR, "Career Opportunities," http://www.stratfor.com/careers (accessed December 10, 2010).

20. Ibid.

21. See iJET, "Careers," http://www.ijet.com/about/careers/index.asp (accessed December 10, 2010).

22. Ibid.

23. See CIA, "Career Opportunities," https://www.cia.gov/careers/opportunities/analytical/open-source-officer-foreign-media-analyst.html (accessed December 10, 2010).

24. See Chenega Corporation, "Job Board," https://jobs.chenega.com (accessed December 10, 2010).

25. See Radiance Technologies, "Careers Index," http://www.radiancetech.com/careers/hr7142.shtm (accessed December 10, 2010).

26. See "Getting into Development," "Interning at IHS Jane's Strategic Advisory Services," September 24, 2010, http://thecareersgroupgid.wordpress.com/2010/09/24/interning-at-ihs-jane%E2%80%99s-strategic-advisory-services (accessed December 10, 2010).

27. Ibid.

28. See U.S. Department of Agriculture's Animal and Plant Health Inspection Service, "Animal Health," http://www.aphis.usda.gov/animal_health/emergingissues/teams/factsheets/GIF_aboutus.pdf (accessed December 10, 2010).

29. Ibid.

30. David Carment and Martin Rudner, ed., *Peacekeeping Intelligence: New Players, Extended Boundaries* (London: Routledge, 2006).

31. Ibid., 1.

32. Ibid., xx.

33. Wies Platje, Dame Pauline Neville-Jones, Ben de Jong, and Robert David Steele, *Peacekeeping Intelligence: Emerging Concepts for the Future* (Oakton, VA: OSS International Press, 2003).

34. Dun & Bradstreet, flier distributed at the 2008 DNI Open Source Conference.

35. Craig S. Fleisher, "Using Open Source Data in Developing Competitive and Marketing Intelligence," *European Journal of Marketing* 42, no. 7–8 (2008): 852–66.

36. Wallace-Wells, "Private Jihad."

37. Ibid.

38. Dun & Bradstreet, flier distributed at the 2008 DNI Open Source Conference.

39. See SOS International, Ltd., "Brief Profile," http://www.sosiltd.com/about_us/default.htm (accessed December 10, 2010).

40. See SOS International, Ltd., "Foreign Media Analysis," http://fma.sosiltd.com/secure/ProductServices.aspx (accessed December 10, 2010).

41. See U.S. Department of Homeland Security, "ICEGangs Database," http://www.dhs.gov/xlibrary/assets/privacy/privacy_pia_ice_icegangs.pdf (accessed December 10, 2010).

42. Martin, "Secret Information in Plain Sight."

43. Ibid.

44. See "Open Source Research" (Solicitation Number MDA908–02-Q-0055, Virginia Contracting Activity, March 11, 2002), https://www.fbo.gov/index?s=opportunity&mode=form&id=6443b3e3c853099f699c3cf114b01ded&tab=core&_cview=1 (accessed December 10, 2010).

45. Ibid.

46. "Open Source Intelligence Support to IO" (Solicitation Number W74V8H-05-T-0253, July 16, 2005), http://www.fbodaily.com/archive/2005/07-July/18-Jul-2005/FBO-00848893.htm (accessed December 10, 2010).

47. "Open Source Research Center" (Solicitation Number GS05T11BM-C0002RFP, October 19, 2010), https://www.fbo.gov/index?s=opportunity&mode=form&id=32545079d3881c9628b0d6f3d518deba&tab=core&_cview=1 (accessed December 10, 2010).

48. Ibid.

49. Ibid.

50. "Foreign Media Analysis/Strategic Information Operations Support" (Solicitation Number FA4600–05-R-0013, April 19, 2005), https://www.fbo.gov/index?s=opportunity&mode=form&id=67d4a8f31d44ebfde767bec23ad6c6fd&tab=core&_cview=1 (accessed December 10, 2010).

51. Ibid.

52. See SOS International, Ltd., "Foreign Media Analysis," http://fma.sosiltd.com/secure/ProductServices.aspx (accessed December 10, 2010).

53. See Foreign Military Studies Office, http://fmso.leavenworth.army.mil (accessed December 10, 2010).

54. "Foreign Media Analysis/Strategic Information Operations Support" (Solicitation Number FA4600–05-R-0013).

55. See IntelCenter, "About Us," http://www.intelcenter.com/aboutus.html (accessed December 10, 2010).

56. See IntelCenter, "Catalog," http://www.intelcenter.com/IntelCenter-Catalog.pdf (accessed December 10, 2010).

57. James S. Major, *Communicating with Intelligence: Writing and Briefing in the Intelligence and National Security Communities* (Lanham, MD: Scarecrow Press, 2008), xxiii.

58. "Transcripts."

59. OSC, pamphlet obtained at the 2008 DNI Open Source Conference.

60. Ibid.

61. Infosphere AB, "Restricted OSINT (Open Source Intelligence) Collection Makes What?," http://www.infosphere.se/extra/pod/?id=177&module_instance=1&action=pod_show (accessed December 11, 2010).

62. Douglas Peak, "The Open Source Academy Helps the Intelligence Community Make the Most of Open Sources," *Military Intelligence Professional Bulletin,*

October–December 2005, http://findarticles.com/p/articles/mi_m0IBS/is_4_31/ai_n16419802/ (accessed December 11, 2010).

63. Ibid.

64. See, for example, Open Source Intelligence Training (UK) Ltd., "OSINT," http://www.opensourceintelligencetraining.com/index.htm; ISS World, "Intelligence Support Systems for Lawful Interception, Criminal Investigations and Intelligence Gathering," http://www.issworldtraining.com/ISS_WASH/register.cfm (accessed December 10, 2010).

65. See OSS.net, "Intelligence Exploitation of the Internet," http://www.oss.net/dynamaster/file_archive/030201/1c0160cde7302e1c718edb08884ca7d7/Intelligence Exploitation of the Internet FINAL 18NOV02.pdf; http://www.fas.org/irp/doddir/army/fmi2-22-9.pdf (accessed December 10, 2010).

66. Fillmore, "Integrating Open Source Intelligence."

67. Remarks and Q&A by the deputy director of national intelligence for analysis and chairman, National Intelligence Council, Thomas Fingar (2008 INSA Analytic Transformation Conference, Orlando, FL, September 4, 2008), 17, http://www.dni.gov/speeches/20080904_speech.pdf (accessed December 11, 2010).

68. See, for example, United American Freedom Foundation, "Military And Government IPS Addresses," http://www.uaff.info/militarytracking.htm (accessed December 10, 2010).

69. See Tor, "Home," http://www.torproject.org (accessed December 10, 2010).

70. See Tor, "Tor Overview," http://www.torproject.org/about/overview (accessed December 10, 2010).

71. Wallace-Wells, "Private Jihad."

72. Ibid.

73. Ellen Nakashima, "Dismantling of Saudi-CIA Web Site Illustrates Need for Clearer Cyberwar Policies," *Washington Post*, March 19, 2010, http://www.washingtonpost.com/wp-dyn/content/article/2010/03/18/AR2010031805464.html (accessed December 11, 2010).

74. Ibid.

75. Ibid.

76. Fillmore, "Integrating Open Source Intelligence."

77. Richards J. Heuer Jr., *Psychology of Intelligence Analysis*, 1999, https://www.cia.gov/library/center-for-the-study-of-intelligence/csi-publications/books-and-monographs/psychology-of-intelligence-analysis/index.html (accessed December 11, 2010).

78. Lowenthal, *From Secrets to Policy*, 62.

79. Major, *Communicating with Intelligence*, 2008.

80. Ibid.

81. Loch K. Johnson, "Glimpses into the Gems of American Intelligence: The President's Daily Brief and the National Intelligence Estimate," *Intelligence and National Security* 23, no. 3 (2008): 333–70.

82. Johnson, *Handbook of Intelligence Studies.*

83. Zegart, *Spying Blind*, 68.

84. Wait, "Intelligence Units Mine the Benefits."

85. Johnson, "Glimpses into the Gems."

86. Ibid.

87. In 2008, then DDNI/A Fingar described the process of producing NIEs. The national intelligence officer (NIO) in charge of assembling the NIE selects two to five drafters. These drafters are, ostensibly, the most knowledgeable members of the intelligence community concerning the topic under investigation. After a draft of the NIE has been assembled based on the most current reporting and analysis available, it is sent to senior NIC officials for an initial approval. Upon receiving approval (usually after extensive revisions to the draft have been made), the document is sent to other agencies within the intelligence community along with a list of the sources used so that the representatives of these agencies can make their own assessments. The representatives usually respond first with written comments. Later, analysts from these agencies hold "coordination sessions" (dubbed by analysts as "struggle sessions"—borrowing a term from the Chinese Communist Party) wherein the analysts debate alternative interpretations. Third, after holding sufficient coordination sessions, the document returns to NIC officials who, upon approval, then distribute it to members of the National Intelligence Board (NIB)— the heads of the analytical organizations throughout the intelligence community. The members of the NIB discuss the document with their respective staffs before convening a meeting to deliberate and modify its contents and format. At this meeting, according to Fingar, there is an ombudsman who observes whether political considerations are being inappropriately used to interpret intelligence or draft the NIE. Finally, once the NIB approves the NIE, the document is printed, briefed to the president and cabinet members, and later disseminated and/or briefed to members of Congress and other policy makers. According to Fingar, this process usually takes between three months and one year. See Thomas Fingar, *National Intelligence Estimates: A Discussion of Process, Analytics, and Structure* (speech before the New America Foundation, June 5, 2008), http://www.newamerica.net/events/2008/national_intelligence_estimates (accessed December 11, 2010).

88. Glasser, "Probing Galaxies."

89. Wallace-Wells, "Private Jihad."

90. Ibid.

91. Ibid.

92. CENTRA Technology, Inc., *Enhancing DHS Information Support to State and Local Fusion Centers: Results of the Chief Intelligence Officer's Pilot Project and Next Steps*, February 20, 2008, http://www.ohs.ca.gov/pdf/fed_reports/DHSInfoSupporttoStateandLocalFusionCenters_02-20-08.pdf (accessed December 11, 2010).

93. Ibid., 21.

94. Ibid., 22.

95. Ibid.

96. The author obtained a copy of the survey.

97. See Open Source Center, https://www.opensource.gov.

Bibliography

9/11: Press for Truth. DVD. Directed by Ray Nowosielski. Los Angeles, CA: Banded Artists, 2006.

9/11 Public Discourse Project. "Final Report of the 9/11 Public Discourse Project." December 12, 2005. http://www.9/11pdp.org/press/2005-12-05_report.pdf (accessed December 4, 2010).

Abrahamsen, Rita, and Michael C. Williams. "Security beyond the State: Global Security Assemblages in International Politics." *International Political Sociology* 3, no. 1 (2009): 1–17.

Aftergood, Steven. "Open Source Center Views Iraqi Election." *Secrecy News*, February 12, 2009. http://www.fas.org/sgp/news/secrecy/2009/02/021209.html (accessed December 4, 2010).

Aftergood, Steven. "The Race to Fix the Classification System." *Secrecy News*, November 29, 2010. http://www.fas.org/blog/secrecy/2010/11/race_to_fix.html (accessed December 4, 2010).

Aftergood, Steven. "Secrecy and Error Correction in Open Source Intel." *Secrecy News*, August 31, 2009. http://www.fas.org/sgp/news/secrecy/2009/08/083109.html (accessed November 21, 2010).

Alvesson, Mats. "Organizational Culture and Discourse." In *The Sage Handbook of Organizational Discourse,* edited by David Grant, Cynthia Hardy, Cliff Oswick, and Linda Putnam, 317–36. London: Sage, 2004.

Anderson, Nate. "Meet the People Who Want Julian Assange 'Whacked.'" *ars technica,* December 3, 2010. http://arstechnica.com/tech-policy/news/2010/12/meet-the-people-who-want-julian-assange-whacked.ars (accessed December 4, 2010).

Andregg, Michael. "Intelligence Ethics: Laying the Foundation for the Second Oldest Profession." In *Handbook of Intelligence Studies,* edited by Loch K. Johnson, 52–63. New York: Routledge, 2007.

Asen, Robert. "A Discourse Theory of Citizenship." *Quarterly Journal of Speech* 90, no. 2 (2004): 189–211.

Bain, Ben. "Officers to Get Guidelines for Open-Source Intell." *Federal Computer Week,* June 18, 2010. http://fcw.com/Articles/2010/06/18/Web-open-source-intell.aspx (accessed December 2, 2010).

Barker, Chris. *Making Sense of Cultural Studies: Central Problems and Critical Debates.* London: Sage, 2002.

Bean, Hamilton. "Communication and Intelligence: Allies or Enemies?" *International Journal of Intelligence and CounterIntelligence* 22, no. 2 (2009): 360–65.

Bean, Hamilton, and Lisa B. Keränen. "The Role of Homeland Security Information Bulletins within Emergency Management Organizations: A Case Study of Enactment." *Journal of Homeland Security and Emergency Management* 4, no. 2 (2007): Article 6.

Best, Richard A., Jr., and Alfred Cumming. "Open Source Intelligence (OSINT): Issues for Congress." Congressional Research Service, December 5, 2007. http://fas.org/sgp/crs/intel/RL34270.pdf (accessed November 21, 2010).

Bizzell, Patricia, and Bruce Herzberg, ed. *The Rhetorical Tradition: Readings from Classic Times to the Present.* Boston: Bedford/St. Martin's, 2001.

Bohannon, John. "Leaked Documents Provide Bonanza for Researchers." *Science* 330, no. 6004 (2010): 575.

Booth, Ken, ed. *Critical Security Studies and World Politics.* Boulder, CO: Lynne Rienner Publishers, 2005.

Bowen, Wyn Q. "Open Source Intelligence and Nuclear Safeguards." In *Spinning Intelligence: Why Intelligence Needs the Media, Why the Media Needs Intelligence,* edited by Robert Dover and Michael S. Goodman, 91–104. New York: Columbia University Press, 2009.

Bratich, Jack Z. *Conspiracy Panics: Political Rationality and Popular Culture.* Albany: State University of New York Press, 2008.

Breitweiser, Kristen. *Wake-Up Call: The Political Education of a 9/11 Widow.* New York: Warner Books, 2006.

Brewin, Bob. "No More Secrets?" *Government Executive,* September 15, 2008. http://www.govexec.com/dailyfed/0908/091508wb.htm (accessed November 21, 2010).

Burger, Timothy J. "Opening Up the CIA," *Time,* August 7, 2005. http://www.time.com/time/magazine/article/0,9171,1090889,00.html (accessed February 23, 2011).

Bye, Kent. "Can Open Source Intelligence Be a Non-Violent Alternative to War?" December 3, 2005. http://www.echochamberproject.com/node/718 (accessed December 3, 2010).

Bye, Kent. "Interview Audio: Congressman Rob Simmons, Chairman of Homeland Security Intelligence and Information Sharing Subcommittee." January 25, 2006. http://www.echochamberproject.com/simmons (accessed December 2, 2010).

Bye, Kent. "Interview Audio: Eliot Jardines, Assistant Deputy Director of National Intelligence for Open Source." January 25, 2006. http://www.echochamberproject.com/jardines (accessed December 2, 2010).

Campbell, Tony. "Bedmates or Sparring Partners? Canadian Perspectives on the Media-Intelligence Relationship in 'The New Propaganda Age.'" In *Spinning Intelligence: Why Intelligence Needs the Media, Why the Media Needs*

Intelligence, edited by Robert Dover and Michael S. Goodman, 165–84. New York: Columbia University Press, 2009.

Carment, David, and Martin Rudner, ed. *Peacekeeping Intelligence: New Players, Extended Boundaries.* London: Routledge, 2006.

CENTRA Technology, Inc. *Enhancing DHS Information Support to State and Local Fusion Centers: Results of the Chief Intelligence Officer's Pilot Project and Next Steps.* February 20, 2008. http://www.ohs.ca.gov/pdf/fed_reports/DHSI nfoSupporttoStateandLocalFusionCe nters_02-20-08.pdf (accessed December 11, 2010).

Cheney, George, Lars Thøger Christensen, Charles Conrad, and Daniel J. Lair. "Corporate Rhetoric as Organizational Discourse." In *The Sage Handbook of Organizational Discourse,* edited by David Grant, Cynthia Hardy, Cliff Oswick, and Linda Putnam, 79–104 (London: Sage, 2004).

Chilton, Paul A. "The Meaning of Security." In *Post-Realism: The Rhetorical Turn in International Relations,* edited by Francis A. Beer and Robert Hariman, 193–216. East Lansing: Michigan State University Press, 1996.

"CIA Launching 'Open Source' Intel Center." *Fox News,* November 8, 2005. http://www.foxnews.com/story/0,2933,174997,00.html (accessed January 13, 2009).

"CIA Mines 'Rich' Content from Blogs," *Washington Times,* April 18, 2006. http://www.washingtontimes.com/news/2006/apr/18/20060418-110124-3694r (accessed November 21, 2010).

Colby, William. *Honorable Men: My Life in the CIA.* New York: Simon and Schuster, 1978.

Commission on the Intelligence Capabilities of the United States Regarding Weapons of Mass Destruction. *Report to the President.* March 31, 2005. http://govinfo.library.unt.edu/wmd/about.html (accessed November 21, 2010).

Commission on the Roles and Capabilities of the United States Intelligence Community. *Preparing for the 21st Century: An Appraisal of U.S. Intelligence.* March 1, 1996. http://www.gpoaccess.gov/int/index.html (accessed November 30, 2010).

Community Open Source Program Office. *Community Open Source Strategic Plan.* February 1995. http://www.oss.net/dynamaster/file_archive/040320/bc201247d9056a4f07e6f5e72 0be9823/OSS1997-02-34.pdf (accessed December 9, 2010).

Constant, David, Sara Kiesler, and Lee Sproull. "What's Mine Is Ours, Or Is It? A Study of Attitudes about Information Sharing." *Information Systems Research* 5, no. 4 (1994): 400–21.

Cooren, François. "Textual Agency: How Texts Do Things in Organizational Settings." *Organization* 11, no. 3 (2004): 373–94.

Croom, Herman L. "The Exploitation of Foreign Open Sources." *Studies in Intelligence* 13, (Summer 1969): 129–36.

Deetz, Stanley. *Democracy in an Age of Corporate Colonization: Developments in Communication and the Politics of Everyday Life.* Albany: State University of New York Press, 1992.

Deetz, Stanley. "Reclaiming Indeterminacy and the Deliberative Process." Paper presented at the Practical Theory, Public Participation, and Community Workshop, Baylor University, January 27–30, 2000. http://www3.baylor.edu/communication_conference/deetz.pdf (accessed December 8, 2010).

Defense Science Board. *Defense Imperatives for the New Administration.* August 2008. http://www.acq.osd.mil/dsb/reports/ADA489102.pdf (accessed December 3, 2010).

Department of Defense. *Instruction 3115.12.* August 24, 2010. http://www.dtic.mil/whs/directives/corres/pdf/311512p.pdf (accessed December 3, 2010).

DiMaggio, Paul J., and Walter W. Powell. "The Iron Cage Revisited: Institutional Isomorphism and Collective Rationality in Organizational Fields." *American Sociological Review* 48, no. 2 (1983): 147–60.

Director of Central Intelligence. *Directive 2/12, Community Open Source Program.* March 1, 1994. http://www.fas.org/irp/offdocs/dcid212.htm (accessed November 30, 2010).

Drake, William Waldo. "I Don't Think They'd Be Such Damned Fools." In *Air Raid, Pearl Harbor! Recollections of a Day of Infamy,* edited by Paul Stillwell, 269–70. Annapolis, MD: U.S. Naval Institute Press, 1981.

Drake, William Waldo. "*Times*' Man, Gets Assignment with Fleet." *Los Angeles Times,* August 1941.

du Gay, Paul. "Against 'Enterprise' (But Not Against 'Enterprise,' for That Would Make No Sense)." *Organization* 11, no. 1 (2004): 37–58.

du Gay, Paul. *Production of Culture/Cultures of Production.* London: Sage, 1997.

du Gay, Paul. "The Tyranny of the Epochal: Change, Epochalism, and Organizational Reform." *Organization* 10, no. 4 (2003): 663–84.

Eden, Lynn. *Whole World on Fire: Organizations, Knowledge, and Nuclear Weapons Devastation.* Ithaca, NY: Cornell University Press, 2004.

Eggen, Dan, and Spencer S. Hsu. "House Bill Backs Additional Reforms from 9/11 Report." *Washington Post,* January 9, 2007. http://www.washingtonpost.com/wp-dyn/content/article/2007/01/08/AR2007010801623.html (accessed December 3, 2010).

Evangelista, Matthew. *Unarmed Forces: The Transnational Movement to End the Cold War.* Ithaca, NY: Cornell University Press, 2002.

Fairclough, Norman. *Discourse and Social Change.* Cambridge: Polity Press, 1992.

Feenberg, Andrew. *Transforming Technology: A Critical Theory Revisited.* Oxford: Oxford University Press, 2002.

Fillmore, Randolph. "Integrating Open Source Intelligence." August 23, 2005. http://drnatsecmgt.blogspot.com/2005/08/mr-eliot-jardines-of-open-source.html (accessed December 10, 2010).

Fingar, Thomas. *National Intelligence Estimates: A Discussion of Process, Analytics, and Structure.* Speech before the New America Foundation, June 5, 2008. http://www.newamerica.net/events/2008/national_intelligence_estimates (accessed December 11, 2010).

Firestone, David. "Kissinger Pulls Out as Chief of Inquiry into 9/11 Attacks." *New York Times,* December 14, 2002. http://www.nytimes.com/2002/12/14/us/threats-responses-investigation-kissinger-pulls-chief-inquiry-into-9-11-attacks.html?pagewanted=1 (accessed December 4, 2010).

Fleisher, Craig S. "Using Open Source Data in Developing Competitive and Marketing Intelligence." *European Journal of Marketing* 42, no. 7–8 (2008): 852–66.

Frank, Larry J. "The United States Navy v. the *Chicago Tribune.*" *Historian* 42, no. 2 (1980): 284–303.

Furubotn, Eirik G. "The New Institutional Economics and the Theory of the Firm." *Journal of Economic Behavior & Organization* 45, no. 2 (2001): 133–53.

Gannon, John C. "Intelligence Challenges for the Next Generation." Remarks, World Affairs Council, Washington, DC, June 4, 1998. http://www.fas.org/irp/cia/product/ddi_speech_060598.html (accessed November 26, 2010).

Gannon, John C. "NIC Chairman Address to Washington College of Law." Remarks, Washington College of Law, American University, Washington, DC, October 6, 2000. https://www.cia.gov/news-information/speeches-testimony/2000/gannon_speech_10062000.html (accessed December 10, 2010).

Gannon, John C. Written Statement, House Committee on Homeland Security, Subcommittee on Intelligence, Information Sharing, and Terrorism Risk Assessment, *Using Open-Source Information Effectively.* 109th Cong., 1st sess., June 21, 2005. http://www.fas.org/irp/congress/2005_hr/062105gannon.pdf (accessed December 2, 2010).

Garud, Raghu, Cynthia Hardy, and Steve Maguire. "Institutional Entrepreneurship as Embedded Agency: An Introduction to the Special Issue." *Organization Studies* 28, no. 7 (2007): 957–70.

Gerber, Brian J., et al. "On the Front Line: American Cities and the Challenge of Homeland Security Preparedness." *Urban Affairs Review* 41, no. 2 (2005): 182–210.

Gibson, Stevyn. "Open Source Intelligence: An Intelligence Lifeline." *RUSI Journal* 149, no. 1 (2004): 16–22.

Gill, Peter, and Mark Phythian. *Intelligence in an Insecure World.* Cambridge: Polity Press, 2006.

Glasser, Susan B. "Probing Galaxies of Data for Nuggets." *Washington Post,* November 25, 2005, A35.

Goodall Jr., H. L. "Why We Must Win the War on Terror: Communication, Narrative, and the Future of National Security." *Qualitative Inquiry* 12, no. 1 (2006): 30–59.

Goodman, Michael. "British Intelligence and the British Broadcasting Corporation: A Snapshot of a Happy Marriage." In *Spinning Intelligence, Why Intelligence Needs the Media, Why the Media Needs Intelligence,* edited by Robert Dover and Michael Goodman, 117–32. New York: Columbia University Press, 2009.

Goodnight, G. Thomas. "Strategic Doctrine, Public Debate and the Terror War." In *Hitting First: Preventive Force in U.S. Security Strategy,* edited by W. W. Keller and G. R. Mitchell, 93–114. Pittsburgh, PA: University of Pittsburgh Press, 2006.

Grant, David, Cynthia Hardy, Cliff Oswick, and Linda Putnam, ed. *The Sage Handbook of Organizational Discourse.* London: Sage, 2004.

Grey, Christopher. "Security Studies and Organization Studies: Parallels and Possibilities." *Organization* 16, no. 2 (2009): 303–16.

Grier, Peter, and Faye Bowers. "Failure of 'Imagination' Led to 9/11." *Christian Science Monitor,* July 23, 2004. http://www.csmonitor.com/2004/0723/p01s03-uspo.html (accessed December 3, 2010).

Hansen, Lene. *Security as Practice: Discourse Analysis and the Bosnian War.* New York: Routledge, 2006.

Hardy, Cynthia. "How Institutions Communicate; or How Does Communicating Institutionalize?" *Management Communication Quarterly* 25, no. 1 (2011): 191–99.

Hardy, Cynthia. "Scaling Up and Bearing Down in Discourse Analysis: Questions Regarding Textual Agencies and Their Context." *Organization* 11, no. 3 (2004): 415–25.

Hardy, Cynthia, Ian Palmer, and Nelson Phillips. "Discourse as a Strategic Resource." *Human Relations* 53, no. 9 (2000): 1227–48.

Harris, Shane. "Intelligence Incorporated." *Government Executive*, May 15, 2005, 40–47.

Harris, Shane. "Intelligence Shop." *Government Executive*, May 1, 2005. http://www.govexec.com/features/0505-01/0505-01na3.htm (accessed August 4, 2008).

Harsch, Joseph C. *At the Hinge of History: A Reporter's Story.* Athens: University of Georgia Press, 1993.

Hartnett, Stephen J., and Jennifer R. Mercieca. "'Has Your Courage Rusted?': National Security and the Contested Rhetorical Norms of Republicanism in Post-Revolutionary America, 1798–1801." *Rhetoric & Public Affairs* 9, no. 1 (2006): 79–112.

Hartnett, Stephen J., and Laura A. Stengrim. *Globalization and Empire: The U.S. Invasion of Iraq, Free Markets, and the Twilight of Democracy.* Tuscaloosa: University of Alabama Press, 2005.

Hastedt, Glenn. "Intelligence Estimates: NIEs vs. the Open Press in the 1958 China Straits Crisis." *International Journal of Intelligence and CounterIntelligence* 23, no. 1 (2010): 104–32.

Heuer, Richards J., Jr. *Psychology of Intelligence Analysis.* 1999. https://www.cia.gov/library/center-for-the-study-of-intelligence/csi-publications/books-and-monographs/psychology-of-intelligence-analysis/index.html (accessed December 11, 2010).

Hitchens, Christopher. *The Trial of Henry Kissinger.* London: Verso, 2001.

Hoffman, Bruce, and Anna-Brit Kasupski. *The Victims of Terrorism: An Assessment of Their Influence and Growing Role in Policy, Legislation, and the Private Sector* (Santa Monica, CA: RAND, 2007).

Holden-Rhodes, J. F. *Sharing the Secrets: Open Source Intelligence and the War on Drugs.* Albuquerque, NM: The University of New Mexico Printing Services, 1994.

House Permanent Select Committee on Intelligence and the Senate Select Committee on Intelligence. *Report of the Joint Inquiry into the Terrorist Attacks of September 11.* Washington, DC: GPO, 2002.

Hulnick, Arthur S. "The Downside of Open Source Intelligence." *International Journal of Intelligence and CounterIntelligence* 15, no. 4 (2002): 565–79.

Hulnick, Arthur S. "Intelligence Reform 2008: Where to from Here?" *International Journal of Intelligence and CounterIntelligence* 21, no. 4 (2008): 621–34.

Hulnick, Arthur S. "OSINT: Is It Really Intelligence?" Paper presented at the annual convention of the American Political Science Association, Boston, MA, August 2008. http://www.allacademic.com//meta/p_mla_apa_research_citation/2/8/1/2/1/pages2 81211/p281211-1.php (accessed November 30, 2010).

Ilardi, Gaetano J. "The 9/11 Attacks—A Study of Al Qaeda's Use of Intelligence and Counterintelligence." *Studies in Conflict & Terrorism* 32, no. 3 (2009): 171–87.

"In Obama White House, New Rules on Day One." *U.S. News & World Report,* January 22, 2009. http://www.usnews.com/articles/news/washington-whispers/2009/01/22/in-obama-white-house-new-rules-on-day-one.html (accessed March 2, 2009).

Information Sharing Environment. *Annual Report to the Congress.* July 2010. http://www.ise.gov/docs/ISE_AR-2010_Final_2010-07-29.pdf (accessed December 5, 2010).

Information Sharing Environment. *ISE Implementation Plan.* 2006. http://www.ise.gov (accessed November 12, 2008).

Infosphere AB. "Restricted OSINT (Open Source Intelligence) Collection Makes What?" http://www.infosphere.se/extra/pod/?id=177&module_instance=1&action=pod_s how (accessed December 11, 2010).

"Inside the Iran NIE." *MSNBC,* December 6, 2007. http://www.msnbc.msn.com/id/22117095 (accessed November 21, 2010).

The Intelligence Reform and Terrorism Prevention Act of 2004. Public Law 108–458. http://www.nctc.gov/docs/pl108_458.pdf (accessed December 3, 2010).

Ivie, Robert L. *Democracy and America's War on Terror.* Tuscaloosa: University of Alabama Press, 2005.

Jacobsen, Kurt. "Interview with Daniel Ellsberg." *Logos* 1, no. 4 (2002): 85–98.

Jardines, Eliot A. Written Testimony, House Committee on Homeland Security, Subcommittee on Intelligence, Information Sharing, and Terrorism Risk Assessment, *Using Open-Source Information Effectively.* 109th Cong., 1st sess., June 21, 2005. http://www.fas.org/irp/congress/2005_hr/062105jardines.pdf (accessed December 2, 2010).

Johnson, Loch K. "Glimpses into the Gems of American Intelligence: The President's Daily Brief and the National Intelligence Estimate." *Intelligence and National Security* 23, no. 3 (2008): 333–70.

Johnson, Loch K. ed. *Handbook of Intelligence Studies.* New York: Routledge, 2007.

Johnston, Rob. *Analytical Culture in the U.S. Intelligence Community: An Ethnographic Study.* Washington, DC: Center for the Study of Intelligence, 2004.

Jones, Calvert. "Intelligence Reform: The Logic of Information Sharing." *Intelligence & National Security* 22, no. 3 (2007): 384–401.

Kean, Thomas, and Lee Hamilton. *Without Precedent: The Inside Story of the 9/11 Commission.* New York: Alfred A. Knopf, 2006.

Keck, Margaret E., and Kathryn Sikkink. *Activists Beyond Borders: Advocacy Networks in International Politics.* Ithaca, NY: Cornell University Press, 1998.

Keller, William W., and Gordon R. Mitchell, ed. *Hitting First: Preventative Force in U.S. Security Strategy.* Pittsburgh: University of Pittsburgh Press, 2006.

Keyton, Joann. *Communication and Organizational Culture: A Key to Understanding Work Experiences.* Thousand Oaks, CA: Sage, 2005.

Kingsbury, Alex. "Spy Agencies Turn to Newspapers, NPR, and Wikipedia for Information: The Intelligence Community is Learning to Value 'Open-Source' Information." *U.S. News & World Report,* September 12, 2008. http://www.usnews.com/articles/news/national/2008/09/12/spy-agencies-turn-to-newspapers-npr-and-wikipedia-for-information.html (accessed April 23, 2009).

Kondra, Alex Z., and Deborah C. Hurst. "Institutional Processes of Organizational Culture." *Culture and Organization* 15, no. 1 (2009): 39–58.

Kuhn, Timothy. "A Communicative Theory of the Firm: Developing an Alternative Perspective on Intra-Organizational Power and Stakeholder Relationships." *Organization Studies* 29, no. 8–9 (2008): 1227–54.

Kuhn, Timothy. "A 'Demented Work Ethic' and a 'Lifestyle Firm': Discourse, Identity, and Workplace Time Commitments." *Organization Studies* 27, no. 9 (2006): 1339–58.

Kuhn, Timothy. "The Discourse of Issues Management: A Genre of Organizational Communication." *Communication Quarterly* 45, no. 3 (1997): 188–210.

Lahneman, William J. "Outsourcing the IC's Stovepipes." *International Journal of Intelligence and CounterIntelligence* 16, no. 4 (2003): 573–93.

Lammers, John C., and Joshua B. Barbour. "An Institutional Theory of Organizational Communication." *Communication Theory* 16, no. 3 (2006): 356–77.

Lathrop, Charles E. *The Literary Spy: The Ultimate Source for Quotations on Espionage and Intelligence.* New Haven, CT: Yale University Press, 2004.

Lawrence, Thomas B., and Roy Suddaby. "Institutions and Institutional Work." In *The Sage Handbook of Organization Studies,* edited by Stewart R. Clegg, Cynthia Hardy, Thomas B. Lawrence, and Walter R. Nord, 215–45. 2nd ed. London: Sage, 2006.

Leetaru, Kalev. "The Scope of FBIS and BBC Open-Source Media Coverage, 1979–2008." *Studies in Intelligence* 54, no. 1 (2010): 17–37.

LexisNexis Open Source Intelligence Roundtable. "OSINT 2020: The Future of Open Source Intelligence." June 17, 2010. http://www.dni.gov/speeches/Speech_OSINT_Roundtable_20100617.pdf (accessed December 3, 2010).

Lindlof, Thomas R., and Bryan C. Taylor, ed. *Qualitative Communication Research Methods.* 2nd ed. Thousand Oaks, CA: Sage 2002.

Loureiro, Pedro A. "U.S. Counterintelligence against Japan in Southern California, 1933–1941." PhD dissertation, San Diego State University, 1987.

Lowenthal, Mark M. *Intelligence: From Secrets to Policy.* 3rd ed. Washington, DC: CQ Press, 2006.

Lowenthal, Mark M. "Open Source Intelligence: New Myths, New Realities." *Intelligencer* 10, no. 1 (1999). http://www.oss.net/dynamaster/file_archive/040319/ ... /OSS1999-P1-08.pdf (accessed November 30, 2010).

Lowenthal, Mark M. "Towards a Reasonable Standard for Analysis: How Right, How Often on Which Issues?" *Intelligence and National Security* 23, no. 3 (2008): 303–15.

Lown, Bernard. *Prescription for Survival: A Doctor's Journey to End Nuclear Madness.* San Francisco: Berrett-Koehler Publishers, 2008.

Lundberg, Kristen. "Piloting a Bi-Partisan Ship: Strategies and Tactics of the 9/11 Commission." Kennedy School of Government Case Program, C15–05–1813.0. Cambridge, MA: President and Fellows of Harvard College, 2005.

Maguire, Steve, Cynthia Hardy, and Thomas B. Lawrence. "Institutional Entrepreneurship in Emerging Fields: HIV/ AIDS Treatment Advocacy in Canada." *Academy of Management Journal* 47, no. 5 (2004): 657–80.

Major, James S. *Communicating with Intelligence: Writing and Briefing in the Intelligence and National Security Communities.* Lanham, MD: Scarecrow Press, 2008.

Marchetti, Victor, and John D. Marks. *The CIA and the Cult of Intelligence.* New York: Dell Publishing, 1974.

Marcus, Alan I. " 'Would You Like Fries with That, Sir?' The Evolution of Management Theories and the Rise and Fall of Total Quality Management within the American Federal Government." *Management & Organizational History* 3, no. 3–4 (2008): 311–38.

Marks, Ronald. "Twittering Intelligence." Open Source Intelligence Forum, February 2009. http://www.osif.us/articlesofinterest.html (accessed November 21, 2010).

Marsh, Pearl-Alice. "Grassroots Statecraft and Citizens' Challenges to U.S. National Security Policy." In *On Security,* edited by Ronnie D. Lipschutz, 124–48. New York: Columbia University Press, 1995.

Martin, Alex, and Peter Wilson. "The Value of Non-Governmental Intelligence: Widening the Field." *Intelligence and National Security* 23, no. 6 (2008): 767–76.

Martin, David. "Secret Information in Plain Sight." *CBS News,* January 10, 2006. http://www.cbsnews.com/stories/2006/01/10/eveningnews/main 1198667.shtml (accessed May 8, 2009).

Martin, Joanne. *Organizational Culture: Mapping the Terrain.* Thousand Oaks, CA: Sage. 2002.

Martin, Joanne, Peter Frost, and Olivia O'Neill. "Organizational Culture: Beyond Struggles for Intellectual Dominance." In *The Sage Handbook of Organization Studies,* edited by Stewart R. Clegg, Cynthia Hardy, Thomas B. Lawrence, and Walter R. Nord, 725–53. 2nd ed. London: Sage, 2006.

Martin, Lauren, and Stephanie Simon. "A Formula for Disaster: The Department of Homeland Security's Virtual Ontology," *Space and Polity* 12, no. 3 (2008): 281–96.

Mercado, Stephen C. "FBIS against the Axis, 1941–1945: Open-Source Intelligence from the Airwaves." *Studies in Intelligence* 11 (Fall–Winter 2001). https://www.cia.gov/library/center-for-the-study-of-intelligence/sci-publications/csi-studies/fall_winter-2001/article04.html (accessed November 29, 2010).

Mercado, Stephen C. "Reexamining the Distinction between Open Information and Secrets. *Studies in Intelligence* 49, no. 2 (2005). https://www.cia.gov/library/center-for-the-study-of-intelligence/csi-publications/csi-studies/studies/Vol49no2/reexamining_the_distinction_3.htm (accessed December 8, 2010).

Mercado, Stephen C. "Sailing the Sea of OSINT in the Information Age." *Studies in Intelligence* 48, no. 3 (2004). https://www.cia.gov/library/center-for-the-study-of-intelligence/csi-publications/csi-studies/studies/vol48no3/article05.html (accessed December 8, 2010).

Mercieca, Jennifer R., and James A. Aune. "A Vernacular Republican Rhetoric: William Manning's Key of Libberty." *Quarterly Journal of Speech* 91, no. 2 (2005): 119–43.

Meyer, John W., and Brian Rowan. "Institutional Organizations: Formal Structure as Myth and Ceremony." *American Journal of Sociology* 83, no. 2 (1977): 340–63.

Milliken, Jennifer. "The Study of Discourse in International Relations: A Critique of Research and Methods." *European Journal of International Relations* 5, no. 2 (1999): 225–54.

Mitchell, Gordon R. "Team B Intelligence Coups." *Quarterly Journal of Speech* 92, no. 2 (2006): 144–73.

Mitchell, Melanthia. "'Net Sleuth' Tells Court of Hunt That Snared Guardsman." *USA Today*, May 15, 2004. http://www.usatoday.com/tech/webguide/internetlife/2004-05-13-netsleuth_x.htm (accessed December 4, 2010).

Nadel, Alan. *Containment Culture: American Narratives, Postmodernism, and the Atomic Age.* Durham, NC: Duke University Press, 1995.

Naquin, Doug. "Remarks by Doug Naquin, CIRA Luncheon, 3 October 2007." *CIRA Newsletter* 32, no. 4 (2007): 3–9. http://www.fas.org/irp/eprint/naquin.pdf (accessed December 2, 2010).

National Commission on Terrorist Attacks upon the United States. *The 9/11 Commission Report.* July 22, 2004. http://www.9-11commission.gov (accessed December 2, 2010).

National Defense Authorization Act for Fiscal Year 2006. Public Law 109–163. http://www.dod.gov/dodgc/olc/docs/PL109-163.pdf (accessed December 2, 2010).

National Intelligence Council. *National Intelligence Estimate, Iran: Nuclear Intentions and Capabilities.* November 2007. http://www.dni.gov/press_releases/20071203_release.pdf (accessed December 5, 2010).

National Intelligence Council. *Open Source Task Force: A Vision for the Future.* January 13, 1992. http://www.oss.net (accessed November 30, 2010).

National Open Source Committee. *National Open Source Strategic Action Plan.* 2009. http://www.fas.org/irp/dni/osc/nossap.pdf (accessed December 3, 2010).

National Strategy for Information Sharing. 2007. http://georgewbush-whitehouse.archives.gov/nsc/infosharing/NSIS_book.pdf (accessed December 5, 2010).

NATO. *Open Source Intelligence Handbook.* November 2001. http://en.wikipedia.org/wiki/NATO_Open_Source_Intelligence_Handbook (accessed December 2, 2010).

Newman, Robert P. "Communication Pathologies of Intelligence Systems." *Speech Monographs* 42 (November 1975): 271–90.

Nolte, William. "Thinking about Rethinking: Reform in Other Professions." *Studies in Intelligence* 52, no. 2 (2008): 19–25.

Noon, David H. "Operation Enduring Analogy: World War II, the War on Terror, and the Uses of Historical Memory." *Rhetoric & Public Affairs* 7, no. 3 (2004): 339–64.

Office of the Director of National Intelligence. *Annual Threat Assessment of the Intelligence Community for the House Permanent Select Committee on Intelligence.* February 7, 2008. http://www.dni.gov/testimonies/20080207_testimony.pdf (accessed December 10, 2010).

Office of the Director of National Intelligence. *Intelligence Community Directive 301, National Open Source Enterprise.* July 11, 2006. http://www.fas.org/irp/dni/icd/icd-301.pdf (accessed December 2, 2010).

Office of the Director of National Intelligence. *Key Facts about Contractors.* 2010. http://www.dni.gov/content/Truth_About_Contractors.pdf (accessed November 21, 2010).

Office of the Director of National Intelligence. *National Intelligence: A Consumer's Guide.* 2009. http://www.dni.gov/reports/IC_Consumers_Guide_2009.pdf (accessed November 21, 2010).

Office of the Director of National Intelligence. *National Open Source Enterprise.* 2006. http://en.wikipedia.org/wiki/National_Open_Source_Enterprise (accessed December 10, 2007).

Office of the Director of National Intelligence. "Remarks and Q&A by Director of National Intelligence Mr. James Clapper, Bipartisan Policy Center (BPC)—The State of Domestic Intelligence Reform." October 6, 2010. http://www.dni. gov/speeches/20101006_speech_clapper.pdf (accessed December 4, 2010).

Office of the Director of National Intelligence. Transcripts from the DNI Open Source Conference 2008, Washington, DC, September 11–12, 2008. http:// www.dni.gov/speeches/20080912_speech.pdf (accessed March 6, 2009).

Office of the Director of National Intelligence. *United States Intelligence Community 500 Day Plan Integration and Collaboration.* 2007. http://www.dni.gov/500-day-plan.pdf (accessed November 26, 2010).

Open Source Center. *Briefing for the UCGIS Winter Meeting 2008.* February 7, 2008. http://www.ucgis.org/winter2008/presentations/Robson.pdf (accessed November 21, 2010).

Peak, Douglas. "The Open Source Academy Helps the Intelligence Community Make the Most of Open Sources." *Military Intelligence Professional Bulletin,* October–December 2005. http://findarticles.com/p/articles/mi_m0IBS/is_4_31/ai_n16419802 (accessed December 11, 2010).

Peiss, Kathy. "Cultural Policy in a Time of War: The American Response to Endangered Books in World War II." *Library Trends* 55, no. 3 (2007): 370–86.

"Pentagon Prepares for Largest Security Breach in U.S Military History as Wikileaks Set to Release 500,000 Iraq Documents," *Mail Online,* October 18, 2010. http://www.dailymail.co.uk/news/article-1321398/WikiLeaks-release-500k-Iraq-documents-US-militarys-largest-security-breach.html (accessed December 4, 2010).

Perkmann, Markus, and André Spicer. "How Are Management Fashions Institutionalized? The Role of Institutional Work." *Human Relations* 61, no. 6 (2008): 811–44.

Pfaff, Tony. "Bungee Jumping Off the Moral Highground: Ethics of Espionage in the Modern Age." In *Ethics of Spying: A Reader for the Intelligence Professional,* edited by Jan Goldman, 66–103. Lanham, MD: Scarecrow Press, 2006.

Phillips, Nelson, and Cynthia Hardy. *Discourse Analysis: Investigating Processes of Social Construction.* Thousand Oaks, CA: Sage, 2002.

Phillips, Nelson, and Namrata Malhotra. "Taking Social Construction Seriously: Extending the Discursive Approach in Institutional Theory." In *The Sage Handbook of Organizational Institutionalism,* edited by Royston Greenwood, Christine Oliver, Kerstin Sahlin, and Roy Suddaby, 702–20. London: Sage, 2008.

Phillips, Nelson, Thomas B. Lawrence, and Cynthia Hardy. "Discourse and Institutions." *Academy of Management Review* 29, no. 4 (2004): 635–52.

Platje, Wies, Dame Pauline Neville-Jones, Ben de Jong, and Robert David Steele. *Peacekeeping Intelligence: Emerging Concepts for the Future.* Oakton, VA: OSS International Press, 2003.

Potter, E. B. *Nimitz.* Annapolis, MD: U.S. Naval Institute Press, 1976.

Poulsen, Kevin, and Kim Zetter. "'I Can't Believe What I'm Confessing to You': The Wikileaks Chats." *Wired,* June 10, 2010. http://www.wired.com/threatlevel/2010/06/wikileaks-chat (accessed December 4, 2010).

Priest, Dana, and William M. Arkin. "Top Secret America." *Washington Post*, July 19, 2010. http://projects.washingtonpost.com/top-secret-america (accessed November 21, 2010).

Pringle, Robert W. "The Limits of OSINT: Diagnosing the Soviet Media, 1985–1989." *International Journal of Intelligence and CounterIntelligence* 16, no. 2 (2003): 280–89.

ProMED. *The 2003 ProMED-Mail Award for Excellence in Outbreak Reporting on the Internet.* http://apex.oracle.com/pls/otn/wwv_flow.accept (accessed August 3, 2008).

Putnam, Linda L., and Michael E. Pacanowsky, ed. *Communication and Organizations: An Interpretive Approach.* Beverly Hills, CA: Sage, 1983.

Randol, Mark A. "Homeland Security Intelligence: Perceptions, Statutory Definitions, and Approaches." Congressional Research Service, January 14, 2009. http://www.fas.org/sgp/crs/intel/RL33616.pdf (accessed December 3, 2010).

Raymond, Matt. "Why the Library of Congress Is Blocking Wikileaks." December 3, 2010. http://blogs.loc.gov/loc/2010/12/why-the-library-of-congress-is-blocking-wikileaks (accessed December 4, 2010).

Remarks and Q&A by the assistant deputy director of national intelligence for open source, Eliot A. Jardines. DNI Open Source Conference, Washington, DC, July 16, 2007. http://www.dni.gov/speeches/20070716_speech_3.pdf (accessed August 15, 2007).

Remarks and Q&A by the deputy director of national intelligence for analysis and chairman, National Intelligence Council, Thomas Fingar. 2008 INSA Analytic Transformation Conference, Orlando, FL, September 4, 2008. http://www.dni.gov/speeches/20080904_speech.pdf (accessed December 11, 2010).

Remarks and Q&A by the deputy director of national intelligence for analysis, Thomas Fingar. DNI Open Source Conference, Washington, DC, July 16, 2007. http://www.dni.gov/speeches/20070717_speech_3.pdf (accessed August 1, 2008).

Remarks and Q&A by the deputy director of national intelligence for collection, Mary Margaret Graham. DNI Open Source Conference, Washington, DC, July 17, 2007. http://www.dni.gov/speeches/20070717_speech_2.pdf (accessed August 3, 2008).

Remarks and Q&A by the director of the Central Intelligence Agency, Michael V. Hayden. DNI Open Source Conference, Washington, DC, September 12, 2008. http://cryptome.org/cia-openspy.pdf (accessed March 1, 2009).

Remarks by the assistant to the president for homeland security and counterterrorism, Frances Fragos Townsend. DNI Open Source Conference, Washington, DC, July 16, 2007. http://www.dni.gov (accessed August 3, 2008).

Right to Know Community. *Moving Toward a 21st Century Right-to-Know Agenda: Recommendations to President-Elect Obama and Congress.* November 2008. http://freegovinfo.info/node/2119 (accessed December 4, 2010).

Rollins, John. "Fusion Centers: Issues and Options for Congress." Congressional Research Service, January 18, 2008. http://www.csmweb.com/Library%20Documents/RL34070.pdf (accessed August 4, 2008).

Roop, Joseph E. "Foreign Broadcast Information Service History Part 1: 1941–1947." Central Intelligence Agency, April 1969. http://www.foia.cia.gov/txt/FBIS_history_part1.pdf (accessed November 30, 2010).

Ross, Andrew. "Containing Culture in the Cold War." *Cultural Studies* 1, no. 3 (1987): 328–48.

Saunders, Kimberly. "Open Source Information: A True Collection Discipline." Master's thesis, Royal Military College of Canada, 2000.

Schiappa, Edward. *Defining Reality: Definitions and the Politics of Meaning.* Carbondale: Southern Illinois University Press, 2003.

Sciolino, Elaine. "C.I.A. Casting About for New Missions." *New York Times,* February 4, 1992, A1.

Scott, W. Richard. *Institutions and Organizations.* Thousand Oaks, CA: Sage, 1995.

Sellnow, Timothy L., Mathew W. Seeger, and Robert R. Ulmer. "Chaos Theory, Informational Needs, and Natural Disasters." *Journal of Applied Communication Research* 30, no. 4 (2002): 269–92.

Semple, Lorenzo, Jr. *Three Days of the Condor.* Motion Picture. Directed by Sydney Pollack. United States: Paramount Pictures, 1975.

Shachtman, Noah. "How to Restore Spies Credibility: Go Open Source." *Wired,* December 14, 2007. http://www.wired.com/dangerroom/2007/12/how-to-restore (accessed November 30, 2010).

Shaffer, Anthony. *Operation Dark Heart: Spycraft and Special Ops on the Frontlines of Afghanistan—and the Path to Victory.* New York: Thomas Dunne Books, 2010.

Shenon, Philip. *The Commission: The Uncensored History of the 9/11 Investigation.* New York: Twelve, 2008.

Shorrock, Tim. *Spies for Hire: The Secret World of Intelligence Outsourcing.* New York: Simon & Schuster, 2008.

Simmons, Robert M. "Open Source Intelligence: An Examination of Its Exploitation in the Defense Intelligence Community." Master's thesis, Joint Military Intelligence College, 1995. http://www.phibetaiota.net/1995/08/history-1995-simmons-open-source-intelligence-an-examination-of-its-exploitation-in-the-defense-intelligence-community (accessed December 1, 2010).

Simon, Jonathan. "Parrhesiastic Accountability: Investigatory Commissions and Executive Power in an Age of Terror." *Yale Law Journal* 14 (2005): 1419–57.

Simpson, Mary, and George Cheney. "Marketization, Participation, and Communication within New Zealand Retirement Villages: A Critical-Rhetorical and Discursive Analysis." *Discourse and Communication* 1, no. 2 (2007): 191–222.

Smircich, Linda. "Concepts of Culture and Organizational Analysis." *Administrative Science Quarterly* 28, no. 3 (1983): 339–58.

Spaulding, Suzanne E. "No More Secrets: Then What?" *Huffington Post,* June 24, 2010. http://www.huffingtonpost.com/suzanne-e-spaulding/no-more-secrets-then-what_b_623997.html (accessed November 21, 2010).

Steele, Robert David. "Fixing the White House and National Intelligence." *International Journal of Intelligence and CounterIntelligence* 23, no. 2 (2010): 353–73.

Steele, Robert David. *Information Operations: All Information, All Languages, All the Time.* Oakton, VA: OSS International Press, 2006.

Steele, Robert David. "The Open Source Program: Missing in Action." *International Journal of Intelligence and CounterIntelligence* 21, no. 3 (2008): 609–19.

Steele, Robert David. "Steele Interview for Military Review." April 16, 2006. http://www.oss.net/dynamaster/file_archive/060417/d0a6e5b9746c0c07 eddbde66 2982b66c/Interview on Academics et al with intelligence 1.1.doc (accessed December 3, 2010).

Steele, Robert David. "United States Marine Corps Comments on Joint Open Source Task Force Report and Recommendations." January 6, 1992. http://www.oss.net/dynamaster/file_archive/060324/9906ba66ee5fe750bb8f e5712 b1e20e7/92 Jan 11 Steele on IC OSINT.pdf (accessed November 30, 2010).

Stiglitz, Joseph E. "On Liberty, the Right to Know, and Public Discourse: The Role of Transparency in Public Life." In *Government Secrecy: Classic and Contemporary Readings,* edited by Susan L. Maret and Jan Goldman, 697–717 (Westport, CT: Libraries Unlimited, 2009).

Strohm, Chris. "Lawmaker Calls for CIA Center to Become Independent Agency." *Government Executive,* June 7, 2006. http://www.govexec.com/dailyfed/0606/060706tdpm1.htm (accessed December 1, 2010).

Stromer-Galley, Jennifer, and Edward Schiappa. "The Argumentative Burdens of Audience Conjectures: Audience Research in Popular Culture Criticism." *Communication Theory* 8, no. 1 (1998): 27–62.

Suchman, Mark C. "Managing Legitimacy: Strategic and Institutional Approaches." *Academy of Management Review* 20, no. 3 (1995): 571–610.

Suddaby, Roy, and Royston Greenwood. "Rhetorical Strategies of Legitimacy." *Administrative Science Quarterly* 50, no. 1 (2005): 35–67.

Symon, Gillian. "Developing the Political Perspective on Technological Change through Rhetorical Analysis." *Management Communication Quarterly* 22, no. 1 (2008): 74–98.

Taylor, Bryan C. "'Our Bruised Arms Hung Up as Monuments': Nuclear Iconography in Post–Cold War Culture." *Critical Studies in Media Communication* 20, no. 1 (2003): 1–34.

Taylor, Bryan C. "Review of *The Boundaries of the New Frontier: Rhetoric and Communication at Fermi National Accelerator Laboratory*, by Joanna S. Ploeger." *Rhetoric & Public Affairs* 41, no. 1 (2011): 14–16.

Taylor, Bryan C., William J. Kinsella, Stephen P. Depoe, and Maribeth S. Metzler, ed. *Nuclear Legacies: Communication, Controversy, and the U.S. Nuclear Weapons Complex.* Lanham, MD: Lexington Books, 2007.

Terkel, Amanda. "Cheney Offers False Excuse for His 'So?' Comment: I Meant, 'What's the Question, Martha?'" *Think Progress,* June 2, 2008. http://thinkprogress.org/2008/06/02/cheney-so-revise (accessed December 4, 2010).

Tovey, Mark, ed. *Collective Intelligence: Creating a Prosperous World at Peace.* Oakton, VA: Earth Intelligence Network, 2008.

Treverton, Gregory F. *The Next Steps in Reshaping Intelligence.* Santa Monica, CA: RAND, 2005.

Trujillo, Nick, and George Dionisopoulos. "Cop Talk, Police Stories, and the Social Construction of Organizational Drama." *Central States Speech Journal* 38, no. 3–4 (1987): 196–209.

U.S. Congress. House of Representatives. Committee on Homeland Security, Subcommittee on Intelligence, Information Sharing, and Terrorism Risk Assessment. *Moving Beyond the First Five Years: Evolving the Office of Intelligence and Analysis to Better Serve State, Local, and Tribal Needs.* 110th Cong., 2nd sess., April 24, 2008. http://www.fas.org/irp/congress/2008_hr/oia.html (accessed November 21, 2010).

U.S. Congress. House of Representatives. Committee on Homeland Security, Subcommittee on Intelligence, Information Sharing, and Terrorism Risk Assessment. *Using Open-Source Information Effectively.* 109th Cong., 1st sess., June 21, 2005. http://www.fas.org/irp/congress/2005_hr/opensource.pdf (accessed November 21, 2010).

U.S. Congress. House of Representatives. Permanent Select Committee on Intelligence. National Security Act of 1992, H.R. 4165. 102nd Cong. 2nd sess., March 4 and 11, 1992.

U.S. Department of Homeland Security. *2008 Strategic Plan.* http://www.dhs.gov/xabout/strategicplan (accessed December 3, 2010).

U.S. Department of Homeland Security. *Intelligence Enterprise Strategic Plan.* January 2006. http://www.fas.org/irp/agency/dhs/stratplan.pdf (accessed December 5, 2010).

U.S. Department of Homeland Security. *Report to Congress on Implementation of Section 705 of the Homeland Security Act and the Establishment of the Office for Civil Rights and Civil Liberties.* 2004. http://www.dhs.gov/xlibrary/assets/CRCL-ReportJun04.pdf (accessed December 3, 2010).

U.S. House of Representatives, Homeland Security Committee. *Giving a Voice to Open Source Stakeholders: A Survey of State, Local, and Tribal Law Enforcement.* September 2008. http://homeland.house.gov/SiteDocuments/OpenSourceReport.pdf (accessed December 3, 2010).

Van Atta, Lee. "L.A. Ship News Reporter Now Official Eyes, Ears of U.S. Fleet." *Los Angeles Times,* August 1, 1941.

Wait, Patience. "Intelligence Units Mine the Benefits of Public Sources: Open Source Center Draws, Analyzes Info from a Variety of Public Databases." *Government Computer News,* March 20, 2006. http://www.gcn.com/print/25_6/40152-1.html (accessed November 21, 2010).

Wallace-Wells, Benjamin. "Private Jihad: How Rita Katz Got into the Spying Business." *New Yorker,* May 29, 2006. http://www.newyorker.com/archive/2006/05/29/060529fa_fact (accessed December 9, 2010).

Wallner, Paul F. "Open Sources and the Intelligence Community: Myths and Realities." *American Intelligence Journal* (Spring/Summer 1993): 19–24.

Warner, Michael. "Reading the Riot Act: The Schlesinger Report, 1971." *Intelligence and National Security* 24, no. 3 (2009): 387–417.

Warrick, Joby. "Leak Severed a Link to Al-Qaeda's Secrets: Firm Says Administration's Handling of Video Ruined Its Spying Efforts." *Washington Post,* October 9, 2007, A1.

Weick, Karl E., Kathleen E. Sutcliffe, and David Obstfeld. "Organizing and the Process of Sensemaking." *Organization Science* 16, no. 4 (2005): 409–21.

Wettering, Frederick L. "OSINT's Primary Advocate." Review of *The New Craft of Intelligence: Personal, Public, and Political* by Robert David Steele. *International Journal of Intelligence and CounterIntelligence* 16, no. 3 (2003): 506–10.

Williams Jody, Stephen D. Goose, and Mary Wareham. *Banning Landmines: Disarmament, Citizen Diplomacy, and Human Security.* Lanham, MD: Rowman and Littlefield, 2008.

Wirtz, James J. "The American Approach to Intelligence Studies." In *Handbook of Intelligence Studies,* edited by Loch. K. Johnson, 28–38. New York: Routledge, 2007.

Wolfers, Arnold. "'National Security' as an Ambiguous Symbol." *Political Science Quarterly* 67, no. 4 (1952): 481–502.

Yeager, Robert C. "To Catch a Terrorist: One Mother's Crusade." *Family Circle,* July 15, 2005. http://www.shannenrossmiller.com/media/hpsc2168.pdf (accessed December 4, 2010).

Zaworski, Martin J. "Automated Information Sharing: Does It Help Law Enforcement Officers Work Better?" *National Institute of Justice Journal* 253 (2006): 25–26.

Zegart, Amy B. *Spying Blind: The CIA, the FBI, and the Origins of 9/11.* Princeton, NJ: Princeton University Press, 2007.

Zuboff, Shoshana. *In the Age of the Smart Machine: The Future of Work and Power.* New York: Basic Books, 1988.

Index

About the Author

HAMILTON BEAN is an assistant professor in the Department of Communication at the University of Colorado Denver. From 2001 to 2005, he served in management positions for a Washington, DC–based open source contractor that supported organizations within the U.S. intelligence community. Since 2005, he has been affiliated with the National Consortium for the Study of Terrorism and Responses to Terrorism (START), a Center of Excellence of the U.S. Department of Homeland Security. His research intersects the fields of communication and national security and appears in *Rhetoric & Public Affairs, Intelligence and National Security*, and *International Journal of Intelligence and CounterIntelligence.*